CBSE Term II 2022

Biology
Class XII

- Complete Theory Covering NCERT
- Case Based Questions
- Short/Long Answer Type Questions
- 3 Practice Papers with Explanations

Author
Rakhi Bisht

ARIHANT PRAKASHAN (School Division Series)

ARIHANT PRAKASHAN (School Division Series)

ꢭ **Administrative & Production Offices**

Regd. Office

'Ramchhaya' 4577/15, Agarwal Road, Darya Ganj, New Delhi -110002
Tele: 011- 47630600, 43518550

ꢭ **Head Office**

Kalindi, TP Nagar, Meerut (UP) - 250002, Tel: 0121-7156203, 7156204

ꢭ **Sales & Support Offices**

Agra, Ahmedabad, Bengaluru, Bareilly, Chennai, Delhi, Guwahati,
Hyderabad, Jaipur, Jhansi, Kolkata, Lucknow, Nagpur & Pune.

ꢭ **ISBN :** 978-93-25796-93-5

ꢭ **PRICE :** ₹125.00

PO No : TXT-XX-XXXXXXX-X-XX

Published by Arihant Publications (India) Ltd.

For further information about the books published by Arihant, log on to www.arihantbooks.com or e-mail at info@arihantbooks.com

Follow us on   

CBSE Term II
2022

Contents

Syllabus

EVALUATION SCHEME

THEORY

Units	Term I	Marks
VI	Reproduction: Chapter - 2, 3 and 4	15
VII	Genetics and Evolution: Chapter – 5 and 6	20
Units	**Term II**	**Marks**
VIII	Biology and Human Welfare: Chapter – 8 and 10	14
IX	Biotechnology and its Applications: Chapter – 11 and 12	11
X	Ecology and Environment: Chapter – 13 and 15	10
Total Theory (Term – I and Term – II)		70
Practicals Term – I		15
Practicals Term – II		15
Total		100

TERM II

Unit-VIII   **Biology and Human Welfare**

Chapter-8   **Human Health and Diseases**

Pathogens; parasites causing human diseases (malaria, dengue, chikungunya, filariasis, ascariasis, typhoid, pneumonia, common cold, amoebiasis, ring worm) and their control; Basic concepts of immunology - vaccines; cancer, HIV and AIDS; Adolescence - drug and alcohol abuse.

Chapter-10   **Microbes in Human Welfare**

Microbes in food processing, industrial production, sewage treatment, energy generation and microbes as bio-control agents and bio-fertilizers. Antibiotics; production and judicious use.

Unit-IX   Biotechnology and its Applications

Chapter-11   Biotechnology - Principles and Processes

Genetic Engineering (Recombinant DNA Technology).

Chapter-12   Biotechnology and its Application

Application of biotechnology in health and agriculture: Human insulin and vaccine production, stem cell technology, gene therapy; genetically modified organisms - Bt crops; transgenic animals; biosafety issues, biopiracy and patents.

Unit-X   Ecology and Environment

Chapter-13   Organisms and Populations

Organisms and environment: Habitat and niche, population and ecological adaptations; population interactions - mutualism, competition, predation, parasitism; population attributes - growth, birth rate and death rate, age distribution.

Chapter-15   Biodiversity and its Conservation

Biodiversity - Concept, patterns, importance; loss of biodiversity; biodiversity conservation; hotspots, endangered organisms, extinction, Red Data Book, Sacred Groves, biosphere reserves, national parks, wildlife sanctuaries and Ramsar sites.

CBSE Circular

Acad - 51/2021, 05 July 2021

Exam Scheme Term I & II

केन्द्रीय माध्यमिक शिक्षा बोर्ड

(शिक्षा मंत्रालय, भारत सरकार के अधीन एक स्वायत संगठन)

CENTRAL BOARD OF SECONDARY EDUCATION

(An Autonomous Organisation under the Ministryof Education, Govt. of India)

Special Scheme for 2021-22

A. Academic session to be divided into 2 Terms with approximately 50% syllabus in each term:

The syllabus for the Academic session 2021-22 will be divided into 2 terms by following a systematic approach by looking into the interconnectivity of concepts and topics by the Subject Experts and the Board will conduct examinations at the end of each term on the basis of the bifurcated syllabus. This is done to increase the probability of having a Board conducted classes X and XII examinations at the end of the academic session.

B. The syllabus for the Board examination 2021-22 will be rationalized similar to that of the last academic session to be notified in July 2021. For academic transactions, however, schools will follow the curriculum and syllabus released by the Board vide Circular no. F.1001/CBSE-Acad/Curriculum/2021 dated 31 March 2021. Schools will also use alternative academic calendar and inputs from the NCERT on transacting the curriculum.

C. Efforts will be made to make Internal Assessment/ Practical/ Project work more credible and valid as per the guidelines and Moderation Policy to be announced by the Board to ensure fair distribution of marks.

Details of Curriculum Transaction

- Schools will continue teaching in distance mode till the authorities permit in-person mode of teaching in schools.
- **Classes IX-X: Internal Assessment** (throughout the year-irrespective of Term I and II) would include the *3 periodic tests, student enrichment, portfolio and practical work/ speaking listening activities/ project*.
- **Classes XI-XII: Internal Assessment** (throughout the year-irrespective of Term I and II) would include end of topic or unit tests/ exploratory activities/ practicals/ projects.
- Schools would create a student profile for all assessment undertaken over the year and retain the evidences in digital format.
- CBSE will facilitate schools to upload marks of Internal Assessment on the CBSE IT platform.
- Guidelines for Internal Assessment for all subjects will also be released along with the rationalized term wise divided syllabus for the session 2021-22.The Board would also provide additional resources like sample assessments, question banks, teacher training etc. for more reliable and valid internal assessments.

Term I Examinations:

- At the end of the first term, the Board will organize **Term I Examination** in a flexible schedule to be conducted between November-December 2021 with a window period of 4-8 weeks for schools situated in different parts of country and abroad. Dates for conduct of examinations will be notified subsequently.

- The Question Paper will have Multiple Choice Questions (MCQ) including case-based MCQs and MCQs on assertion-reasoning type. Duration of test will be **90 minutes** and it will cover only the rationalized syllabus of **Term I only** (i.e. approx. 50% of the entire syllabus).

- Question Papers will be sent by the CBSE to schools along with marking scheme.

- The exams will be conducted under the supervision of the External Center Superintendents and Observers appointed by CBSE.

- The responses of students will be captured on OMR sheets which, after scanning may be directly uploaded at CBSE portal or alternatively may be evaluated and marks obtained will be uploaded by the school on the very same day. The final direction in this regard will be conveyed to schools by the Examination Unit of the Board.

- Marks of the **Term I** Examination will contribute to the final overall score of students.

Term II Examination/ Year-end Examination:

- At the end of the second term, the Board would organize **Term II or Year-end Examination** based on the rationalized syllabus of Term II only (i.e. approximately 50% of the entire syllabus).

- This examination would be held around **March-April 2022** at the examination centres fixed by the Board.

- The paper will be of **2 hours duration** and have questions of different formats (case-based/ situation based, open ended- short answer/ long answer type).

- In case the situation is not conducive for normal descriptive examination **a 90 minute MCQ based exam** will be conducted at the end of the Term II also.

- Marks of the Term II Examination would contribute to the final overall score.

केन्द्रीय माध्यमिक शिक्षा बोर्ड

(शिक्षा मंत्रालय, भारत सरकार के अधीन एक स्वायत संगठन)

CENTRAL BOARD OF SECONDARY EDUCATION

(An Autonomous Organisation under the Ministryof Education, Govt. of India)

6. **Assessment / Examination as per different situations**

A. **In case the situation of the pandemic improves and students are able to come to schools or centres for taking the exams.**

Board would conduct Term I and Term II examinations at schools/centres and the theory marks will be distributed equally between the two exams.

B. **In case the situation of the pandemic forces complete closure of schools during November-December 2021, but Term II exams are held at schools or centres.**

Term I MCQ based examination would be done by students online/offline from home - in this case, the weightage of this exam for the final score would be reduced, and weightage of Term II exams will be increased for declaration of final result.

C. **In case the situation of the pandemic forces complete closure of schools during March-April 2022, but Term I exams are held at schools or centres.**

Results would be based on the performance of students on Term I MCQ based examination and internal assessments. The weightage of marks of Term I examination conducted by the Board will be increased to provide year end results of candidates.

D. **In case the situation of the pandemic forces complete closure of schools and Board conducted Term I and II exams are taken by the candidates from home in the session 2021-22.**

Results would be computed on the basis of the Internal Assessment/Practical/Project Work and Theory marks of Term-I and II exams taken by the candidate from home in Class X / XII subject to the moderation or other measures to ensure validity and reliability of the assessment.

In all the above cases, data analysis of marks of students will be undertaken to ensure the integrity of internal assessments and home based exams.

Dr. Joseph Emmanuel
Director (Academics)

CHAPTER 01

Human Health and Diseases

In this Chapter...

- Health
- Disease
- Common Infectious Diseases in Humans
- Immunity
- Vaccination and Immunisation
- Allergies
- Autoimmunity
- Immune System in the Body
- Acquired Immuno Deficiency Syndrome (AIDS)
- Cancer
- Drugs and Alcohol Abuse

Health

According to World Health Organisation (WHO), **health** is a state of complete physical, mental and social well-being and not merely the absence of disease or physical fitness. Health is mainly affected by

- **Genetic disorders** which the child inherits from parents by birth and deficiencies with which a child is born.
- **Infections** caused by pathogens.
- **Lifestyle** including the food and water we take, rest and exercise, habits that we have or lack, etc.

Disease

The condition of improper functioning or any condition which interferes with the normal functioning of one or more organ or organ systems of the body and causes disorder of mind or body is called disease. It is characterised by various signs and symptoms.

Types of Diseases

Diseases can be classified as shown below

1. **Congenital diseases** These diseases are present in human since birth (genetic disorders) or are caused due to mutation, e.g. Down's syndrome, sickle-cell anaemia, etc.

2. **Acquired diseases** These diseases develop after birth and are not transferred from parents to offspring. Acquired diseases are further categorised into

   (i) **Infectious diseases or Communicable diseases** These diseases are easily transmitted from a diseased person to a healthy person either by direct transmission or by indirect transmission. The infectious diseases are very common, e.g. common cold, etc.

   (ii) **Non-infectious diseases or Non-communicable diseases** These diseases cannot be transmitted from a diseased person to a healthy person. These diseases occur either due to nutritional deficiencies or malfunctioning of organs, e.g. cancer, diabetes, etc.

Common Infectious Diseases in Humans

Infectious diseases occur either by **pathogen** which cause disease in human, e.g. bacteria, viruses, fungi, protozoans, helminthes, etc., or by **vectors** which spread diseases as they act as carriers to transmit the pathogen from an infected person to a healthy person, e.g. female *Anopheles* mosquito.

Some common diseases and their pathogenic members are discussed as follows

Bacterial Diseases

Some common bacterial diseases are as follows

1. **Typhoid** is caused by a bacterium called *Salmonella typhi*. *S. typhi* enters the small intestine through contaminated food and water and migrates to other organs through blood.

   Symptoms are high fever (39-40°C), weakness, stomach pain, constipation, headache and loss of appetite. In severe cases, intestinal perforation and death may occur.

   Widal test is the confirmatory test for diagnosis of typhoid.

2. **Pneumonia** is caused by *Streptococcus pneumoniae* and *Haemophilus influenzae*. These bacteria infect alveoli of the lungs. The alveoli get filled with fluid which causes decrease in respiratory efficiency of the lungs.

   Pneumonia spreads by inhaling droplets/aerosol from infected individuals, sharing glasses and utensils with an infected person.

   Symptoms are fever, chills, cough, headache, etc. In severe cases, the lips and finger nails may turn grey-bluish in colour.

3. **Plague** is caused by *Pasteurella/Yersinia pestis* and is also called **black death**.

4. **Diphtheria** is caused by *Corynebacterium diphtheriae* and is characterised by difficulty in breathing due to infection in the mucous membrane of upper respiratory tract.

Viral Diseases

Some common viral diseases are as follows

1. **Common cold** occurs due to a group of viruses called **rhinoviruses**. These viruses infect the nose and the respiratory passage, but not the lungs.

   The infection occurs when droplets from cough or sneeze of an infected person are either inhaled directly or transmitted through contaminated objects such as pen, books, cups, computer's keyboard or mouse, etc.

   Symptoms include nasal congestion and discharge, sore throat, hoarseness, cough, headache, tiredness, etc., which generally last for 3-7 days.

2. **Dengue** is caused by *Flavivirus* and transmitted by *Aedes aegypti* mosquito bite.

   Symptoms are high fever, severe front headache, joint pain, nausea and vomiting.

Treatement for dengue is provided through analgesic medicines as not a vaccine is available for its treatment yet.

Dengue can be prevented by elimination of mosquitoes and their eggs.

3. **Chikungunya** is caused by chikungunya virus and is transmitted by *Aedes aegypti* mosquito bite.

   Symptoms include onset of fever, crippling joint pain, lymphadenopathy, etc.

   Chikungunya can be prevented by elimination of mosquitoes and their eggs.

Protozoan Diseases

Some common protozoan diseases are as follows

1. **Malaria** is caused by different species of the protozoan *Plasmodium* (*vivax*, *malariae* and *falciparum*). Its transmitting agent is female *Anopheles* mosquito that transfers the sporozoites of *Plasmodium*.

   Different species of *Plasmodium* (*P. vivax*, *P. malariae* and *P. falciparum*) are responsible for different types of malaria as given below

Plasmodium species	Types of malaria
P. vivax	Benign tertian malaria
P. falciparum	Malignant/pernicious malaria (Most serious)
P. malariae	Quartan malaria
P. ovale	Mild tertian malaria

The **life cycle** of *Plasmodium* in its host(s) is described below

(i) *Plasmodium* enters the human body as **sporozoites** through the bite of an infected female *Anopheles* mosquito.

(ii) These **sporozoites** reach the liver through blood and multiply asexually within the liver cells and attack the Red Blood Cells (RBCs) where they multiply again resulting in their rupture.

(iii) The rupturing of RBCs is associated with the release of a toxin called **haemozoin**, which is responsible for the high fever recurring every 3/4 days and chill (shivering).

(iv) Gametocytes (sexual stages) develop in the RBCs of human host.

(v) The gametocytes of parasite then enters the mosquito's body alongwith the blood when female *Anopheles* mosquito bites the infected person.

(vi) Further development occurs in the stomach wall of the mosquito and the gametes fuse to form a zygote.

(vii) The zygote undergoes further development in the body of the mosquito to form sporozoites.

(viii) These sporozoites are then transported and stored in its salivary glands and are transferred into another human body through saliva.

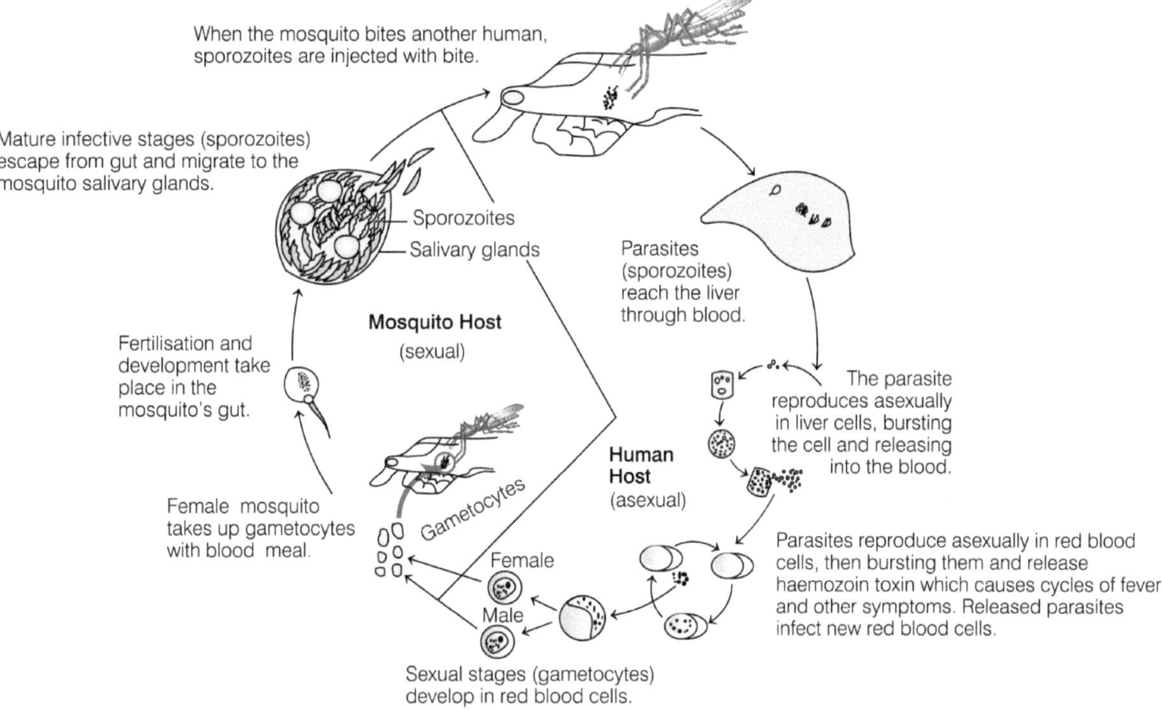

Stages in the life cycle of *Plasmodium*

Symptoms include influenza like illness, shaking chills, headache, muscle ache, nausea, vomiting and diarrhoea.

Malaria can also lead to anaemia and jaundice and can also be life-threatening if left untreated.

2. **Amoebiasis** (amoebic dysentery) is caused by an intestinal endoparasite, *Entamoeba histolytica*, which is a protozoan parasite of the large intestine of humans.

Carrier of pathogens is housefly. It transmits the parasite from faeces of an infected person to the food. Infection takes place through the contaminated food and water.

Symptoms are abdominal pain, constipation, cramps, faeces with excess mucus and blood clots.

Helminthic Diseases

Some common helminthic diseases are as follows

1. **Ascariasis** is caused by an intestinal endoparasite of human, *Ascaris lumbricoides* commonly called as **roundworm**.

Infection occurs as the eggs of parasite excreted along with faeces of infected person, contaminate water and soil. Infection reaches human beings through contaminated vegetables, fruits and water.

Symptoms are abdominal pain, indigestion, muscular pain, fever, anaemia, nausea, headache and blockage of intestinal passage.

2. **Filariasis/Elephantiasis** is caused by filarial worms *Wuchereria bancrofti* and *Wuchereria malayi. Culex* mosquito (female) is the vector.

Symptoms are chronic inflammation of organs in which they live, blockage of lymph vessels of lower limbs resulting in swelling. Genital organs also get affected leading to their deformation.

Fungal Disease

Common fungal disease in humans is ringworm. **Ringworm** is caused by fungi of the genera– *Microsporum*, Trichophyton and *Epidermophyton*.

Infection occurs through contact with an infected person or from soil, through the use of towels, clothes, combs, etc., of an infected person.

Symptoms are appearance of dry, scaly lesions on various parts of the body such as skin, nails and scalp accompanied by intense itching.

Heat and moisture help these fungi to grow in regions like folds as in groin or between the toes.

Prevention and Control of Infectious Diseases

Maintenance of personal and public hygiene is extremely important for prevention and control. Some of the preventive measures that can be taken are as follows

1. **For personal hygiene** Keeping the body clean, consumption of clean drinking water, food, vegetables, fruits, etc.

2. **For public hygiene** Proper disposal of waste and excreta, periodic cleaning and disinfection of water reservoirs, pools, cesspools and tanks and observing standard practices of hygiene in public catering.

3. **For vector borne diseases such as malaria** Eradication of vectors and destroying their breeding sites, e.g. using mosquito nets and repellents, avoiding stagnation of water, regular cleaning of coolers, etc., introducing fishes like *Gambusia* in ponds that feed on mosquito larvae, spraying of insecticides in ditches, drainage areas and swamps, etc.

4. **For air-borne diseases** Avoid contact with infected persons or their belongings.

5. **Vaccination and immunisation** These programmes for diseases should be strictly followed.

Immunity

The ability of the body (host) to fight against the disease causing agents is called immunity. It is of two types as shown below

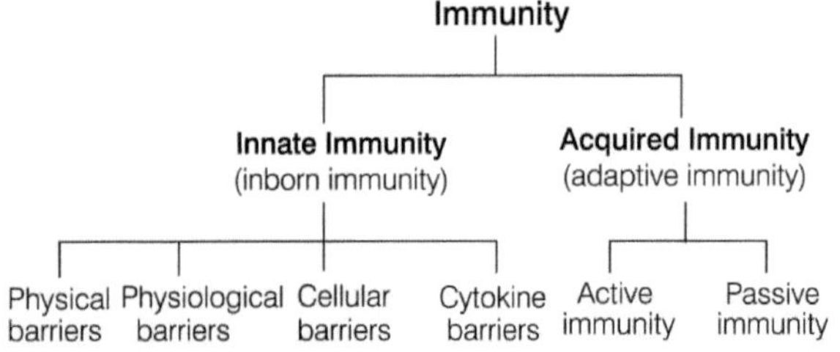

Innate Immunity

It refers to non-specific type of defence elements with which an individual is born and which are always available to protect the body. It is a non-specific type of defence. It consists of four types of barrier systems that prevent the entry of pathogen or foreign element into the body.

Types of Barriers in Innate Immunity

Various types of barriers are as given below

(i) **Physical barriers** Skin is the first line of defence. It prevents the entry of the pathogens into the body. Mucus coating of epithelium lining the respiratory, gastrointestinal and urogenital tracts also helps in trapping microbes.

(ii) **Physiological barriers** Tears from the eyes, saliva in the mouth, acid in the stomach, etc., prevent the growth of microbes.

(iii) **Cellular barriers** These include the special types of cells in our body which kill the disease causing agents. These are WBCs like Poly Morpho Nuclear Leukocytes (PMNL–neutrophils), monocytes and natural killer cells (type of lymphocytes) in the blood and macrophages in tissues.

(iv) **Cytokine barriers** Cells which are virus-infected release proteins called **interferons** that protect non-infected cells from further viral infection.

Acquired Immunity

It is pathogen specific immunity. It is not present from birth and develops during an individual's lifetime. This type of immunity is acquired, either by encountering the disease or by vaccination. It has the following characters

(i) **Specificity** It has the ability to distinguish many different foreign molecules.

(ii) **Memory** It is a unique feature, which helps in producing an intensive secondary/ anamnestic response when the pathogen attacks the second time.

(iii) **Discrimination between self and non-self** This type of immunity is able to recognise and respond to foreign molecules (non-self) and can avoid response to those molecules that are present within the body (self).

Types of Acquired Immunity

Acquired immunity can be classified as

Active Immunity

It is the immunity developed by the body when it is exposed to the antigens which may be in the form of living or dead microbes or other proteins. Antibodies are produced by the body in this case. Introduction of pathogens or microbes either during immunisation or by any infection induces active immunity. It is slow, but long lasting and has no side effects. This immunity may be

(i) **Artificial immunity** developed by vaccination.

(ii) **Natural immunity** developed during natural infection.

Passive Immunity

It is the immunity bestowed by antibodies that are directly given to the body. It is fast but lasts only for few days. Some examples of passive immunity are

(i) Antibodies received by foetus from mother through placenta.

(ii) Antibodies in the colostrum (IgA rich). **Colostrum** is a yellowish fluid secreted by mother during the initial days of lactation.

Immune Responses

Following are two major types of immune responses

1. **Primary response** It is the response generated when a body encounters a pathogen for the first time. It is of low intensity. After every primary response, cell memory stores the details of the encounter.

2. **Secondary/Anamnestic response** Subsequent encounters of the same pathogen elicits secondary response. It is highly intense. The memory of the first encounter helps in the intense secondary response. It has the capacity to distinguish between self and foreign molecules/cells.

Primary and secondary responses are carried out with the help of two types of lymphocytes, i.e. B-lymphocytes and T-lymphocytes which are classified as

Humoral Immune Response

It is mediated immune response. It includes

(i) **B-lymphocytes** or **B-cells** which produce an army of proteins called **antibodies** in response to pathogens. These antibodies are found in blood.

(ii) **T-lymphocytes** or **T-cells** help B-lymphocytes to produce antibodies.

Cell-Mediated Immune (CMI) Response

- It is mediated by T-lymphocytes. It plays an important role in organ transplantation and is responsible for body's ability to differentiate between 'self' and 'non-self'.

- In case of transplantation, the chances of graft rejection are very high. Hence, tissue matching and blood group matching are essential before transplantation of any organ or tissue. Even after successful transplant, the patient has to take immuno-suppressants throughout his/her life. There are two groups of T-lymphocytes responsible for CMI

    (i) **Cytotoxic/Killer T-cells** which kill the specific target cells by a variety of mechanisms.
    (ii) **Helper T-cells** which activate the specific B-cells to produce antibodies.

Antigens and Antibodies

Antigens (Immunogens) These are substances which when enter the body, stimulate the production of antibodies.

Antibodies These are immunoglobulins (class of proteins) produced in response to antigenic stimulation.

Each antibody molecule has four peptide chains, out of which; two small chains are called **Light** (L) **chains** and two large chains are called **Heavy** (H) **chains.**

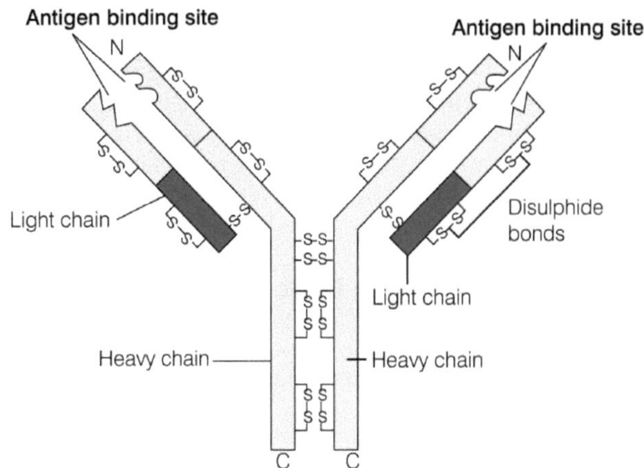

Structure of an antibody molecule

An antibody is represented as H_2L_2. In our body, different types of antibodies are produced such as IgG, IgA, IgM, IgE and IgD.

Types of Antibodies

Types	Functions
IgG	• Most prevalent class of antibody constitute, 75-80% of total antibodies.
	• Protects against fungi, bacteria, toxins, etc.
	• It can cross placenta from mother to child and provides immune protection to newborns.
	• Responsible for Rh-factor in blood.
IgA	• Second most prevalent antibody.
	• It is about 15% of the total antibodies.
	• Secreted through parts lined by mucous system.
	• Found in secretions from nose, eyes, lungs and digestive tract, saliva, tears, etc.
	• Also found in colostrum, i.e. breast milk for newborn's immune protection.
IgM	• Third most common antibody.
	• It constitutes 5-10% of total antibodies.
	• They are first to be produced in response to encounter with a pathogen.
	• Responsible for blood transfusion reactions in ABO blood system.
IgE	• The least common antibody.
	• It makes upto only 0.002% of total antibodies and is involved in allergic reactions.
IgD	• Their function is not well understood yet.

Vaccination and Immunisation

The basic principle of immunisation is based on the property of memory of the immune system. In **vaccination**, an antigen or antigenic protein or pathogen which is in inactive form is introduced in the body which induces very mild immune response. The vaccine thus, generates antibodies that neutralise pathogen during actual infection. It also generates memory B- and T-cells that recognise the pathogen on subsequent exposure and elicit a massive immune response.

Recombinant DNA Vaccine

Recombinant DNA technology has led to the production of antigenic polypeptides of pathogen via bacteria or yeast cells. It helps in the production of recombinant DNA vaccines on a large scale, e.g. hepatitis-B vaccine (produced from yeast). The vaccines contain a specific gene (segment of DNA). These vaccines are more advantageous as they are pure, specific, etc.

Passive Immunisation

It refers to the introduction of antibodies or antitoxins directly for quick immune response, e.g. in tetanus, preformed antibodies are directly injected and in case of snake bites, antitoxin (contain antibodies to the toxin) against venom is directly given.

Allergies

- The exaggerated or hypersensitive response of the immune system to certain agents in the environment is called **allergy** and its causing elements are called **allergens**. Dust, mites, pollens, animal dander (old skin scales which are constantly shed), etc., are some common allergens. The antibodies produced in response to allergens are of IgE type.
- **Symptoms of allergic reaction** includes sneezing, watery eyes, rashes, running nose, difficulty in breathing, etc.
- Allergy occurs due to the release of chemicals like histamine and serotonin from the mast cells. Drugs like anti-histamine, adrenaline and steroids quickly reduce the symptoms of allergy.
- Now-a-days, allergies are very common especially in children of metropolitan cities which is a result of high sensitivity and lowering of immunity. It is due to the protected environment provided early in life.
- For determining the cause of allergy, the patient is exposed to or injected with very small doses of possible allergens and the reactions are studied.

Autoimmunity

It is the state, where body loses the ability to distinguish between self and non-self cells. The body's immune system goes off the track and starts destroying self cells and molecules. This causes damage to the body resulting in **autoimmune diseases**, e.g. rheumatoid arthritis, Addison's disease, Hashimoto's disease, etc.

Immune System in the Body

The main function of immune system is to recognise the foreign molecules (antigens), respond to them and to keep memory of these encounters. It also plays a crucial role in organ transplants, allergic reactions and autoimmune diseases. Human immune system consists of antibodies, immune cells, lymphoid organs and tissues. It has unique features of memory and identification of a large number of pathogens.

Lymphoid Organs

Organs where lymphocytes originate, proliferate and get matured are known as lymphoid organs. They can be categorised as

Primary Lymphoid Organs

In primary lymphoid organs, immature lymphocytes differentiate to mature antigen sensitive lymphocytes and after maturation, lymphocytes migrate to secondary lymphoid organs.

The two primary lymphoid organs are

(i) **Bone marrow** It is the main lymphoid organ where all the blood cells including lymphocytes are produced. It is the site of B-lymphocytes maturation.

(ii) **Thymus** It is a lobed organ, located near the heart and beneath the breast bone. It is large at the time of birth, but with age, the size keeps on reducing and becomes very small on attaining puberty. Growth and maturation of T-lymphocytes takes place here.

Secondary Lymphoid Organs

These organs provide the sites for the interaction of lymphocytes with the antigen, which then proliferate to become effector cells.

The secondary lymphoid organs are

(i) **Spleen** It is a large bean-shaped organ containing lymphocytes, phagocytes and large number of erythrocytes. It filters the blood by trapping blood-borne microorganisms.

(ii) **Lymph nodes** These are small solid structures located at different points along the lymphatic system. Their function is to trap the microorganisms or other antigens that enter the lymph and tissue fluid. The trapped antigens in the lymph nodes are responsible for the activation of lymphocytes present there and cause the immune response.

(iii) **Mucosal Associated Lymphoid Tissue (MALT)** It is located within the lining of major tracts in the body like respiratory, digestive, urogenital tracts. MALT constitutes about 50% of the lymphoid tissue in human body.

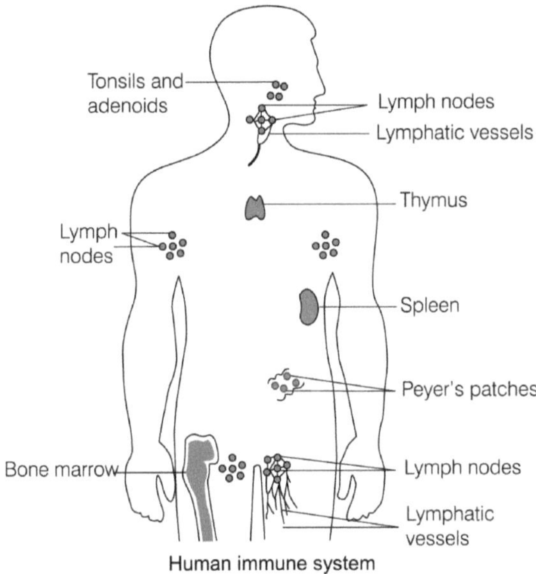

Human immune system

Note (i) **Bursa of fabricus** *is the primary lymphoid organ in birds that is considered equivalent to mammal's bone marrow.*

(ii) *Both bone marrow and thymus provide micro-environments for the development and maturation of T-lymphocytes.*

(iii) *Peyer's patches of small intestine, tonsils and appendix are also considered as secondary lymphoid organs.*

Acquired Immuno Deficiency Syndrome (AIDS)

- It refers to the deficiency of the immune system, acquired during the lifetime of an individual, indicating that it is not a congenital disease. It was first reported in 1981 in USA.
- The causative agent is **Human Immunodeficiency Virus** (HIV). It belongs to the group of viruses called **retrovirus**. It has single-stranded RNA genome enclosed in an envelope.
- HIV is transmitted by
  - Sexual contact with an infected person.
  - Transfusion of contaminated blood.
  - Sharing infected needles.
  - Infected mother to unborn child through placenta.

- Individuals who are susceptible to infection are
  - Drug addicts due to intravenous drug injections.
  - Involved with multiple sexual partners.
  - Require repeated blood transfusion.
  - Children born to HIV positive mother.
- HIV/AIDS spreads only through body fluids. There is always a time-lag between the infection and appearance of AIDS symptoms, i.e. it varies from a few months to many years (usually 5-10 years).

Mode of HIV Infection

Virus enters the macrophage after entering the body of a person. RNA gets replicated to form viral DNA by enzyme reverse transcriptase. Viral DNA gets incorporated into the host cell DNA and directs the infected cells to produce new viruses. Macrophages continue to produce virus particles and act like HIV factory.

These virus particles enter helper T-lymphocytes (T_H cells) in the blood, where they continue to replicate and produce viral progeny. The number of helper T-lymphocytes progressively decreases in the body of the infected people.

As the number of T-cells decrease, immunity also decreases. As a result, the person cannot produce any immune response even against common bacteria like *Mycobacterium*, parasites like *Toxoplasma* viruses and fungi. During this period, person suffers from fever, diarrhoea and weight loss.

Treatment and Diagnosis

Enzyme Linked Immuno-Sorbent Assay (ELISA) is used as a diagnostic test for AIDS.

Treatment of AIDS with anti-retroviral drugs is only partially effective. These can only prolong the life of the patient, but cannot prevent death.

Prevention of AIDS

As AIDS has no cure, prevention is the best option. Preventive measures for HIV infection are

- Ensure use of disposable syringes and needles.
- Ensure keeping blood banks safe from HIV.
- Free distribution of condoms.
- Prevention of drug abuse.
- Discouraging unsafe sex and encouraging regular checkups.

To prevent the spread of HIV infection WHO has started many programmes. In India organisations like National AIDS Control Organisation (NACO) and other NGO's educate peoples about AIDS in rural and urban areas.

Cancer

It is the major cause of death all over the globe. It is caused by the breakdown of normal regulatory mechanisms of cell growth.

Normal cells show a property called **contact inhibition** by virtue of which contact with other cells inhibit their uncontrolled growth. Cancerous cells, however lose this property and continue to divide giving rise to masses of cells called **tumours**.

Tumours are of two types, i.e. **benign** and **malignant**.

(i) **Benign tumours** normally remain confined to their original location and do not spread to other parts of the body and cause little damage.

(ii) **Malignant tumours** are a mass of proliferating cells called **neoplastic** or **tumour cells**. These cells grow very rapidly, invading and damaging the surrounding normal tissues. As these cells actively divide and grow, these also starve the normal cells by competing for vital nutrients. Cells sloughed from malignant tumours reach distant sites through blood flow and wherever they get lodged in the body, they start a new tumour there. This property is called **metastasis**.

Causes of Cancer

Carcinogens are cancer-causing agents. These are

(i) **Chemical** Cigarette smoke (cause lung cancer) benzopyrene, dyes, paints, etc.

(ii) **Biological** Oncogenic viruses, some parasites, etc. Cancer causing viruses called **oncogenic viruses** have genes called **viral oncogenes**. Normal cells have genes called **cellular oncogenes** (C-onc) or **proto-oncogenes** which are present in inactive state, but under certain conditions (like mutation) get activated to cancer-causing oncogenes.

(iii) **Physical** Ionizing radiations like X-rays and γ-rays, non-ionizing radiations like UV-rays (cause DNA damage leading to neoplastic transformation).

Cancer Detection and Diagnosis

Cancer can be detected by the following methods

(i) **Blood** and **bone marrow tests** To know elevation in number of cell counts.

(ii) **Biopsy** of a piece of suspected tissue done by cutting thin sections, which are then stained and examined under microscope.

(iii) **Radiography** By X-rays to detect cancer of the internal organs.

(iv) **Computed tomography** Using X-rays to generate a 3D image of internal tissue.

(v) **Resonance imaging** involves use of non-ionizing radiation and strong magnetic field to detect pathological and physiological changes in living tissue.

(vi) **Monoclonal antibodies** Against cancer-specific antigens are also used for cancer detection.

(vii) **Molecular biology** Technique to detect genes in individual with inherited susceptibility to certain cancers.

Treatment of Cancer

Treatment of cancer involves the following methods

(i) **Surgery** Tumours are removed by surgery to check further spread of cancer cells.

(ii) **Radiation therapy** Tumour cells are irradiated by a lethal dose of radiation while protecting the surrounding normal cells.

(iii) **Chemotherapy** Several chemotherapeutic drugs are used to kill cancer cells. But, their side effects like hair loss, anaemia is also reported.

(iv) **Immunotherapy** Biological modifiers like α-interferons are used to activate the immune system and help in destroying the tumour.

Drugs and Alcohol Abuse

The use of drugs and alcohol has risen especially among the youth. This is a cause of concern as it results in many harmful effects.

The drugs which are commonly abused are as follows

Opioids

These are the drugs which bind to specific opioid receptors present in our central nervous system and gastrointestinal tract. These have narcotic, analgesic, sedative and astringent effects.

Some of them are

Heroin is a common opioid and is also called as **smack**. It is chemically diacetylmorphine, white, odourless, bitter crystalline compound.

- It is obtained from the acetylation of morphine, which is extracted from the latex of poppy plant, *Papaver somniferum.*

- It is taken either by snorting or through injection.

- Heroin is a depressant which slows down the body functions.

Morphine is an effective sedative, painkiller and very useful in patients who have undergone surgery.

Cannabinoids

These are a group of chemicals which interact with cannabinoid receptors present mainly in brain. Cannabinoids are obtained from the inflorescence of the plant *Cannabis sativa*. Leaves, flower tops, resins of *C. sativa* in various combinations produce hashish, charas, marijuana and ganja.

These are inhaled or ingested orally. These drugs affect cardiovascular system of the body.

Coca Alkaloids or Cocaine

It has a potent stimulating action on the central nervous system, producing a sense of euphoria and increased energy. Cocaine is derived from the leaves and young branches of a South American plant called *Erythroxylum coca*.

Its mode of intake is either sniffing or snorting. It is a strong stimulant and when taken in overdose causes headache, convulsions, hallucination and death due to cardiovascular or respiratory failure.

Hallucinogens

These are psychedelic drugs which affect the cerebrum and sense organs. These are obtained from plants like *Atropa belladonna* and *Datura* species. Lysergic acid diethylamide (LSD) is derived from the fungus, *Claviceps purpurea*.

Effect of these drugs occurs on thoughts, feelings and perceptions of an individual. Drugs like barbiturates, amphetamines, benzodiazepines, etc., normally used as medicines.

Tobacco

It contains nicotine which stimulates the adrenal gland to release adrenaline and nor-adrenaline which in turn increases the blood pressure and heart rate. It is obtained from tobacco plant.

Its mode of intake is smoking, chewing or can be used as a snuff.

Tobacco can induce lung cancer, bronchitis, emphysema, coronary heart disease, cancer of throat, oral cancer, urinary bladder cancer, etc.

Smoking of tobacco leads to increase in carbon monoxide content of blood and reduces the concentration of haem-bound oxygen. This leads to oxygen deficiency in the body.

Adolescence and Drug/Alcohol Abuse

Adolescence is the period during which a child becomes mature in terms of his/her attitudes and beliefs for independent participation in the society.

Age between 12-18 years is called **adolescent period**. Adolescence is accompanied by several biological and behavioural changes. It is a vulnerable phase of mental and psychological development of an individual.

In this age use of drugs or alcohol occurs out of curosity or experimentation which later turns to addiction.

Addiction and Dependence

Addiction is the psychological attachment to certain effects such as euphoria and a temporary feeling of well-being associated with drugs and alcohol.

Dependence on drug/alcohol is the tendency of the body to manifest a characteristic and unpleasant **withdrawl syndrome**, if regular dose of drugs/alcohol is discontinued abruptly. Withdrawl symptoms are characterised by anxiety, shakiness, nausea and sweating.

Effects of Drug/Alcohol Abuse

The common warning signals of drug/alcohol addiction are
- Drop in academic performance.
- Isolation from family and friends.
- Lack of interest in personal hygiene.
- Aggressive and rebellious behaviour.
- Reckless behaviour, vandalism and violence.

Prevention and Control

The preventive measures are
- Avoid undue peer pressure.
- Accept failures and disappointments as part of life.
- Seek help from parents and peers.
- Seek professional and medical help for de-addiction.
- Look for danger signs.

Chapter Practice

Objective Questions

• Multiple Choice Questions

1. .... is a complete state of physical, mental and social well-being of a person.

   (a) Disease (b) Health
   (c) Infection (d) Nutrition

Ans. (*b*) Health is a complete state of physical, mental and social well-being and not merely the absence of disease or infirmity.

2. Disease which can easily transmit from one person to another is called

   (a) non-infectious disease (b) infectious disease
   (c) viral disease (d) congenital disease

Ans. (*b*) Disease which can easily transmit from one person to another is called infectious diseases. These are also called communicable disease.

3. Common cold differs from pneumonia because

   (a) pneumonia is a communicable disease, whereas the common cold is a nutritional deficiency disease
   (b) pneumonia can be prevented by a live attenuated bacterial vaccine, whereas the common cold has no effective vaccine
   (c) pneumonia is caused by a virus, while the common cold is caused by the bacterium, *Haemophilus influenzae*
   (d) pneumonia pathogen infects alveoli, whereas the common cold affects nose and respiratory passage but not the lungs

Ans. (*d*) Pneumonia is caused by the bacteria, *Streptococcus pneumoniae* and *Haemophilus influenzae* which infect the alveoli of lungs.

On the other hand, common cold is caused by a variety of viruses, most commonly by rhinovirus (RNA virus) and affects the upper respiratory tract, but not the lungs.

4. Where will you look for the sporozoites of the malarial parasite?

   (a) RBCs of humans suffering from malaria
   (b) Spleen of infected person
   (c) Salivary glands of freshly moulted female *Anopheles* mosquito
   (d) Saliva of infected female *Anopheles* mosquito

Ans. (*d*) When an infected female *Anopheles* bites a healthy person, *Plasmodium* in the form of 'sporozoites' are transmitted from saliva of mosquito into the human body. Thus, one can look for the sporozoites of the malarial parasite in the saliva of the infected female, *Anopheles* mosquito.

5. Which one of the following disease is spread by housefly?

   (a) Dengue
   (b) Filariasis
   (c) Amoebiasis
   (d) Ascariasis

Ans. (*c*) Amoebiasis is spread by housefly which acts as mechanical carrier the protozoan parasite, *Entamoeba histolytica*.

6. The group of diseases carried (transmitted) by insects are

   (a) typhoid, jaundice, tuberculosis
   (b) mumps, measles, smallpox
   (c) scabies, ringworm, swine flu
   (d) malaria, filaria, yellow fever

Ans. (*d*) The group of disease carried by insects are malaria (by female *Anopheles* mosquitoes). Filaria by female *Culex* mosquito and yellow fever by female *Aedes*.

Thus, option (d) is correct.

7. The following table shows certain diseases, their causative organisms and symptoms.

Diseases	Causative organisms	Symptoms
I. Filariasis	*A*	Inflammation of lymphatic vessels
II. Typhoid	*B*	High fever, stomach pain
III. *C*	Rhinoviruses	Nasal congestion and discharge
IV. Ascariasis	*Ascaris*	*D*

The correct option regarding *A*, *B*, *C* and *D* is

(a) A–*Wuchereria*, B–*Salmonella typhi*, C–Common cold, D–Internal bleeding, fever, anaemia

(b) A–*Salmonella typhi*, B–*Ascaris*, C–Typhoid, D–Stomach pain, headache

(c) A–*Ascaris*, B–*Entamoeba histolytica*, C–Pneumonia, D–Constipation, fever

(d) A–*Entamoeba histolytica*, B–*Salmonella typhi*, C–Common cold, D–Nasal discharge, high fever

Ans. (*a*) A–*Wuchereria*, B–*Salmonella typhi*, C–Common cold, D–Internal bleeding, fever, anaemia.

8. Which of the following immune responses is responsible for rejection of kidney graft?

(a) Humoral immune response

(b) Inflammatory immune response

(c) Cell-mediated immune response

(d) Autoimmune response

Ans. (*c*) Cell-mediated immune response is responsible for the rejection of kidney graft.

9. Active immunity development is related to

(a) natural killer cells   (b) memory cells

(c) helper T-cells   (d) suppressor T-cells

Ans. (*b*) Active immunity development is related to memory cells formed when B-cells and T-cells are activated by a pathogen.

10. Choose the correct option regarding a antibody.

(a) IgA–Helps in allergic reaction

(b) IgG–Cross placenta

(c) IgE–Found in secretions

(d) IgM–Exists as dimer

Ans. (*b*) Option (b) is correct regarding antibody.

IgG antibody can cross placenta and provides natural passive immunity to the developing foetus.

11. Vaccination protects a person from disease because it

(a) helps in better digestion

(b) increases RBC count

(c) stimulates production of antibodies

(d) improves healing system

Ans. (*c*) Vaccination protects a person from disease because it stimulates production of antibodies.

12. Consider the following statements.

I. IgE antibodies are produced in an allergic reaction.

II. B-lymphocytes mediate cell-mediated immunity.

III. The yellowish fluid colostrum has abundant IgE antibodies.

IV. Spleen is a secondary lymphoid organ.

Choose the correct option.

(a) Only I is correct

(b) I and II are correct

(c) II and III are correct

(d) I and IV are correct

Ans. (*d*) Statements I and IV are correct, while II and III are incorrect. Incorrect statements can be corrected as

- Cell-mediated immunity is mediated by T-lymphocytes.

- The yellowish fluid colostrum has abundant IgA antibodies.

13. Match the following columns.

	Column I (Cancer causing agents)		Column II (Examples)
A.	Chemical agent	1.	Benzopyrene in cigarette smoke
B.	Physical agent	2.	X-rays
C.	Biological agent	3.	Oncogenic viruses

Codes

	A	B	C			A	B	C
(a)	1	2	3		(b)	3	2	1
(c)	3	1	2		(d)	1	3	2

Ans. (*a*) A–1, B–2, C–3

14. Opioids are drugs that bind to specific opioid receptors present in our

(a) central nervous system

(b) urinogenital system

(c) gastrointestinal tract

(d) Both (a) and (c)

Ans. (*d*) Opioids are drugs, which bind to specific opioid receptors present in our central nervous system and gastrointestinal tract.

Thus, option (d) is correct.

15. Smoking addiction is harmful because smoke produces polycyclic aromatic hydrocarbons, which cause

(a) reduction in oxygen transport

(b) increase in blood pressure

(c) cancer

(d) retardation of growth of foetus

Ans. (*c*) Smoking addiction is harmful because smoke produces polycyclic aromatic hydrocarbons, currently classified as human carcinogens as these cause cancer.

• Assertion-Reasoning MCQs

Direction (Q. Nos. 1-5) *Each of these questions contains two statements, Assertion (A) and Reason (R). Each of these questions also has four alternative choices, any one of which is the correct answer. You have to select one of the codes (a), (b), (c) and (d) given below.*

(a) Both A and R are true and R is the correct explanation of A

(b) Both A and R are true, but R is not the correct explanation of A

(c) A is true, but R is false

(d) A is false, but R is true

1. Assertion (A) AIDS and hepatitis-B are sexually transmitted diseases.

Reason (R) There is no permanent cure for both of them.

Ans. (*b*) Both A and R are true, but R is not the correct explanation of A.

2. Assertion (A) Interferons help to eliminate the viral infections.

Reason (R) They released by infected cells, reach the nearby uninfected cells and make them resistant to viral infection.

Ans. (*a*) Both A and R are true and R is the correct explanation of A.

Virus infected cells secrete proteins called interferons, which protect non-infected cells from further viral infection.

3. Assertion (A) Antibody mediated immune response is provided by B-cells.

Reason (R) B-cells work chiefly by secreting substances called antibodies into the body fluids.

Ans. (*a*) Both A and R are true and R is the correct explanation of A.

Antibody mediated immune response occurs due to antibodies produced in the blood. These antibodies are chiefly secreted by B-cells into the body fluids. When an antigen (pathogen) enters the body the B-cells produce antibodies (immunoglobulins) in response to it.

4. Assertion (A) Dope test is used to estimate the level of alcohol by analysing the breathe of alcohol drinking person.

Reason (R) Athletes undergo dope test before major tournaments or a match.

Ans. (*d*) A is false, but R is true. A can be corrected as

Dope test is not releated with alcohol. It is the blood test used to estimate whether a person taking part in a competition used any drug to make their performance better. Thus, athletes undergo dope test before major tournaments or a match.

5. Assertion (A) Repeated use of drugs, increases the tolerance level of receptors in our body.

Reason (R) Addiction occurs as receptors respond only to higher doses of drugs.

Ans. (*b*) Both A and R are true, but R is not the correct explanation of A.

Repeated use of drugs, increase the tolerance level of receptors in our body because consumption or use of drugs for a longer period of time increases the number of receptors at neural junction which inturn, increases the tolerance level. Consequently, receptors respond only to higher doses of drugs thereby causing addiction.

• Case Based MCQ

1. Observe the type of plant shown below and answer the questions that follows.

(i) A type of drug is obtained from the plant whose one flowering branch is shown above.

Choose the correct statement(s) regarding the figure.

 I. It is a hallucinogen.

 II. It is a stimulant.

 III. It produces euphoria and increased energy.

 IV. It induced behavioural abnormalities by changing thoughts, feelings and perceptions.

Codes

(a) I and III   (b) II and IV

(c) I and IV   (d) II and III

Ans. (*c*) Statements I and IV are correct.

(ii) The diagram shown above represents the flowering branch of which plant?

(a) *Cannabis sativa*   (b) *Datura*

(c) Opium poppy   (d) None of these

Ans. (*b*) The diagram shown above is flowering branch of *Datura*.

(iii) Which one of the following fungi-contains hallucinogens?

(a) *Morchella esculenta*   (b) *Amanita muscaria*

(c) *Neurospora* sp.   (d) *Ustilago* sp.

Ans. (*b*) *Amanita muscaria* is a fungus which is known for containing hallucinogenic properties.

(iv) Drugs that are normally used as medicines to help the patients cope with mental illness are

(a) barbiturates   (b) amphetamines
(c) benzodiazepines   (d) All of these

Ans. (*d*) Drugs like barbiturates, amphetamines, benzodiazepines, LSD and other similar drugs are normally used as medicines to help patients cope with mental illness like depression and insomnia.

Thus, option (d) is correct.

(v) Nicotine intake stimulates the release of hormones known as ....

(a) adrenaline and nor-adrenaline
(b) thyroxine and parathyroxine
(c) oestrogen and progesterone
(d) All of the above

Ans. (*a*) Nicotine acts on the adrenal gland to stimulate the release of adrenaline and nor-adrenaline into the blood circulation.

PART 2
Subjective Questions

• Short Answer (SA) Type Questions

1. What are lifestyle diseases? How are they caused? Name any two such diseases.   (**NCERT Exemplar**)

Ans. Lifestyle diseases are ailments that are primarily based on the day-to-day habits of people.

Lifestyle diseases are caused by specific food habits, work related posture or exposure to harmful radiations or substances, lack of physical exercise, mental stress, etc. Two lifestyle diseases are

- Hypertension
- Heart disease

2. Mention any four symptoms of dengue fever.

Ans. Four characteristic features of dengue fever are high fever, severe front headache, joint pain, nausea and vomiting.

3. *Plasmodium falciparum* is the causative agent of the most severe form of malaria. It is distributed throughout the tropics. Explain why malaria is restricted to the tropics?

Ans. Malaria is transmitted by *Anopheles* mosquito, which is insect vector for the *Plasmodium falciparum* parasite.

This parasite needs warm conditions with temperatures above 20° C to complete its life cycle in the mosquito. Therefore, mosquitoes breed in warm conditions of tropics and in areas of stagnant water. Hence, malaria is restricted to the tropics.

4. The harmful allele of sickle-cell anaemia has not been eliminated from human population. Such afflicted people derive some other benefit? Discuss.   (**NCERT Exemplar**)

Ans. Sickle-cell anaemia still persists in the population despite being harmful because this mutation can also be beneficial in certain conditions. The mutant Hb type haemoglobin is found at high frequencies (upto 20% and above) in the tropical Africa.

It is known that heterozygotes ($Hb^S\ Hb^A$), having both types of haemoglobin show resistance to malarial infection as the body targets the *Plasmodium falciparum* infected cell for destruction. In contrast, individuals homozygous for normal haemoglobin ($Hb^A\ Hb^A$) suffer high mortality rates in early childhood due to malarial infection. Thus, the allele for sickle-cell has been maintained because heterozygotes have a higher reproductive success than either of the two possible homozygotes.

5. Name a human disease, its causal organism, symptoms (any three) and vector that spread by intake of water and food contaminated by human faecal matter.   (**All India 2017**)

Ans. The disease with given characteristics is amoebiasis. Causative agent is a parasite, *Entamoeba histolytica*, which is found in the large intestine of human. The transmitting agent of the pathogen is housefly.
Symptoms include constipation, abdominal pain, cramps and stools with excess mucus and blood clots.

6. How does the transmission of each of the following take place?

Ringworm, Malaria, Ascariasis, Pneumonia. (**NCERT**)

Ans. The mode of transmission of the above diseases are

Diseases	Modes of transmission
Ringworm	Transmitted through soil or by using towels, combs, clothes of an infected individual.
Malaria	It is also a vector-borne disease that is usually spread by the bitting of female *Anopheles* mosquito.
Ascariasis	Transmitted by contaminated food and water.
Pneumonia	It spreads by droplets/ aerosols released during nasal secretions of infected person.

7. Compare the symptoms of ascariasis, amoebiasis and elephantiasis. **(Delhi 2020)**

Ans. Comparison between the symptoms of ascariasis, amoebiasis and elephantiasis are as follows

Ascariasis	Amoebiasis	Elephantiasis
Caused by *Ascaris lumbricoides*.	Caused by *Entamoeba histolytica*.	Caused by *Wuchereria bancrofti*.
Symptoms include abdominal pain, indigestion, muscular pain, fever, anaemia, nausea, headache and blockage of intestinal passage.	Symptoms are abdominal pain, constipation, cramps, faeces with excess mucus and blood clots.	Symptoms include inflammation of organs in which they live for many years, normally affect lymph vessels of lower limbs resulting in swelling of feet and genitals, hence called elephantiasis.

8. What measures would you take to prevent the water-borne diseases? **(NCERT)**

Ans. To prevent water-borne diseases, water bodies, like ponds, water tanks, reservoirs in the city or village should be cleaned periodically. The proper disposal of domestic waste, excreta, sewage should be done. At personal level, boiling of water, using water purifier, washing hands before meals should be practiced.

9. 'Prevention is better than cure'. Comment. **(NCERT Exemplar)**

Ans. Prevention is always better than cure because some diseases cause extensive damage to the body tissues or organs and have a

(i) negative effect on their capacity to function.

(ii) permanent or long term debilitating effect.

(iii) negative mental and psychological effect.

(iv) financial burden.

Hence, it is said that prevention is easier and effective than cure of a disease.

10. Why is it that during changing weather, one is advised to avoid closed, crowded and air conditioned places like cinema halls, etc? **(NCERT Exemplar)**

Ans. During changing weather, one is advised to avoid crowded places because changing seasons are the time when infectious agents are more active as moist conditions favours the growth of pathogens. Also, people are more vulnerable as their body system is busy in adapting to the changing environmental conditions of temperature, humidity, etc. Thus, this increases the chances of getting easily infected by various pathogens.

11. Community service department of your school plans a visit to a slum area near the school with an objective to educate the slum dwellers with respect to health and hygiene.

(i) Why is there a need to organise such visits?

(ii) Write the steps you will highlight as a member of this department, in your interactions with them to enable them to lead a healthy life. **(All India 2014)**

Ans. (i) Slums are generally unauthorised and encroached colonies having no public facilities. Due to lack of public facilities and education, the living standards there are very low and people are always at risk. Thus, there is a need to organise visits to educate people of slum about sanitation and other health related issues.

(ii) Development of healthy life is a bidirectional process and needs the cooperation of both authorities and public of slum area. Interacting with people, understanding their needs, availability of funds, interaction with all concerned authorities, making a concrete plan of development are required to handle the situation of slums.

12. Explain any three preventive measures to control microbial infections. **(NCERT Exemplar)**

Ans. Preventive measures to control microbial infections are as follows

1. **Personal hygiene** Keeping the body clean, consumption of clean drinking water, food, vegetables, fruits, etc.

2. **Public hygiene** Proper disposal of waste and excreta, periodic cleaning and disinfection of water reservoirs, pools, cesspools and tanks and observing standard practices of hygiene in public catering.

3. **For vector borne diseases such as malaria** Eradication of vectors and destroying their breeding sites, e.g. using mosquito nets and repellents, avoiding stagnation of water, regular cleaning of coolers, etc., introducing fishes like *Gambusia* in ponds that feed on mosquito larvae, spraying of insecticides in ditches, drainage areas and swamps, etc.

13. 'Maintenance of personal and public hygiene is necessary for prevention and control of many infectious diseaes'. Justify the statement giving suitable examples.

Ans. Diseases which are easily transmitted from one person to another, are called infectious diseases.

For prevention and control of such diseases, maintenance of personal and public hygiene is necessary, for this purpose, some common preventive measures should be taken as follows

(i) **Education** People should be educated about communicable disease to protect themselves from such diseases.

(ii) **Isolation** The infected person should be kept isolated to minimise the spread of infection.

(iii) **Vaccination** People should get vaccination on time to avoid infection.

(iv) **Sanitation** The sanitation should be improved to avoid infection from polluted water, contaminated food, etc.

(v) **Eradication of Vectors** The breeding places of vectors must be destroyed and adult vectors should be killed by suitable methods.

(vi) **Sterilisation** The patient's surroundings and articles of use should be completely sterilised to reduce the chances of infection.

14. Certain attributes of innate immunity are given in the table below. Identify A, B, C, D, E and F respectively in it.

	Types of barriers	Examples of the barriers	Functions
(i)	A	B	Prevent microbial growth
(ii)	C	Polymorpho nuclear leukocytes	D
(iii)	Cytokine	E	F

(Delhi 2016C)

Ans. (i) A–Physiological barriers, B–Acid in stomach.

(ii) C–Cellular barriers, D–Phagocytose and destroy microbes

(iii) E–Interferons, F–Prevention of viral infections

15. Many microbial pathogens enter the gut of humans along with food. What are the preventive barriers to protect the body from such pathogens? What type of immunity do you observe in this case?

Ans. Many microbial pathogens enter the gut of humans along with food. The preventive barriers to protect the body from such pathogens are as follows

(i) The mucus coating of the epithelium lining of the gut helps in trapping microbes entering the body.

(ii) Saliva in the mouth and hydrochloric acid in gastric juice secreted by stomach prevent microbial growth.

This type of immunity is innate immunity. It is present from birth and is inherited from parents. The innate immunity remains throughout the life.

16. (i) It is generally observed that the children who had suffered from chickenpox in their childhood may not contact the same disease in their adulthood. Explain giving reasons the basis of such an immunity in an individual. Name this kind of immunity.

(ii) What are interferons? Mention their role.

(All India 2016)

Ans. (i) When the boy suffered from chickenpox, first time his body's immune system exhibited primary response. Along with that, the memory of chickenpox virus was stored by the immune system. Now, whenever the same virus will attack this boy, the immune system will produce an intense response, preventing the body from getting chickenpox again. Thus, protecting the boy from getting infected by chickenpox ever again in life. It is known as acquired immunity.

(ii) Interferons are special kind of proteins secreted by virus infected cells. These protect the healthy cells from the virus attack.

17. What does the term 'memory of the immune system' mean? (NCERT Exemplar)

Ans. Memory of the immune system is an unique feature, which helps in producing an intensive secondary/anamnestic response when the pathogen attacks the second time.

18. Name the types of acquired immune responses and the special types of lymphocytes involved in providing them. (Delhi 2020)

Ans. Types of acquired immune responses are

(i) Humoral immune response provided by B-lymphocytes.

(ii) Cell-mediated immune response provided by T-lymphocytes.

19. Differentiate between active immunity and passive immunity.

Ans. Differences between active immunity and passive immunity are as follows

Active immunity	Passive immunity
It is developed due to contact with pathogen or its antigen.	It is developed when readymade antibodies are injected into the body.
It has no side effects.	It may cause a reaction.
It is slow but long lasting.	It is fast but lasts only for few days.
It takes time to develop its response.	It is used when the immune response has to be faster.
e.g. vaccination for polio, etc.	e.g. administration of tetanus antitoxins, etc.

20. (i) What is the functional difference between B and T-cells?

    (ii) Name the source used to produce hepatitis-B vaccine using *r*DNA technology. **(Delhi 2020)**

Ans. (i) Functional differences between B and T-cells are as follows

B-cells	T-cells
They form humoral or Antibody-Mediated Immune System (AMIS).	They form Cell-Mediated Immune System (CMIS).
They defend against viruses and bacteria that enter the blood and lymph.	They defend against pathogens including protists and fungi that enter the cells.
They form plasma cells and memory cells by the division.	They form killer, helper and suppressor cells by the division of lymphoblasts.

    (ii) Hepatitis-B vaccine is produced from surface antigens of transgenic yeast by *r*DNA technology. The antigens represent whole protein vaccine.

21. For an organ transplant, it is an advantage to have an identical twin. Why?

Ans. For an organ transplant, it is an advantage to have an identical twin because the organ will have same surface markers and therefore, the recipient's immune system will not identify it as foreign and will not react against it. In case of different surface markers, the immune system starts a reaction, kills the foreign tissue or rejects it.

22. Why is mother's milk considered the most appropriate food for a newborn infant?

                                    (NCERT Exemplar)

Or

Why is colostrum a boon to the newborn baby?

                                    (All India 2015C)

Ans. Mother's milk is considered most appropriate or a boon for a newborn infant as it provides immunity in the initial period of baby's life. The yellowish fluid colostrum secreted by mother during the initial days of lactation has abundant antibodies (IgA) to protect the infant.

23. What is the basic principle of vaccination? How do vaccines prevent microbial infections? Name the organism from which hepatitis-B vaccine is produced. **(NCERT Exemplar)**

Ans. The basic principle of immunisation is based on the property of memory of the immune system. In vaccination, an antigen or antigenic protein or pathogen which is in inactive form is introduced in the body which induces very mild immune response. The vaccine thus, generates antibodies that neutralise pathogen during actual infection. It also generates memory B and T-cells that recognise the pathogen on subsequent exposure and elicit a massive immune response. Yeast cells help in production of hepatitis-B vaccine.

24. (i) List any two situations, when a medical doctor would recommend injection of preformed antibodies into the body of a patient. Name this kind of immunisation and mention its advantages.

    (ii) Name the kind of immunity attained when instead of antibodies, weakened antigens are introduced into the body.

Ans. (i) The two situations in which doctor will recommend injection of preformed antibodies into the body can be

       (a) in case of snake bite

       (b) in case of tetanus

    This type of immunisation is called passive immunisation.

    Advantages of passive immunisation are as follows

       (a) It helps to prevent and slow down the course of disease.

       (b) Passive immunisation with preformed antibodies leads to promote the availability of large amount of antibody thus act quickly.

    (ii) Passive immunity attained when instead of antibodies, weakened antigens are introduced into the body.

25. Following a road accident four injured persons were brought to a nearby clinic. The doctor immediately injected them with tetanus antitoxin.

    (i) What is tetanus antitoxin?

    (ii) Why were the injured immediately injected with this antitoxin?

    (iii) Name the kind of immunity this injection provided. **(All India 2020)**

Ans. (i) Tetanus antitoxin is a preparation containing antibodies to the toxin. Produced by tetanus bacteria, *Clostridium tetani*.

    (ii) The injured persons are immediately injected with tetanus antitoxin for preventing any infection and septic. Antitoxins neutralise the toxin produced by bacteria.

    (iii) Tetanus antitoxin represents artificial passive immunisation where quick response is generated in the body.

26. In the metropolitan cities of India, many children are suffering from allergy/asthma. What are the main causes of this problem? Give some symptoms of allergic reactions. **(NCERT Exemplar)**

Ans. In metropolitan cities, lifestyle is responsible for lowering of immunity and high sensitivity to allergens. The polluted environment of cities, which affect the respiratory system is the reason of allergy/asthma in childrens.

Some symptoms of allergic reactions are sneezing, watery eyes, running nose and difficulty in breathing.

27. A person shows strong unusual hypersensitive reactions when exposed to certain substances present in the air. Identify the condition. Name the cells responsible for such reactions. What precaution should be taken to avoid such reactions.

Ans. If a person is hypersensitive to certain substance present in the air, he may be allergic to it.

Mast cells release certain chemicals, e.g. histamine and serotonin, in response to this substance that results in allergic reaction.

Precaution taken to prevent such reaction is to avoid the allergens responsible for particular allergy.   (2)

28. Lymph nodes are secondary lymphoid organs. Explain the role of lymph nodes in our immune response.

Ans. Immune system of human beings consists of lymphoid organs, where the maturation and proliferation of lymphocytes occur. Lymphoid organs are of two types. These are as follows

(i) **Primary lymphoid organs** which include bone marrow and thymus where B-and T- lymphocytes mature and acquire their antigen-specific receptor.

(ii) **Secondary lymphoid organs** which include spleen, lymph nodes, tonsils, Peyer's patches of small intestine and appendix where lymphocytes interact with the antigen and proliferate to become effector cells.

Lymph nodes are small solid structures present at different points along the lymphatic system. They trap the microorganisms or other antigens that enter the lymph and tissue fluid. Antigens trapped in the lymph nodes activate the lymphocytes and produce an immune response.

29. Answer the following.

(i) Highlight the role of thymus as a lymphoid organ.

(ii) Give the name of the cells that are released from the above mentioned gland. Mention how they help in immunity?   **(Delhi 2012)**

Ans. (i) Thymus is a primary lymphoid organ. It is lobe-shaped and is known to be the site for the growth and differentiation of antigen sensitive T-lymphocytes.

(ii) Thymus releases T-lymphocytes, which are involved in cell-mediated immunity and also help B-lymphocytes to produce antibodies.

30. How does spleen act as lymphoid organ? Explain.

Ans. Spleen is a large bean-shaped organ containing lymphocytes, phagocytes and large number of erythrocytes. It filters the blood by trapping blood-borne microorganisms.

B-cells become activated and produce antibodies in it. Spleen acts as a graveyard of RBCs.

31. The following are some well-known abbreviations, which have been used in this chapter. Expand each one to its full form.

   (i) MALT   (ii) CMI   (iii) AIDS

   (iv) NACO   (v) HIV   **(NCERT)**

Ans. (i) **MALT**–Mucosal Associated Lymphoid Tissue

(ii) **CMI**–Cell-Mediated Immunity

(iii) **AIDS**–Acquired Immuno Deficiency Syndrome

(iv) **NACO**–National AIDS Control Organisation

(v) **HIV**–Human Immunodeficiency Virus

32. The immune system of a person is suppressed. In the ELISA test, he was found positive to a pathogen.
                          (NCERT Exemplar)

(i) Name the disease, the patient is suffering from.

(ii) What is the causative organism?

(iii) Which cells of body are affected by the pathogen?

Ans. (i) The patient is suffering from AIDS.

(ii) AIDS is caused by Human Immunodeficiency Virus (HIV). It is a retrovirus containing RNA as genetic material.

(iii) Macrophages and helper T-cells are affected by the pathogen.

33. (i) What precaution(s) would you recommend to a patient requiring repeated blood transfusion?

(ii) If the advise is not followed by the patient, there is an apprehension that the patient might contract a disease that would destroy the immune system of his/her body.

Explain with the help of schematic diagram only how the immune system would get affected and destroyed.   **(Delhi 2017)**

Ans. (i) Repeated blood transfusion may result in contracting diseases like AIDS. The recipient must ensure that the donor's blood is being screened for HIV and other pathogens.

(ii) In the absence of such measures, the patient can get infected by HIV (Human Immmunodeficiency Virus) which causes AIDS. It is a threatening disorder that weakens the immune system by attacking helper T-cells in the body.

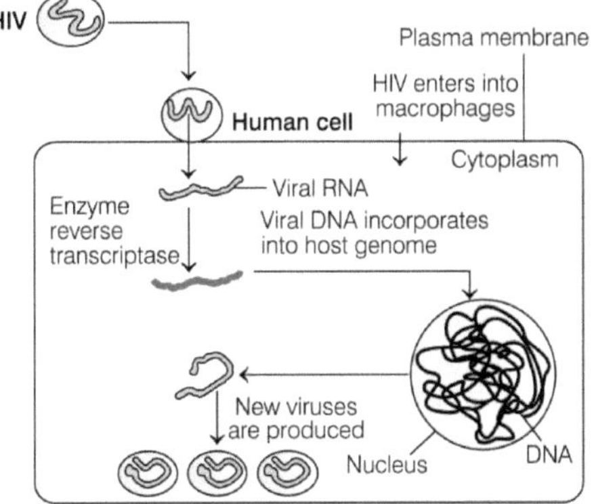

34. Differentiate between benign tumour and malignant tumour. **(NCERT Exemplar; All India 2015C)**

Ans. Differences between benign and malignant tumour are as follows

Benign tumour	Malignant tumour
Limited adherence occurs amongst cells of benign tumour.	There is no adherence amongst cells. They tend to slip past one another.
Benign tumour does not show metastasis and is non-invasive.	It shows metastasis and thus invades other body parts.
It stops growth after reaching a certain size.	Malignant tumour shows indefinite growth.
It is less fatal to the body.	It is more fatal to the body.

35. What is cancer? How is a cancer cell different from the normal cell? How do normal cells attain cancerous nature?

Ans. An abnormal and uncontrolled division of cells is termed as cancer. Genes called cellular oncogenes (c-onc) or proto-oncogens present in normal cells when activated under certain conditions lead oncogenic transformation of the normal cells leading cancer.

A cancer cell is different from the normal cell in following ways

Cancer cell	Normal cell
Cancer cells divide in an uncontrolled manner.	Normal cells divide in a controlled manner.
The cells do not show contact inhibition.	The cells show contact inhibition.
Lifespan is indefinite.	Lifespan is definite.

36. Give the full form of CT and MRI. How are they different from each other? Where are they used? **(NCERT)**

Ans. **CT** is Computed Tomography which uses X-rays to generate 3D images of internal organs.

MRI is Magnetic Resonance Imaging which uses strong magnetic fields and non-ionising radiations to detect pathological and physiological changes in the living tissue accurately.

Both are used in cancer detection.

37. How are morphine and heroin related? Mention the effect each one of them has on the human body? **(All India 2014C)**

Ans. Heroin is obtained from acetylation of morphine. They both affect the central nervous system and gastrointestine tract. Thus, both are related. Morphine, is as an effective sedative and painkiller while heroin acts as depressant and slows down body functions.

38. Name two drugs obtained from poppy plant. 'These drugs are medically useful, but are often abused'. Taking the mentioned examples justify by giving reasons. **(Delhi 2016 C)**

Ans. Both morphine and heroin are extracted from the latex of plant *Papaver somniferum*.

Morphine acts as an effective sedative and painkiller, while heroin acts as depressant and slows down body functions. When taken in excess amounts, these drugs alter the moods or induce sleep.

39. Write the scientific name of the source plant of the drugs-marijuana and hashish also mention their effect on human body. **(Delhi 2014C)**

Ans. The scientific names of the source plant of drugs marijuana and hashish is *Cannabis sativa*. They usually effect the cardiovascular system of human body.

40. Name the blank spaces *A, B, C* and *D* in the table given below.

Names of the drugs	Plant sources	Organ systems affected
A	Coca plant	*B*
Charas	*C*	*D*

(Foreign 2008)

Ans. *A*–Cocaine, *B*–Central nervous system, *C*–*Cannabis sativa*, *D*–Cardiovascular system

41. 'Many secondary metabolites of plants have medicinal properties. It is their misuse that creates problems'. Justify the statement with an example. **(NCERT Exemplar)**

Ans. Many secondary metabolites obtained from plants are used for their medicinal properties, e.g. opiates derived from poppy plant are used as drugs to relieve pain.

The problem starts when these metabolites are misused for having pleasure and are taken in doses above the prescribed limit, e.g. opium addict loses weight, fertility and interest in work.

42. Explain why using tobacco in any form is injurious to health.

Ans. Consumption of tobacco is injurious to health in the following ways
(i) It can cause cancer of lungs, throat, urinary bladder and oral cavity.
(ii) Emphysema, bronchitis and coronary heart diseases can be caused.
(iii) Gastric ulcer can occur.
(iv) Smoking tobacco increases carbon monoxide levels in the blood, which leads to the oxygen deficiency in body.

43. The tobacco smoking is associated with the rise in blood pressure and emphysema (oxygen deficiency in the body). Explain.

Ans. Tobacco smoking increases the concentration carbon monoxide (CO) in blood and reduces the concentration of haemoglobin bound oxygen. Thus, leading to oxygen deficiency (emphysema) and high blood pressure in the body.

44. Why is that once a person starts taking alcohol or drugs, it is difficult to get rid of this habit? Discuss it with your teacher.

Ans. It is difficult to get rid of alcohol or drugs once a person starts taking them because their repeated use lead to addiction. It increases the tolerance level of these substances in the body and then the receptors respond only to higher doses of alcohol and drugs which in turn increases the dosage and it becomes difficult to get rid of the habit.

45. Do you consider passive smoking is more dangerous than active smoking? Why?

(**NCERT Exemplar**)

Ans. Passive smoking can be equally dangerous because it exposes the person to the same harmful effects of smoke. Passive smoking means being in the same room or place, where someone is smoking and getting exposed to smoke in the surrounding area.

Once inhaled, the smoke can trigger mucus release in the bronchioles that blocks the airways. This induces coughing. But prolonged exposure can lead to bronchitis, emphysema, respiratory tract infections and eventually lung cancer.

46. What happens to an individual when a regular dose of drugs/alcohol is abruptly discontinued? What characteristics manifest in the individual under such a situation? (**Outside Delhi 2016C**)

Or If a regular dose of drug or alcohol is not provided to an addicted person, he shows some withdrawal symptoms. List any four such withdrawal symptoms.

Ans. If the regular dose of drug or alcohol in an addicted person is discontinued abruptly, the body exhibits characteristic and unpleasant symptoms called 'withdrawal syndrome'.

The 'withdrawal syndrome' is characterised by symptoms like anxiety, shakiness, nausea and excessive sweating.

47. Why cannabinoids are banned in sports and games?

(**NCERT Exemplar**)

Or Intake of cannabinoids should be banned. Justify giving reasons. (**Delhi 2014**)

Ans. Cannabinoids are banned in sports as athletes were misusing these drugs in order to enhance their performance. These can have a serious negative effect on their general health and in long term, can hamper the normal functioning of organ systems.

Hence, intake of cannabinoids should be banned.

48. Do you support 'dope test' being conducted on sports persons participating in a prestigious athletic meet? Give three reasons in support of your answer.

(**All India 2014C**)

Ans. Yes, the 'dope test' should be conducted on sports persons participating in prestigious athletic meet.

This is done to find out whether any participant had taken any kind of performance enhancing drugs.

The use of drugs in sports should be banned as

 (i) they increase muscle strength.

 (ii) promote aggressiveness.

 (iii) increase athletic performance.

Because of above reasons, use of such drugs, e.g. steroids, analgesics, diuretics should be banned for participants as it would be unfair to the other participants (not consuming such drugs).

49. (i) Why is there a fear amongst the guardians that their adolescent wards may get trapped in drug/alcohol abuse?

 (ii) Explain 'addiction' and 'dependence' in respect of drug/alcohol abuse in youth. (**All India 2017**)

Ans. (i) The age between 12-18 years of age is called adolescent period. There is always a fear amongst guardians that their adolescents may get trapped in drug/alcohol abuse due to following reasons

  (a) Adolescence is accompanied by several biological and behavioural changes. It is a vulnerable phase of mental and psychological development of an individual in which an individual may get addicted to alcohol/drugs very easily.

  (b) In this age, the first use of drugs or alcohol may be out of curiosity or experimentation, which later on turns to addiction.

  (c) Adolescents usually take drugs due to social pressure, need of adventure, excitement, to avoid stress, depression and frustration.

 (ii) **Addiction** It is a psychological attachment to certain effects such as euphoria and temporary feeling of well-being associated with drugs and alcohol. It makes the person to take up drugs on regular basis, even when they are not needed or even when their use becomes self-destructive.

Dependence It is the tendency of the body to show unpleasant and characteristic withdrawal syndrome, if the dose of alcohol or drug is discontinued abruptly. Dependency pushes the person away from social norms and leads to social adjustment problems.

50. Due to under peer pressure, a group of adolescents started using opioids intravenously. What are the serious problems they might face in future?

Ans. Serious problems, they might face in future are

(a) Higher risk of infections like AIDS and hepatitis-B which transmits through sharing of infected needle and syringes or sexual contact.

(b) Since, the tolerance levels of the receptors present in our body to these drugs elevates, they respond only to higher doses of drugs leading to greater intake and addiction.

• Long Answer (LA) Type Questions

1. Explain the adaptive immunity with emphasis on its properties, activation and its role in vaccination.

Ans. Adaptive immunity is pathogen specific immunity. It is not present from birth and develops during an individual's lifetime. This type of immunity is acquired, either by encountering the disease or by vaccination. It has the following characters

(i) **Specificity** It is the ability to distinguish different foreign molecules.

(ii) **Memory** It is a unique feature, which helps in producing an intensive secondary/ anamnestic response when the pathogen attacks the second time.

(iii) **Discrimination between self and non-self** This type of immunity is able to recognise and respond to foreign molecules (non-self) and can avoid response to those molecules that are present within the body (self).

Vaccination is based on the property of memory of adaptive immune system. In vaccination, an antigen or pathogen which is in inactive form is introduced in human body which induces mild immune response. The vaccine is therefore generating antibodies along with memory B and T-cells that recognise the pathogen on subsequent exposure.

2. What are recombinant DNA vaccines? Give two examples of such vaccines. Discuss their advantages. **(NCERT Exemplar)**

Ans. Recombinant DNA vaccines are made up of a small circular DNA (plasmid) that has very tiny piece of pathogen DNA incorporated in it to produce one or two specific proteins of the pathogen.

This recombinant DNA is introduced into the bacteria or yeast cells, where it can use cell's machinery to produce polypeptides of pathogen. These are used as vaccines to trigger a range of immune responses. Vaccines produced by using this approach allow large scale production, e.g.

(i) Hepatitis-B vaccine produced from yeast.

(ii) Bird flu DNA vaccine.

Advantages

(i) Recombinant DNA vaccines are advantageous over killed or attenuated vaccines, since they do not get virulent or mutated again as it is seen in case of attenuated vaccines.

(ii) Secondly these are highly pure, specific and elicit show strong immune response.

3. Explain the process of replication of a retrovirus after it gains entry into human body. **(All India 2014)**

Or What is the mechanism by which the AIDS virus causes deficiency of immune system of the infected person? **(NCERT)**

Ans. The process by which retrovirus gains entry into human host body or the mechanism by which AIDS virus causes immunodeficiency is as follows

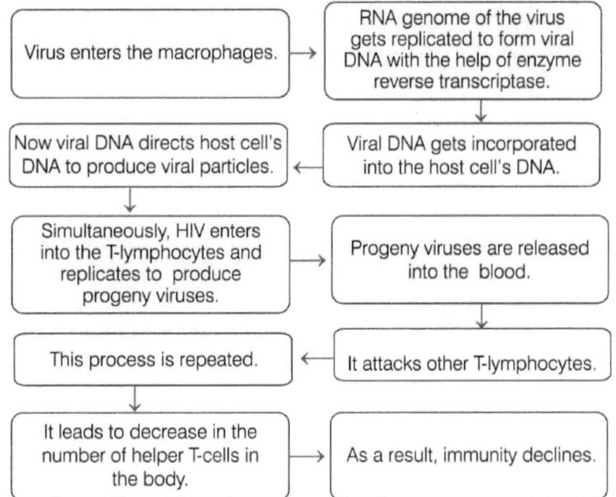

4. (i) Cancer is one of the most dreaded disease. Explain 'contact inhibition' and 'metastasis' with respect to the disease.

(ii) Name the group of genes that have been identified in normal cells that could lead to cancer. How do these genes cause cancer?

(iii) Name any two techniques that are useful in detecting cancers of internal organs.

(iv) Why are cancer patients often given α-interferon as part of the treatment? **(Delhi 2014)**

Ans. (i) **Contact inhibition** Normal cells have the property of contact inhibition (stoppage of growth on coming in contact with other cells), but cancer cells do not have this property. As a result, cancer cells divide continuously to give rise to a mass of cells (tumours).

Metastasis This property is exhibited by malignant tumours. It is the pathological process of spreading of cancerous cells to different parts of the body. These cells divide uncontrollably, forming a mass of cells called tumour.

From the tumour, some cells get sloughed off and enter the bloodstream. From the bloodstream, these cells reach near by as well as distant parts of the body therefore, initiating the formation of new tumours by dividing actively.

(ii) There are cancer causing viruses called oncogenic **viruses**. They have genes called **viral oncogenes**. Certain other genes called **cellular oncogenes** (c-onc) or **proto-oncogenes** have been identified in normal cells, which when activated can lead to tumour formation.

(iii) Techniques that are useful in detecting cancers of internal organs are

    (a) **Computed Tomography** (CT) is done to generate a 3-D image of internal tissue. It uses X-rays.

    (b) **Magnetic Resonance Imaging** (MRI) involves the use of non-ionizing radiations and strong magnetic fields to detect pathological and physiological changes in a living tissue.

(iv) The biological response modifiers such as α-interferons are given to cancer patients as a part of their treatment because it activates patients's immune system and helps in destroying the tumour.

5. Drugs like LSD, barbiturates, amphetamines, etc., are used as medicines to help patients with mental illness. However, excessive doses and abusive usage are harmful. Enumerate the major adverse effects of such drugs in humans. **(NCERT Exemplar)**

Ans. Harmful effects of drugs like LSD, barbiturates, etc., are

(i) Anxiety, shakiness, nausea and sweating, loss of mind control.

(ii) Reckless behaviour, vandalism and violence.

(iii) Lack of interest in personal hygiene, fluctuations in weight and appetite.

(iv) Social adjustment problems.

(v) Withdrawal, isolation, depression, fatigue, aggressive behaviour.

(vi) Withdrawal symptoms can be severe and life threatening.

(vii) Excessive doses of drugs may lead to coma and death due to respiratory failure, heart failure or cerebral haemorrhage.

6. In your view what motivates youngsters to take alcohol or drugs and how can this be avoided? **(NCERT)**

Or Why do some adolescents start taking drugs. How can this be avoided? **(NCERT Exemplar)**

Ans. Adolescents take drugs/alcohol due to following reasons

(i) Social and peer pressure.

(ii) Curiosity and need for adventure, excitement and experiment.

(iii) To avoid stress, depression and frustation.

(iv) To overcome hardships.

(v) Avoid unsupportive or unstable family structure.

(vi) Perception that it is cool or progressive. This perception is further promoted by TV, movies, newspapers and internet.

This can be avoided by

(i) **Avoid undue peer pressure** Parents must understand the abilities and personality type of the child. A child should not be pushed unduly for studies or sports or other activities. Pressure from parents and teacher beyond threshold is not healthy for children.

(ii) **Education and counselling** Parents and teachers should educate and counsel the child to face difficult situations as part of life. Stress, disappointments and failure must be taken in a healthy way. Involvement in extracurricular activities is a good distraction from daily stress. It channelises the child's energy in right direction.

(iii) **Seeking help from parents and peers** In case of any academic or emotional problem, advice and guidance should be sought out from parents or trusted friends. Besides solving problems, it also helps in venting out feelings of anxiety, fear and guilt.

(iv) **Looking for danger signs** Danger signs must be brought in light and must be told to parents and teachers if they find someone using drugs or alcohol. There should be no hesitation in informing the same to the elders. This helps in preventing the person from drug abuse and initiating remedial steps.

(v) **Seeking professional and medical help** Affected people have a lot of help available in the form of doctors, psychologists, psychiatrists and rehabilitation programmes. An addicted person can get completely rid of the problem and lead a perfectly normal and healthy life by getting help.

• Case Based Questions

1. Refer to the diagram given below and answer the questions that follows.

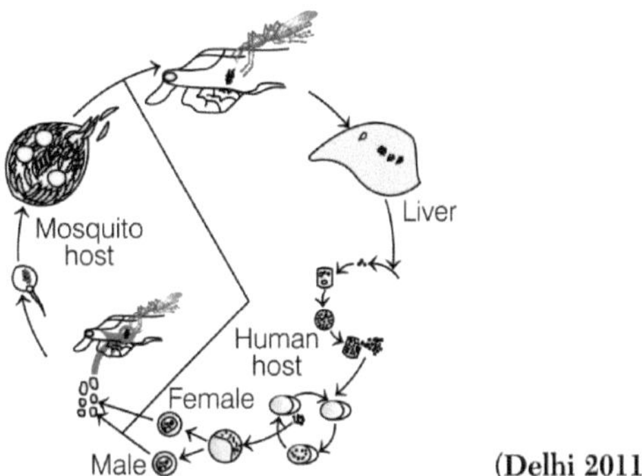

(Delhi 2011)

(i) The parasite in above diagram reproduces in human host by which method?

Ans. The parasite reproduces in human host by asexual method.

(ii) The sexual stages of parasite are referred to as?

Ans. The sexual stages of parasite are gametocyte.

(iii) Where does the fertilisation and development of parasite take place in mosquito body?

Ans. In mosquito's body, fertilisation and development of parasite take place in stomach.

(iv) What are sporozoites?

Ans. The mature infective stage of mosquito is called sporozoite.

(v) What is the cause of cycles of fever during malaria?

Ans. At regular intervals, the parasite reproduces and causes bursting of RBCs. This releases haemozoin and causes periodic cycles of fever.

2. Direction *Read the following passage and answer the questions that follows.*

The principle of immunisation or vaccination is based on the property of memory of the immune system. In vaccination, a preparation of antigenic proteins of pathogen or inactivated/ weakened pathogen (vaccine) are introduced into the body.

The antibodies would neutralise the pathogenic agents during the infection. The vaccine also generates memory B and T-cells that recognise the pathogen quickly on subsequent exposure and overwhelm the invaders with a massive production of antibodies.

(i) Hepatitis-B vaccine is produced from which microbes?

Ans. Hepatitis-B vaccine is produced from transgenic yeast by recombinant DNA technology. It is the first commercially available human vaccine that is produced by the genetic engineering technology.

(ii) In which type of immunity, a quick immune response is needed as in tetanus infection, preformed antibodies or antitoxin is injected into the patient body?

Ans. Passive immunity refers to when antibodies are directly injected into the body to generate quick immune response.

Thus, if a person is infected with some deadly microbes to which quick immune response is required as in tetanus, we directly inject the preformed antibodies or antitoxin into the body of the infected person. This is passive immunisation.

(iii) Antivenom injection contains preformed antibodies while polio drops that are administered into the body contain which forms of pathogens?

Ans. Oral polio vaccine contains five polio strains in attenuated forms (pathogens).

(iv) Use of vaccines and immunisation programmes have controlled which of the infectious diseases?

Ans. Vaccines and immunisation programmes were successful for tetanus, diphtheria, pneumonia, etc., are infectious diseases.

3. Direction *Read the following passage and answer the questions that follows.*

Once Gita asked Sarita about her adrenaline and steroid medication. Sarita told Gita that she is allergic to pollens and mites. Sarita also mentioned that she became allergic due to the protected environment provided to her in early life. Upon further conversation, Gita discussed that she is suffering from an autoimmune disease.

(i) Name the antibody which is produced in response to allergens.

Ans. IgE antibody is released in allergic reactions.

(ii) Mention few symptoms of allergic reactions.

Ans. Watery eyes, running nose, wheezing, sneezing, etc., are some symptoms of allergy.

(iii) How adrenaline and steroids would help Gita to relieve allergy?

Ans. Adrenaline and steroids help to suppress histamine and serotonin from the mast cells upon the entry of allergens in body. Thus, the allergic symptoms are either suppressed or reduced.

(iv) What is an autoimmune disease?

Ans. Autoimmune diseases are those in which the body begin to attack self-cells.

(v) Give two examples of autoimmune diseases.

Ans. Examples of autoimmune diseases are rheumatoid arthritis and type I diabetes.

4. The outline structure of a drug is given below.

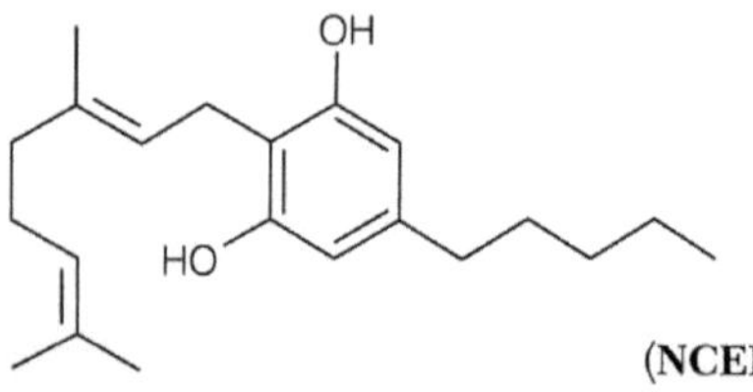

(NCERT Exemplar)

(i) Which group of drugs does this represent?

Ans. The given structure represents cannabinoids group of drugs.

(ii) What are the modes of consumption of these drugs?

Ans. Mode of consumption of these drugs is inhalation or oral ingestion.

(iii) Name the organ of the body which is affected by consumption of these drugs.

Ans. Organ affected by consumption of these drugs is heart. It affects the cardiovascular system.

Chapter Test

Multiple Choice Questions

1. Which one of the following is not correctly matched?
  - (a) *Glossina palpalis* – Sleeping sickness
  - (b) *Culex pipiens* – Filariasis
  - (c) *Aedes aegypti* – Chikungunya
  - (d) *Anopheles culicifacies* – Dengue

2. Which of the following is a symptom of ringworm?
  - (a) Chronic inflammation
  - (b) Abdominal pain
  - (c) Dry and scaly lesions on skin
  - (d) Muscular pain

3. Transplantation of organs in a patient is declared failed. Choose the option which indicates the type of immune response responsible for this reaction.
  - (a) Autoimmunity
  - (b) Humoral immunity
  - (c) Cell-mediated immunity
  - (d) Cytotoxins

4. Which of the following types of vaccine matches with its correct examples?
  - I. Toxoids –Tetanus vaccine
  - II. Attenuated vaccine – BCG vaccine
  - III. Inactive vaccine – MMR vaccine
  - IV. Combinations – DPT vaccine

  Codes
  - (a) I, II and III
  - (b) II, III and IV
  - (c) I, II and IV
  - (d) I, III and IV

5. Which one of the following is correct match?
  - (a) Heroin – Depressant
  - (b) Cocaine – Opiatic narcotic
  - (c) Morphine – Hallucinogenic
  - (d) Tobacco – Psychedelic drug

Assertion-Reasoning MCQs

Direction (Q. Nos. 1-3) *Each of these questions contains two statements, Assertion (A) and Reason (R). Each of these questions also has four alternative choices, any one of which is the correct answer. You have to select one of the codes (a), (b), (c) and (d) given below.*

  - (a) Both A and R are true and R is the correct explanation of A
  - (b) Both A and R are true, but R is not the correct explanation of A
  - (c) A is true, but R is false
  - (d) A is false, but R is true

1. **Assertion** (A) Interferons are a type of antibodies produced by body cells infected by bacteria.

  Reason (R) They interfere with viral replication at the site of injury.

2. **Assertion** (A) AIDS is a disorder caused by HIV.

  Reason (R) HIV is a virus that damages immune system of its host.

3. **Assertion** (A) Cancer cells are virtually immortal until the body in which they reside, die.

  Reason (R) Cancer is caused by damage to gene regulation of the cell division cycle.

Short Answer Type Questions

1. Which causative organisms are responsible for ringworm? List any two symptoms of the disease.

2. List all the types of antibodies produced in our body. Among all, which antibodies are produced during?
  - (i) Allergic reactions
  - (ii) Transfusion reaction/rejection

3. (i) Which agents cause allergy?
  (ii) How does the human body respond to allergens?

4. What are hallucinogens? Give two examples. Mention their clinical use, if any.

5. What are the side effects of anabolic steroids in adult males and adolescents?

Long Answer Type Questions

1. How HIV transmitted in humans? What are the treatment and prevention of AIDS?

2. Explain the effects of alcohol on the
  - (i) kidney
  - (ii) brain
  - (iii) heart
  - (iv) liver
  - (v) immunity

Answers

Multiple Choice Questions

  1. (d)   *2. (c)*   *3. (c)*   *4. (c)*   *5. (a)*

Assertion-Reasoning MCQs

  1. (d)   *2. (a)*   *3. (a)*

For Detailed Solutions
Scan the code

CHAPTER 02

Microbes in Human Welfare

In this Chapter...

- Microbes in Household Products
- Microbes in Industrial Products
- Microbes in Sewage Treatment
- Microbes in Production of Biogas
- Microbes as Biocontrol Agents
- Microbes as Biofertilisers

- **Microbes** are microscopic, single-celled, minute organisms that individually are too small to be seen with naked eyes, i.e. can be seen only under a microscope.
- Microbes constitute major groups of biological systems on the earth, which are present almost everywhere, i.e. in soil, air, water, plants and animals and also even inside our body. These can be found in extreme conditions of pH (alkaline and acidic soil) and temperature (thermal vents or geysers and below the several metre thick snow layers).
- Microbes are diverse group of organisms including protozoans, bacteria, fungi, microscopic plants, viruses, viroids and prions (proteinaceous infectious agents), etc.
- Some microbes cause infections and diseases in human beings, animals and plants. But several microbes are useful to man in diverse ways.
- The microbes like fungi and bacteria can be cultured in laboratory on nutritive media to form colonies that can be seen with the naked eyes.

Microbes in Household Products

Microbes and their products are used in everyday life, e.g. production of curd, formation of dough, cheese, toddy, etc.

Some products produced by microbes are given below

Curd

- Microorganisms like *Lactobacillus* and others commonly called **Lactic Acid Bacteria** (LAB) grow in milk and convert it into curd. We have seen at home that a starter is added to milk which turns it into curd. This starter is known as **inoculum**, which contains millions of LAB.
- During growth, LAB produce acids that coagulate and partially digest the milk proteins. Thus, converting milk to curd. They also improve nutritional quality by increasing vitamin-B_{12} content of the curd. A number of organic acids can also be found in curd.
- LAB also play a beneficial role in checking disease causing microbes in our stomach.

Dough

Microbes are used in making foods such as dosa and idli. The puffed up appearance of their dough is due to the production of CO_2 gas through fermentation by bacteria. In bread making, dough is fermented using baker's yeast, (*Saccharomyces cerevisiae*). It convertes the present sugar into CO_2.

Toddy

It is a traditional drink of some parts of Southern India. It is made by fermenting sap from palm trees, coconut, etc. Microbes are also used to ferment fish, soybean, bamboo shoots, etc., to make food.

Cheese

It is formed by partial degradation of milk by different microorganisms. Different varieties of cheese are known by their texture, flavour and taste. This specificity comes from the microbes used. For example,

(i) **Swiss cheese** with large holes is produced by *Propionibacterium shermanii*. Holes are created due to the production of large amount of CO_2 by this bacterium.

(ii) **Roquefort cheese** are ripened by growing a specific fungi, *Penicillium roqueforti* on them, which gives them a particular flavour.

Microbes in Industrial Products

In industry, microbes are used to make a number of products such as beverages, enzymes and antibiotics, etc., valuable to human beings. Industrial scale production requires growing microbes in very large vessels called **fermentors**.

Fermented Beverages

- Large scale production of beer, brandy, whisky, rum, etc., is done by fermenting malted cereals and fruit juices using unicellular fungi *Saccharomyces cerevisiae* (brewer's yeast).
- Different types of alcoholic drink like wine and beer are produced without distillation. Whisky, brandy and rum are produced by distillation of the fermented broth.

Antibiotics

- These are the chemical substances which are produced by some microbes to kill or retard the growth of other disease causing microbes. **Penicillin** was the first antibiotic to be discovered by **Alexander Fleming**.
- Alexander Fleming observed that if a mould of *Penicillium notatum* grows on a nutrient medium, it does not let a bacterium, *Staphylococcus* grow around it. He then

isolated the chemical produced by the mould and named it penicillin. However, its full potential as an effective antibiotic was established later on by **Ernst Chain** and **Howard Florey**. Penicillin was extensively used in treating American soldiers wounded in World War-II. For this discovery, **Fleming**, **Chain** and **Florey** were awarded the Nobel Prize in 1945.

- Antibiotics are widely used in treating human and animal bacterial diseases. Deadly diseases like plague, whooping cough (kali khansi), diphtheria, leprosy (kusht rog) are completely curable diseases now due to the use of antibiotics.
- One of the most productive sources of antibiotics has been the genus–*Streptomyces* from which many antibiotics have been derived. Some of them are streptomycin, tetracycline, erythromycin, terramycin, which are obtained from *Streptomyces griseus*, *S. aureofaciens*, *S. erethreus* and *S. remosus*, respectively.

Chemicals, Enzymes and Other Bioactive Molecules

Microbes are being used for commercial and industrial production of certain chemicals like alcohols, organic acids, enzymes and other bioactive molecules (which are functional in living systems or can interact with their components). Some of them are given below

Organic Acids Produced by Microbes

Organic acids	Microorganisms
Citric acid	*Aspergillus niger* (fungus)
Acetic acid	*Acetobacter aceti* (bacterium)
Butyric acid	*Clostridium butylicum* (bacterium)
Lactic acid	*Lactobacillus* (bacterium)

Enzymes and their Uses

Enzymes	Uses
Lipases	Used in detergent formulations. They are helpful in removing oily stains from the laundry.
Pectinases and proteases	Used in bottled juices, for clearing of juices.
Streptokinase	Obtained from genetically modified form of bacterium *Streptococcus*. It is used as a 'clot buster' for removing clots from the blood vessels of heart patients, who have undergone myocardial infarction leading to heart attack.

Bioactive Molecules and their Uses

Bioactive molecules (Products)	Micro-organisms	Uses
Cyclosporin-A	*Trichoderma polysporum* (fungus)	As immunosuppressive agent in organ transplant patients.
Statins	*Monascus purpureus* (yeast)	As blood cholesterol lowering agents. It acts by competitively inhibiting enzyme responsible for cholesterol synthesis.

Microbes in Sewage Treatment

- Sewage is the municipal wastewater generated everyday in cities and towns. It contains large amounts of organic matter and many pathogenic microbes. That is why before being disposed, in water bodies, it needs to be treated in **Sewage Treatment Plants** (STPs) to make it less polluting.
- Certain heterotrophic microbes naturally present in sewage are used in its treatment. This treatment is carried out in two stages, i.e. primary treatment and secondary treatment.

Primary Treatment

- In primary treatment, physical removal of particles, i.e. large and small, is done from the sewage through filtration and sedimentation. All solids that settle down, form the **primary sludge** and the supernatant forms the **effluent**, which is taken for secondary treatment.

Secondary Treatment

- In secondary treatment or biological treatment, the primary effluent is passed into large aeration tanks where it is constantly agitated mechanically. This allows the growth of the aerobic microbes into **flocs** (masses of bacteria associated with fungal filaments to form mesh-like structures) which consume the major part of the organic matter in the effluent that significantly reduces the **BOD** (Biochemical Oxygen Demand) of the effluent.
- BOD is the amount of oxygen that would be consumed, if all the organic matter in one litre of water were oxidised by bacteria. The sewage water is treated till the BOD is reduced. The greater is the BOD of wastewater, more is its polluting potential.
- The effluent is then passed into a **settling tank** where the bacterial flocs are allowed to sediment. This sediment is called **activated sludge** as it contains active microbes. From here
  - A small part of the activated sludge is pumped back into the aeration tank to serve as the inoculum.
  - The remaining major part of the sludge is pumped into large tanks called **anaerobic sludge digesters**. Here,

lack of oxygen kills the aerobic bacteria which are digested along with the other biomass by anaerobic bacteria and fungi.
  - The effluent from the secondary treatment plant is generally released into natural water bodies like rivers and streams.
- During digestion of organic matter, bacteria produce a mixture of gases such as methane, hydrogen sulphide and carbon dioxide. These gases form **biogas**, which is inflammable and can be used as a fuel.

River Action Plan

- The ministry of environment and forests has initiated the **Ganga Action Plan** and **Yamuna Action Plan** to save these major rivers of our country from pollution. These plans propose to build a large number of sewage treatment plants, so that only treated sewage may be discharged into the rivers.
- The states involved in Ganga Action Plan are Uttarakhand, UP, Bihar, West Bengal and Jharkhand.

Microbes in Production of Biogas

- **Biogas** is a mixture of gases, but the major content is methane gas. It is produced by the anaerobic microbial activity during digestion of biomass with the help of certain bacteria. Biogas is used as fuel.
- The type of gas produced by microbes during their growth and metabolism depends upon the microbes and the organic substrates they utilise. Certain bacteria, which grow anaerobically on cellulosic material, produce large amount of methane along with CO_2 and H_2. These bacteria are called **methanogens** and one such common bacterium is *Methanobacterium*. Methanogens produce large amount of biogas [CH_4 (50-70%), CO_2 (30-40%) and H_2 (remaining)].
- Methanogens are also present in anaerobic sludge during sewage treatment. They are also present in rumen (a part of stomach) of cattle, where they help in breakdown of cellulosic material in the food and thus, play important role in nutrition of cattle.

Biogas Plant

- The excreta of cattle commonly called **gobar,** is rich in methanogenic bacteria. Thus, cattle dung can be used for generation of biogas, commonly called **gobar gas**.
- **Cattle dung** is available in large quantities in rural areas hence, biogas plants are mostly functional in rural areas.
- **Biogas plant** consists of a concrete tank (10-15 feet deep) in which biowastes are collected and slurry of dung is fed. A floating cover is placed over the slurry, which keeps on rising, as the gas is produced in the tank due to the microbial activity.

- *Methanobacterium* in the dung acts on the biowaste to produce biogas. An outlet is also present which connects to a pipe that supply biogas to the nearby houses. The biogas thus produced is used for cooking and lighting.
- There is another outlet from which spent slurry is removed that can be used as fertiliser. Biogas production technology was developed in India mainly by **Khadi and Village Industries Commission** (KVIC) and **Indian Agricultural Research Institute** (IARI).

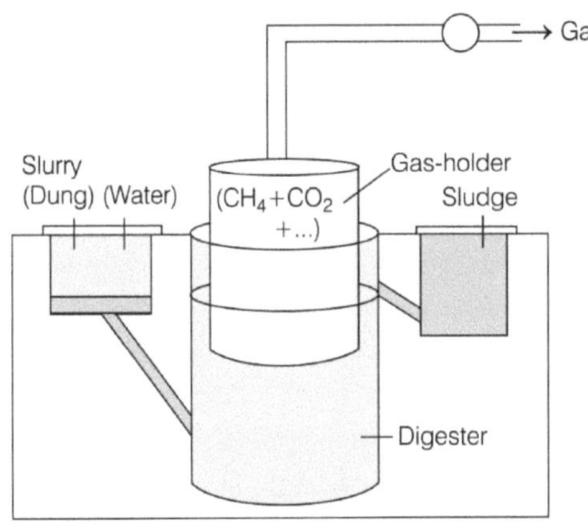

A typical biogas plant

Microbes as Biocontrol Agents

Biocontrol refers to the use of biological methods for controlling various plant diseases and pests. This method is employed because the long time use of chemical insecticides, pesticides and weedicides has been proved to be harmful for all living organisms and the environment (air, water, soil, etc).

Biological Control of Pests and Diseases

- The use of biocontrol measures has become more preferable since it greatly reduces our dependence on toxic chemicals. Here, pests can be controlled by making use of natural predation rather than chemicals.
- Biocontrol involves creation of a system where the insects/pests are not eradicated rather are kept at manageable levels by a system of check and balances within ecosystem. Various microbes can be used as **biocontrol agents**, e.g.
  - Aphids and mosquitoes can be controlled by ladybird beetle and dragonflies, respectively.
  - Butterfly caterpillars can be killed by using the bacteria *Bacillus thuringiensis* (*Bt*). *Bt* is available as dried spores which are mixed with water and sprayed on to plants such as brassicas and fruit trees, where these are eaten by the insect larvae. In the gut of the larvae, the toxin is released and the larvae get killed. This will kill the caterpillars, but leave other insects unharmed.

  - **Fungi** (like *Trichoderma* sp., a free-living fungi that are common in root ecosystems) are effective against several fungal plant pathogens.
  - **Viruses** (like baculoviruses belonging to genus-*Nucleopolyhedrovirus*) are excellent for species specific narrow spectrum insecticides. These do not have negative impact on non-target insects and have narrow spectrum insecticidal applications.
- **Integrated Pest Management** (IPM) is an environmentally sensitive and effective approach of pest management that uses information on life cycles of organisms and their interaction with environment. The integrated pest management is done to control insects and pests of plants, animals and humans.

Microbes as Biofertilisers

- To cut down the pollution caused by chemical fertilisers, it is important to switch to **organic farming** (raising crops through the use of components of biological origin, e.g. **biofertilisers**).
- Biofertilisers are organisms, e.g. bacteria, fungi and cyanobacteria that enrich the nutrient quality of the soil.

The main sources of biofertilisers are as follows

Bacteria

Nitrogen-fixing bacteria fix atmospheric nitrogen into organic form, which is used by the plant as nutrient, e.g. *Rhizobium* is a symbiotic bacterium that lives in the root nodules of legumes and fixes atmospheric nitrogen into organic compounds.

Azotobacter and *Azospirillum* are free-living bacteria, which absorb free nitrogen from the soil, air and convert it into salts of nitrogen compounds.

Fungi

They also form symbiotic association with plants, i.e. **mycorrhiza**, which absorb phosphorus from soil and passes it to the plants. Many members of genus–*Glomus* form mycorrhiza. Plants with mycorrhizal association show other benefits also such as
  (i) Resistance to root-borne pathogens.
  (ii) Tolerance to salinity and drought.
  (iii) Increase in plant growth and development.

Cyanobacteria

These are autotrophic microbes found in aquatic and terrestrial environments. Most of them fix atmospheric nitrogen, e.g. *Anabaena, Nostoc, Oscillatoria*, etc. In paddy fields, cyanobacteria serve as important biofertiliser. Blue-Green Algae (BGA) also add organic matter to the soil. Thus, increasing its fertility, but still BGA are not very popularly used.

Chapter Practice

Objective Questions

• Multiple Choice Questions

1. Curd is formed by adding a small amount of curd to milk. This small amount is referred to as inoculum
(a) True
(b) False
(c) Cannot say
(d) Partially true or false

Ans. (a) Given statement is true as

Curd is formed by adding a small amount of curd to milk. This small amount of curd is referred to as starter or inoculum, which contains million of Lactic Acid Bacteria (LAB).

2. Conversion of milk to curd improves its nutritional value by increasing the amount of
(a) vitamin-D
(b) vitamin-E
(c) vitamin-B_{12}
(d) vitamin-A

Ans. (c) Milk is converted to curd by certain bacteria called lactic acid bacteria.

These bacteria, during the process of curdling of milk, also increase its nutritive value by increasing the amount of vitamin-B_{12}.

3. Big holes in Swiss cheese are formed as a result of
(NCERT Exemplar)
(a) machine used for making the cheese
(b) a bacterium producing a large amount of carbon dioxide
(c) a bacterium that is visible to naked eyes
(d) a fungus that produces large amount of carbon dioxide

Ans. (b) Big holes in Swiss cheese are formed by a large amount of carbon dioxide (CO_2) produced by a bacterium called *Propionibacterium shermanii*.

4. Match the following columns.

	Column I		Column II
A.	*Lactobacillus*	1.	Roquefort cheese
B.	*Saccharomyces cerevisiae*	2.	Swiss cheese
C.	*Propionibacterium shermanii*	3.	Bread
D.	*Penicillium roqueforti*	4.	Milk into curd

Codes

	A	B	C	D			A	B	C	D
(a)	4	3	2	1		(b)	3	2	1	4
(c)	4	1	2	3		(d)	1	4	3	2

Ans. (a) A–4, B–3, C–2, D–1

5. Which of the following organisms is used in the production of beverages like wine, beer, whisky brandy or rum?
(a) *Clostridium butylicum*
(b) *Aspergillus niger*
(c) *Saccharomyces cerevisiae*
(d) *Penicillium notatum*

Ans. (c) A yeast, *Saccharomyces cerevisiae* is used in the production of alcoholic beverages like wine, beer, whisky, brandy or rum. It is also known as Brewer's yeast.

6. Which one of the following antibiotics was extensively used to treat American soldiers wounded in World War-II?
(a) Streptokinase
(b) Neomycin
(c) Stains
(d) Penicillin

Ans. (d) During World War-II, penicillin was used to treat the wounds of American soldiers.

7. The BOD test measures the rate of uptake of oxygen by microbes in water bodies. The greater BOD of sample water, indicates that
(a) it is highly polluted
(b) it is not polluted
(c) it is moderately polluted
(d) pollution level cannot be determined

Ans. (*a*) BOD is a measure of the organic matter present in water. Thus, greater the value of BOD in a sample of water, more will be its polluting potential. This indicates that the water body is highly polluted.

8. In the sewage treatment, bacterial flocs are allowed to sediment in a settling tank. This sediment is called as
(a) activated sludge (b) primary sludge
(c) anaerobic sludge (d) secondary sludge

Ans. (*a*) In the sewage treatment, when Biochemical Oxygen Demand (BOD) of sewage has reduced, the effluent is passed into settling tank. Here, the bacterial flocs settle and the sediment thus formed is called activated sludge.

9. Given below is the flowchart of sewage treatment. Identify *A*, *B*, *C*, *D* and *E* and select the correct option.

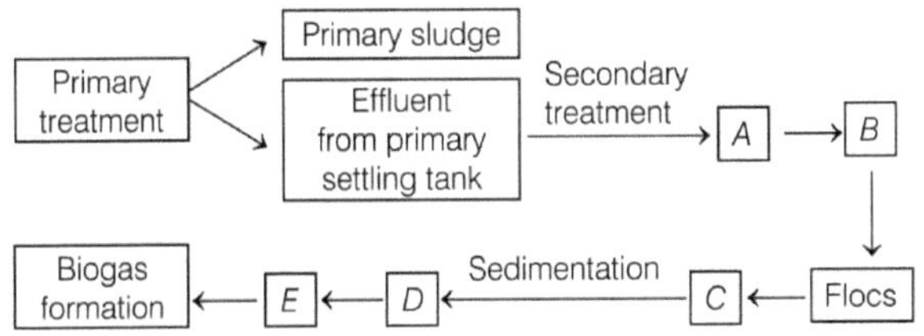

(a) *A*–Small aeration tank, *B*–Microbial digestion, *C*–High BOD, *D*–Activated sludge, *E*–Aerobic sludge digesters
(b) *A*–Large aeration tank, *B*–Mechanical agitation, *C*–Increased BOD, *D*–Activated sludge, *E*–Aerobic sludge digesters
(c) *A*–Small aeration tank, *B*–Microbial digestion, *C*–Low BOD, *D*–Activated sludge, *E*–Anaerobic sludge digesters
(d) *A*–Large aeration tank, *B*–Mechanical agitation, *C*–Reduced BOD, *D*–Activated sludge, *E*–Anaerobic sludge digesters

Ans. (*d*)

10. The most flammable gaseous component of biogas is
(a) methane
(b) methane, CO_2, H_2 and H_2S
(c) CO_2, H_2 and H_2S
(d) CO, methane and N_2

Ans. (*a*) The most flammable gaseous component of biogas is methane.

11. The diagram given below represents a typical biogas plant. Select the correct option for *A*, *B* and *C*, respectively.

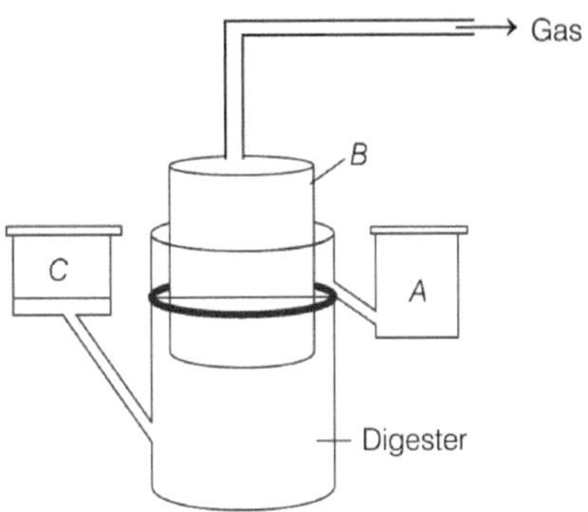

(a) *A*–Sludge, *B*–Dung + Water, *C*– Gas holder
(b) *A*–Dung + Water, *B*–Sludge, *C*–$CH_4 + CO_2$
(c) *A*–Sludge, *B*–Gas holder, *C*–Dung + Water
(d) *A*–$CH_4 + CO_2$, *B*–Dung + Water, *C*–Sludge

Ans. (*c*)

12. Organic farming includes
(a) use of fertilisers and pesticides of biological origin
(b) IPM (Integrated Pest Management)
(c) locally developed pest resistant varieties
(d) All of the above

Ans. (*d*) Organic farming includes several methods to enhance soil fertility. In such farming, methods of biological origin are used, e.g. biopesticides, biofertilisers, IPM (Integrated Pest Management), locally developed pest resistant varieties, green manure, etc.

Thus, option (d) is correct.

13. Which weed has been eradicated by biological control?
(a) *Parthenium*
(b) Cactus
(c) *Eichhornia*
(d) *Chrysanthemum*

Ans. (*b*) Cactus has been eradicated by the method of biological control. It was done by introducing the cochineal insect, *Cactoblastis cactorum*. The insect is a type of moth which exceptionally feeds on the cactus plant.

14. Which one of the following is not a nitrogen-fixation organism?

(a) *Anabaena*   (b) *Nostoc*
(c) *Azotobacter*   (d) *Pseudomonas*

Ans. (*d*) *Pseudomonas* is a denitrifying bacteria, which converts ammonia and nitrates into free nitrogen, i.e. librate free nitrogen in the environment through nitrogen cycle. Therefore, it is not a nitrogen-fixation organism.

15. Blue-green algae are mainly used as biofertilisers in the field of which crop?

(a) Gram   (b) Millet   (c) Rice   (d) Maize

Ans. (*c*) Blue-green algae used as biofertilisers in the field of rice or paddy. It increases the fertility by nitrogen-fixation.

• Assertion-Reasoning MCQs

Direction (Q. Nos. 1-5) *Each of these questions contains two statements, Assertion (A) and Reason (R). Each of these questions also has four alternative choices, any one of which is the correct answer. You have to select one of the codes (a), (b), (c) and (d) given below.*

(a) Both A and R are true and R is the correct explanation of A

(b) Both A and R are true, but R is not the correct explanation of A

(c) A is true, but R is false

(d) A is false, but R is true

1. Assertion (A) Yeasts such as *Saccharomyces cerevisiae* are used in baking industry.

Reason (R) Carbon dioxide produced during fermentation causes bread dough to rise by thermal expansion.

Ans. (*b*) Both A and R are true and R is not the correct explanation of A.

2. Assertion (A) Beer and wine are called soft liquours.

Reason (R) These beverages have lower percentage of alcohol.

Ans. (*a*) Both A and R are true and R is the correct explanation of A.

3. Assertion (A) Biogas is used as fuel for cooking and lighting.

Reason (R) It is considered as an ecofriendly and a pollution free source of energy.

Ans. (*b*) Both A and R are true, but R is not the correct explanation of A.

Biogas is used as fuel for heating, cooking, lighting because it is flammable. It is an alternative of firewood, kerosene, etc., and acts as an ecofriendly and a pollution free source of energy.

4. Assertion (A) Disadvantages of synthetic pesticides can be overcome by the use of biopesticides.

Reason (R) Biopesticides control weeds and pest without causing any damage to living organisms.

Ans. (*a*) Both A and R are true and R is the correct explanation of A.

Synthetic pesticides are chemicals which have several disadvantages such as their high cost, long term pollution, toxicity and tendency to accumulate in living organisms, etc. These disadvantages can be overcome by the use of biopesticides that are simple components of biological origin because these cause no damage or toxicity in living organisms.

5. Assertion (A) Chemical pesticides are preferred over biopesticides.

Reason (R) These are mostly expensive, hazardous and pollute the atmosphere.

Ans. (*d*) A is false, but R is true. A can be corrected as Chemical pesticides are not preferred over biopesticides. This is because chemical fertilisers are generally more expensive and hazardous in nature. These unnecessarily pollute the natural resources like soil and water.

• Case Based MCQ

1. Direction *Read the following passage and answer the questions that follows.*

In modern agricultural system, the farmers have increased the use of chemicals such as insecticides, weedicides, etc., to control plant diseases and pests. These chemicals however, are harmful and toxic for human beings, animals and have been polluting environment (soil, groundwater), fruits, vegetables and crop plants, with their increased use. Thus, it is better to use biological agents to save our crop plants from pests, etc. Biocontrol refers to the use of biological methods for controlling plant diseases and pests.

(i) Which of the following can be used as a biocontrol agent in the treatment of plant disease?

(a) *Chlorella*   (b) *Anabaena*
(c) *Lactobacillus*   (d) *Trichoderma*

Ans. (*d*) *Trichoderma* can be used as a biocontrol agent of several plant pathogens. It is a filamentous soil fungus having mycoparasitic activity.

(ii) *Bacillus thuringiensis* is used as

(a) biofungicide   (b) biopesticide
(c) biocontrol agent   (d) bioweapon

Ans. (*c*) *Bacillus thuringiensis* is a soil bacterium used as biocontrol agent that can control infestations by insect pests such as butterfly, caterpillars, ants, moths, etc. Some strains of these bacteria can kill animal and plant parasitic nematodes, snails, protozoans, etc.

(iii) A biocontrol agent to be a part of an integrated pest management should be
    (a) species-specific and symbiotic
    (b) free-living and broad spectrum
    (c) narrow spectrum and symbiotic
    (d) species-specific and inactive on non-target organisms

Ans. (*d*) For a biocontrol agent to be a part of an Integrated Pest Management (IPM) programme, it should be species-specific and inactive or have no negative impacts on non-target organisms like plants, mammals, birds, fish and even another non-target insects. It should kill only targeted insects/pests (organisms).

(iv) Which of the following statements is correct with reference to biocontrol agents?
    (a) Ladybird and dragonflies help in getting rid of aphids and mosquitoes, respectively
    (b) *Nucleopolyhedrovirus* are considered the best candidates to be the part of IPM
    (c) *Trichoderma* are free-living fungi
    (d) All of the above

Ans. (*d*) All the given statements are correct with reference to biocontrol agents.

(v) **Assertion** (A) Biocontrol refers to the use of biological methods for controlling pests and diseases.

Reason (R) Our dependence on toxins and chemicals will remain same even after introduction of biocontrol agents.
    (a) Both A and R are true and R is the correct explanation of A
    (b) Both A and R are true, but R is not the correct explanation of A
    (c) A is true, but R is false
    (d) Both A and R are false

Ans. (*c*) A is true, but R is false because

Biocontrol is the use of biological methods for controlling pests and diseases. Adopting biocontrol agents will actually reduce our dependence on toxins and chemicals which cause harm to the environment.

PART 2
Subjective Questions

• Short Answer (SA) Type Questions

1. In which food would you find lactic acid bacteria? Mention some of their useful applications. **(NCERT)**

Ans. Generally, Lactic Acid Bacteria (LAB) are found in milk and its products.

Some useful applications of LAB are
- LAB play very beneficial role in checking disease causing microbes in our stomach.
- They also improve nutritional quality by increasing vitamin-B_{12} content of the curd.

2. Write the name of bacterium which is involved in setting milk into curd. Explain the process they carry in doing so. Write another beneficial role played by such bacteria.

Ans. Microorganisms like *Lactobacillus* and other commonly called Lactic Acid Bacteria (LAB) grow in milk and convert it into curd.

In this process, a small amount of starter is added to milk which turns it into curd. This starter is known as **inoculum**, which contains millions of LAB. These LAB produce acids that coagulate and partially digest the milk proteins. Thus, converting milk to curd. These bacteria also improve the nutritional quality by increasing vitamin-B_{12} content in curd. A number of organic acids can also be found in curd.

LAB also play very beneficial role in checking disease causing microbes in our stomach.

3. Name some traditional Indian food made of wheat, rice and Bengal gram, which involve use of microbes. **(NCERT)**

Ans. Some Indian traditional food made of wheat, rice and Bengal gram are
Wheat–Bhature and nan
Rice–Idli and dosa
Bengal gram–Dhokla and khandvi

4. Make a list of three household products along with the names of the microorganisms producing them. **(All India 2016)**

Ans. The three household products along with the names of the microorganisms producing them are as given below

    Items Microorganisms
    (i) Curd – *Lactobacillus*
    (ii) Bread – *Saccharomyces cerevisiae*
    (iii) Swiss cheese – *Propionibacterium shermanii*

5. Give examples to prove that microbes release gases during metabolism.

Ans. Release of gases by microbes during metabolic activities can be justified by the following examples
    (i) Puffed up appearance of dough, is due to the production of CO_2 gas through fermentation by bacteria.
    (ii) Swiss cheese has large holes due to production of CO_2.
    (iii) Methanogens produce methane.

6. Write a note on fermentation by microbes and its applications.

Ans. Fermentation is the process of conversion of carbohydrates to alcohol and CO_2 by some microorganisms in the absence of O_2. Microbes *via* fermentation are utilised for the synthesis of a number of products valuable for human beings.

Some of the applications of fermentation by microbes are

(i) Production of bread using baker's yeast.

(ii) Microbes are used to ferment fish, soybean, bamboo shoots, etc.

(iii) Different varieties of cheese are produced by fermentation *via* microbes.

(iv) Wine, beer and other alcoholic drinks are also produced by fermentation.

(v) Vinegar is also produced by fermentation.

7. In which way, microbes have played a major role in controlling diseases caused by harmful bacteria? **(NCERT)**

Ans. Microbes play major role in controlling diseases by harmful bacteria as they are used in preparing medicines. The most important medicines for which microbes are used, are antibiotics. These are chemical compounds produced by some microbes, which are used to kill or to subside the growth of other diseases causing microbes. Streptomycin, tetracycline and penicillin are some of the commonly used antibiotics. Antibiotics have significantly contributed towards the welfare of the human society.

8. Read the statements given below and identify them as true or false. Also, correct the statements which are false.

(i) *Lactobacillus acidophilus* is used in fermentation of milk.

(ii) LAB is grown on molasses and sold as a food flavouring agent.

(iii) Ernst Chain and Howard Florey discovered antibiotic penicillin.

Ans. (i) True

(ii) False, yeast is grown on molasses and sold as a flavouring agent because it produces a characteristic smell and taste in food.

(iii) False, Alexander Fleming discovered penicillin. Ernst Chain and H Florey discovered the full potential of this antibiotic.

9. Following is the list of some commercially important products. Give the name of microorganisms responsible for producing each of these products.

(i) Citric acid

(ii) Acetic acid

(iii) Butyric acid

(iv) Lactic acid

Ans. Microorganisms (microbes) responsible for producing each of these products are

	Organic acids	Microorganisms (Microbes)
(i)	Citric acid	*Aspergillus niger* (fungus)
(ii)	Acetic acid	*Acetobacter aceti* (bacterium)
(iii)	Butyric acid	*Clostridium butylicum* (bacterium)
(iv)	Lactic acid	*Lactobacillus* (bacterium)

10. Which enzymes play an important role in detergents that we use for washing clothes?

Ans. Enzymes like lipases are used in detergents formulations which causes breakdown of oils and thus help in removing oily and greasy stains from the clothes. These enzymes are obtained from *Candida lipolytica* and *Geotrichum candidum*.

11. Name the enzyme produced by *Streptococcus* bacterium. Explain its importance in medical sciences.

Ans. Streptokinase enzyme is produced by the bacterium, *Streptococcus*. It is modified by genetic engineering and is used as a clot buster for removing clots from the blood vessels of patients who have suffered from myocardial infarction.

12. Why are some molecules called bioactive molecules? Give two examples of such molecules. **(All India 2011)**

Ans. Bioactive molecules are produced from microbes that are useful to other living organisms in modifying their metabolism, e.g. streptokinase, cyclosporin-A, statins, etc.

13. Find out the name of microbes from which cyclosporin-A and statins are obtained. **(NCERT)**

Ans. (i) Cyclosporin-A is obtained from the fungus, *Trichoderma polysporum*.

(ii) Statins is obtained from yeast, *Monascus purpureus*.

14. How has fungus, *Trichoderma polysporum* proved to be very essential to organ transplant patients?

Ans. Fungus, *Trichoderma polysporum* is used to produce cyclosporin-A which act as an immunosuppressive agent during transplantation. They supress the immune system of patient, so that it does not act against the organ transplanted.

15. (i) Match the microbes listed under Column I with the products mentioned under Column II.

	Column I		Column II
A.	*Penicillium notatum*	1.	Statin
B.	*Trichoderma polysporum*	2.	Ethanol
C.	*Monascus purpureus*	3.	Antibiotic
D.	*Saccharomyces cerevisiae*	4.	Cyclosporin-A

(ii) Why is distillation required for producing certain alcoholic drinks?

Ans. (i) The correct matches are as follows

Column I		Column II
A. *Penicillium notatum*	1.	Antibiotic
B. *Trichoderma polysporum*	2.	Cyclosporin-A
C. *Monascus purpureus*	3.	Statin
D. *Saccharomyces cerevisiae*	4.	Ethanol

(ii) Distillation is required to increase the alcohol content in alcoholic drinks. Whiskey, brandy and rum are produced by this process.

16. How do bioactive molecules of fungal origin help in restoring good health of humans?

Ans. Some bioactive molecules of fungal origin have been reported for their role in restoring good health of humans. For example, **cyclosporin-A** that is used as an immunosuppressive agent in organ transplant patients is produced by the fungus, *Trichoderma polysporum*. **Statins** produced by yeast, *Monascus purpureus* have been commercialised as blood cholesterol lowering agents.

17. What is sewage? In which way, it is harmful for us?
(**NCERT**)

Ans. Sewage is the municipal wastewater collected from city or town homes that contain toilet, bathroom and kitchen waste. It contains large amounts of organic matter and many pathogenic microbes which are harmful to humans as they can cause diseases like cholera, typhoid, polio, etc.

18. During the secondary treatment of primary effluents, how does a significant decrease in BOD occur? (**Delhi 2009**)

Or

List the events that reduce the Biological Oxygen Demand (BOD) of a primary effluent during sewage treatment. (**Delhi 2016**)

Ans. During secondary treatment, the primary effluent is passed into large aeration tanks where it is constantly agitated mechanically and air is pumped into it which allows vigorous growth of useful aerobic microbes into flocs, i.e. masses of bacterial cells in association with fungal filaments, forming mesh-like structure. As they grow, the microbes consume a major part of the organic matter in the effluent, which significantly reduces BOD.

19. Distinguish between the roles of flocs and anaerobic sludge digesters in sewage treatments. (**Delhi 2016**)

Ans. In sewage treatment, flocs consume major part of the organic matter, converting it into microbial biomass and releasing lot of minerals. It reduces the BOD of sewage. While in anaerobic sludge digesters, many anaerobic bacteria are present, which digest the organic mass as well as aerobic microbes. During this digestion, methane, CO_2, etc., are produced.

20. Why is aerobic degradation more important than anaerobic degradation for the treatment of large volumes of wastewaters rich in organic matter. Discuss.

Ans. Aerobic degradation is more important than anaerobic degradation because naturally occurring aerobic and facultative microbes (bacteria, fungi, Protozoa and others) in the wastewater can rapidly oxidise soluble organic and nitrogenous compounds. Mechanical addition of oxygen makes the process faster and most of the pathogenic content of the effluent is removed.

21. 'Determination of Biological Oxygen Demand (BOD) can help in suggesting the quality of a water body'. Explain.

Ans. BOD refers to the amount of oxygen that would be consumed if all the organic matter in one litre of water were oxidised by bacteria. The microbes biodegrade the major part of the organic matter in the effluent by using the dissolved oxygen. It reduces the BOD of the effluent.

When the BOD of sewage is reduced significantly the effluent is passed into a settling tank where the bacterial flocs are allowed to sediment forming the activated sludge. Thus, higher the value of BOD, more is the water polluted and more is the amount of biodegradable matter.

22. How is primary sludge is different from activated sludge?

Ans. Primary sludge is different from activated sludge as primary sludge includes all solid substances which get setteled after primary treatment. It traps lots of microbes and debris while activated sludge is the sediment formed from effluent after secondary treatment which contains bacterial flocs. (2)

23. What is the key difference between primary and secondary sewage treatment? (**NCERT**)

Ans. Differences between primary and secondary sewage treatment are as follows

Primary sewage treatment	Secondary sewage treatment
It is a physical process.	It is a biological process.
It involves physical removal of solid material.	It involves the action of microbes.
It is less complicated and not expensive.	It is a complicated and an expensive process.

24. Give the name of the two different categories of microbes naturally occurring in sewage water. Explain their role in cleaning sewage water into usable water. (**Delhi 2012**)

Ans. Two different categories of microbes naturally occurring in sewage water are aerobic and anaerobic microbes.

(i) **Role of aerobic microbes in cleaning water**
Aerobic microbes grow excessively in the aeration

tank and consumes a major part of the organic matter. It helps in reducing the BOD of the effluent.

(ii) **Role of anaerobic microbes in cleaning water** In the settling tank, anaerobic microbes digest the aerobic bacteria and fungi and produce gases like CH_4, CO_2, H_2S, etc. It makes the water less polluted to be released in the water bodies.

25. (i) What would happen if a large volume of untreated sewage is discharged into a river?

(ii) In what way, anaerobic sludge diagestion is important in sewage treatments?

Ans. (i) If untreated sewage is discharged directly into rivers it will lead to serious pollution of the waters with organic matter and pathogenic bacteria, Protozoa and many other diseases.
This water, if used, will cause outbreaks of water borne diseases.

(ii) In anaerobic sludge digestion, anaerobic bacteria, digest the aerobic bacteria and the fungi in the sludge and the remaining organic matter.

During this digestion, bacteria produce a mixture of gases such as methane, hydrogen sulphide and carbon dioxide. These gases (biogas) can be used as source of energy as it is inflammable.

26. Do you think microbes can be used as a source of energy? If yes how? **(NCERT)**

Ans. Yes, microbes can be used as a source of energy, e.g. methanogens like *Methanobacterium* are used to produce biogas, which is a source of energy.

27. Why are biogas plants considered more beneficial in rural areas?

Ans. The raw material for the biogas plant is mainly cow dung, which is available in plenty in rural areas where cattle are used. The biogas is used for lighting and cooking in these areas, as distribution is only in short distances. The spent slurry from the biogas plant is used as manure in agriculture; hence biogas plants are more suitable in rural areas.

28. What are methanogens? How do they help to generate biogas? **(All India 2015)**

Ans. Bacteria which grow anaerobically on cellulosic material, produce large amounts of methane along with CO_2 and H_2 are called **methanogens** (one of the common bacterium is *Methanobacterium*).

Methanogens are found in anaerobic sludge and in rumen of cattle. These methanogens are grown in slurry which comprises of cattle dung, they act upon it by breaking it down and release gases like methane and CO_2. Hence, methanogens help to generate biogas.

29. Name a genus of baculovirus. Why are they considered good biocontrol agents? **(All India 2016)**

Or Describe the role of *Nucleopolyhedrovirus*, in the integrated pest management programmes.
(All India 2011)

Ans. A genus of baculoviruses is *Nucleopolyhedrovirus*.

They are considered good biological control agents because of their species-specific and narrow spectrum insecticidal applications. They do not have any negative impact on plants, mammals, birds, fish or even on non-target insects.

Thus, making them useful in overall integrated pest management programme.

30. Given below is a list of six microorganisms. State their usefulness to humans.

(i) *Nucleopolyhedrovirus*
(ii) *Saccharomyces cerevisiae*
(iii) *Monascus purpureus*
(iv) *Trichoderma polysporum*
(v) *Penicillium notatum*
(vi) *Propionibacterium shermanii* **(Delhi 2016)**

Ans. (i) *Nucleopolyhedrovirus* is widely used biopesticide in crop fields.

(ii) *Saccharomyces cerevisiae* commonly called **brewer's yeast**, is used for fermenting malted cereals and fruit juices to ethanol.

(iii) Statins are produced by yeast, *Monascus purpureus*. These have been commercialised as blood cholesterol lowering agents.

(iv) Cyclosporin-A is produced by the fungus, *Trichoderma polysporum* and it is used as an immunosuppressive agent in case of organ transplants.

(v) *Penicillium notatum* is used for the production of penicillin.

(vi) *Propionibacterium shermanii* is used to produce Swiss cheese.

31. Why do organic farmers do not recommend eradication of insect-pests? Explain giving reason. **(Delhi 2009)**

Ans. Organic farmers do not recommend eradication of insect-pests as without them, the beneficial predatory and parasitic insects which depend upon pests as food or hosts would not be able to survive.

32. (i) How do organic farmers control pests? Give two examples.

(ii) State the difference in their approach from that of conventional pest control methods. **(All India 2016)**

Ans. (i) The organic farmers control pests by the use of insect pests resistant varieties. The two examples are

(a) The Pusa Gaurav variety of *Brassica* is resistant to aphids.

(b) Pusa Sawani variety of okra is resistant to shoot and fruit borer.

(ii) The use of resistant variety is safer to control the pests as it does not involve chemical pesticides which are used in conventional method of controlling pests. Thus, it is environmental friendly method and reduce soil pollution.

33. Microbes can be used to decrease the use of chemical fertilisers and pesticides. Explain how this can be accomplished. **(NCERT)**

Ans. Microbes can be used to decrease the use of chemical fertilisers and pesticides as

(i) Microbes play an important role in organic farming, which reduce the use of chemical fertilisers and pesticides, etc.

(ii) They act as biofertilisers which help in increasing the fertility of the soil. They also help in improving plant growth by supplying plant nutrients. Many species of bacteria and cyanobacteria help in fixing the nitrogen in the soil.

(iii) Many biological agents like ladybird and *Bacillus thuringiensis*, etc., are useful in eradicating pests.

34. How do biofertilisers enrich the fertility of the soil? **(NCERT)**

Ans. The main sources of biofertilisers are bacteria, fungi and cyanobacteria. They help in enriching the fertility of the soil in many ways

(i) *Rhizobium* that forms nodules on the roots of leguminous plants (a symbiotic association) fixes atmospheric nitrogen into organic forms, which is used by the plant as nutrient.

(ii) *Azospirillum* and *Azotobacter* fix atmospheric nitrogen, while living freely and enriching the nitrogen content of the soil.

(iii) Many members of the genus–*Glomus* (fungi) form symbiotic associations with plant known as mycorrhiza that

(a) absorb phosphorus from soil and pass it to the plant.

(b) help the plants to develop resistance to root-borne pathogens.

(iv) *Cyanobacteria* autotrophic microbes, e.g. *Anabaena, Nostoc, Oscillatoria* can fix atmospheric nitrogen in aquatic and terrestrial environment and also add organic matter to the soil and increase its fertility.

35. Why is *Rhizobium* categorised as a symbiotic bacterium? How does it act as a biofertiliser? **(Delhi 2012)**

Ans. *Rhizobium* lives in the root nodules of leguminous plants and fixes the atmospheric nitrogen in the soil as nitrogenous compounds that can be utilised by the plants as nutrients. Since, both are mutually benefitted, it is called symbiotic bacterium. Hence, *Rhizobium* acts as a biofertiliser.

36. How does the application of the fungal genus– *Glomus*, to the agricultural farm increase the farm output?

Ans. The application of *Glomus* to agricultural field increases the farm output by increasing the nutrient availability to the crops. *Glomus* develops symbiotic association with the roots of plants, called mycorrhiza. It absorbs phosphorus from the soil and passes it to the plants it associates with. In return, it derives sugars from the host plant cells for its survival.

37. How does the application of cyanobacteria help to improve agricultural output?

Ans. Cyanobacteria are autotrophic microbes found in aquatic and terrestrial environments. Most of these fix atmospheric nitrogen, e.g. *Anabaena, Nostoc, Oscillatoria*, etc.

In paddy fields, cyanobacteria serve as important biofertiliser. They also add organic matter to the soil, thus increasing the fertility.

38. Name two organisms belonging to two different kingdoms that are commonly used as biofertilisers and how ? **(Delhi 2020)**

Ans. The two microorganisms belonging to two different kingdoms that are commonly used as biofertiliser are

1. **Fungi**

Many members of genus–*Glomus* form mycorrhiza. Plants with mycorrhizal association show benefits such as

(i) Resistance to root-borne pathogens.

(ii) Tolerance to salinity and drought.

(iii) Increase in plant growth and development.

2. **Bacteria**

Nitrogen-fixing bacteria fix atmospheric nitrogen into organic form, which is used by the plant as nutrient, e.g. *Rhizobium* is a symbiotic bacterium that lives in the root nodules of legumes and fixes atmospheric nitrogen into organic compounds. *Azotobacter* and *Azospirillum* are free-living bacteria, which absorb free nitrogen from the soil, air and convert it into salts of nitrogen compounds.

39. Choose any three microbes, from the following, which are suited for organic farming which is in great demand these days for various reasons. Mention one application of each one chosen.

Mycorrhiza, *Monascus, Anabaena, Rhizobium Methanobacterium, Trichoderma*   **(Delhi 2015)**

Ans. The three microbes that can be chosen for organic farming are

(i) ***Rhizobium*** The nodules on the roots of leguminous plants are formed by the symbiotic association of *Rhizobium* bacteria. These bacteria fix atmospheric nitrogen into organic forms, which is used by the plants as nutrient.

(ii) **Mycorrhiza** Fungi form symbiotic association with plants called mycorrhiza. The fungal symbiont absorbs phosphorus from soil and passes it to the plant. Such plant shows resistance to root-borne pathogens, tolerance to salinity and drought and overall increase in plant growth and development.

(iii) ***Anabaena*** It is a cyanobacteria that is used as a biofertiliser. It fixes atmospheric nitrogen.

• Long Answer (LA) Type Questions

1. Explain the process of sewage water treatment before it can be discharged into natural water bodies. Why is this treatment essential?

(All India 2014)

Ans. The sewage treatment is essential before being released into water bodies as it leads to water pollution and as a consequence increased incidence of waterborne diseases.

This treatment is carried out in two stages

Primary Treatment
It is also known as **physical treatment** because it basically involves physical removal of small and large, floating and suspended solids from sewage through filtration and sedimentation. Initially, floating debris is removed by sequential filtration.

Then, the **grit** (soil and small pebbles) are removed by sedimentation in settling tanks. Aluminium or iron sulphate is added in certain places for flocculation.

All solids that settle form the **primary sludge**. It traps lots of microbes and debris. The supernatant forms the **effluent**. This effluent is then taken from the primary settling tank for secondary treatment.

Secondary Treatment
This treatment is also known as **biological treatment** because it involves the use of microbes or microbiota for the treatment of sewage.

• The effluent from primary treatment is passed into large aeration tanks, where it is constantly, mechanically agitated and air is pumped into it which helps in the growth of useful aerobic microbes into **flocs**. While growing, these microbes consume major part of the organic matter converting it into microbial

biomass and releasing lot of minerals. This significantly reduces the **Biochemical Oxygen Demand** (BOD). The sewage water is treated till the BOD is reduced.

• When the BOD of effluent is reduced significantly, it is then passed into a settling tank, where the bacterial 'flocs' are allowed to sediment. This sediment is called **activated sludge**. A small part of the activated sludge is then pumped back into the aeration tank to serve as the inoculum.

• The remaining part of the sludge is pumped back into large tanks called **anaerobic sludge digesters**, in which other anaerobic bacteria (methanogens) are also present.
They digest the organic mass as well as **aerobic microbes** (bacteria and fungi of the sludge). During the digestion, mixture of gases like methane (CH_4), hydrogen sulphide (H_2S), carbon dioxide (CO_2), etc., are produced.

• These gases form **biogas** that is used as a source of energy because it is inflammable. The effluent from secondary treatment plant is released into natural water bodies like rivers and streams.

2. (i) Name the category of microbes naturally occurring in sewage and making it less polluted during the treatment.

(ii) Explain the different steps involved in the secondary treatment of sewage.   **(Foreign 2014)**

Ans. (i) Hetrotrophic microbes are naturally occurring in sewage which make it less polluted during sewage treatment.

(ii) Refer to Long Q. No. 1.

3. Describe the main idea behind the biological control of pests and diseases.

Ans. The main idea behind the biological control of pests and diseases is to use is a method of controlling pests in agriculture that relies on natural predation and not on chemicals.

Organic farmers believe that 'biodiversity furthers health'. The more diversity a landscape has, the more sustainable it is.

Therefore, they work to create a system where the insects (pests) are not eradicated, but kept at manageable levels by a complex system of checks and balance within a living and vibrant ecosystem.

It is different from 'conventional' farming practices that use chemical methods to kill both useful and harmful life forms. This is a holistic approach, as it seeks to develop an understanding of the webs of interaction between the myriad of organisms, including both flora and fauna in the field.

Biological farming approach requires familiarity with various life forms, their habitat, predators as well as pest, their life cycle, patterns of feeding, etc., to use them in biocontrol measures and reduce the dependence on chemicals and pesticides.

Examples of biological control agents are

(i) Ladybird and dragonflies are useful to get rid of aphids and mosquitoes, respectively.

(ii) To control butterfly caterpillars, bacteria such as *Bacillus thuringiensis* are used in the form of sprays or sachets as dry spores.

4. What are biofertilisers? Name the categories of organisms used as biofertilisers with an example for each. How do they function in organic farming?

Ans. Biofertilisers are organisms that enrich the nutrient quality of soil by enhancing the availability of nutrients to the crops.

The categories of organisms used as biofertilisers are as given below

(i) **Bacteria** Nitrogen-fixing bacteria fix atmospheric nitrogen into organic form, which is used by the plant as nutrient, e.g. *Rhizobium* is a symbiotic bacterium that lives in the root nodules of legumes and fixes atmospheric nitrogen into organic compounds.

(ii) **Fungi** They also form symbiotic association with plants, i.e. mycorrhiza, which absorb phosphorus from soil and passes it to the plants. Many members of genus–*Glomus* form mycorrhiza. Plants with mycorrhizal association show other benefits also such as

  (i) Resistance to root-borne pathogens.

  (ii) Tolerance to salinity and drought.

  (iii) Increase in plant growth and development.

(iii) **Cyanobacteria** These are autotrophic microbes found in aquatic and terrestrial environments. Most of them fix atmospheric nitrogen, e.g. *Anabaena, Nostoc, Oscillatoria*, etc. In paddy fields, cyanobacteria serve as important biofertiliser. Blue-Green Algae (BGA) also add organic matter to the soil. Thus, increasing its fertility.

All of these play a vital role in organic farming as there is no indulgence of chemicals fertilisers and hence, no polluting water bodies.

• Case Based Questions

1. Direction *Read the following passage and answer the questions that follows.*

Microbes or microorganisms form a big part of the biological systems of the world. They are present everywhere–within the soil, around us, in water, both in and around our body. They are microscopic in nature and have variable shapes and sizes. People are of the belief that all microorganisms are harmful for us. However, it is to be made sure that not all microbes are harmful, some useful microbes benefit humans in a variety of ways.

Microbes and their products are used in everyday life in different fields of work. Surprisingly, microbes like fungi and bacteria can be cultured in laboratory on nutritive media to form colonies.

(i) Microorganisms are termed as 'ubiquitous'. Explain.

Ans. Ubiquitous means present or found everywhere. Since, microbes can be found anywhere around us from air, water to the soil, they are called 'ubiquitous'.

(ii) Name the different types of microorganisms.

Ans. The different types of microorganisms include algae, bacteria, fungi, virus and Protozoa.

(iii) There is no life without microorganisms? Discuss.

Ans. Microorganisms, especially bacteria, help in decomposing the dead and decaying matter and are also responsible for oxygen in the air which is essential for our survival.

(iv) Explain the role of microorganisms in various fields (Any two).

Ans. Microbes and their products are used in everyday life in different fields such as

(a) *Saccharomyces cerevisiae* is used for fermenting malted cereals and fruit juices to produce ethanol.

(b) Some microorganisms also work as biocontrol agents, e.g. *Bacillus thuringiensis*, to control butterfly, catterpillars.

(v) Name the toxic released by *Bacillus thuringiensis*.

Ans. Thurioside is released by *Bacillus thuringiensis*.

2. Direction *Read the following passage and answer the questions that follows.*

Antibiotics are the chemical substances, produced by some microbes that can kill or retard the growth of other disease causing microbes. The first antibiotic discovered was penicillin. Alexander Fleming, while working on Staphylococci bacteria, found a mould growing in one of his culture plates. This mould produced a chemical, which inhibits the bacterial growth.

However, the production of antibiotics has become widespread by the pioneering efforts of Ernst Chain and Howard Florey on chemotherapeutic effectiveness of penicillin during 1939-41. Penicillin was extensively used in treating American soldiers wounded in World War-II.

(i) Who coined the term 'antibiotics'?

Ans. The term antibiotics was coined by Waksman in the year 1942.

(ii) From which microorganism, penicillin was obtained?

Ans. Penicillin was extracted from *Penicillium notatum*. It was extracted by Alexander Fleming in the year 1929.

(iii) Name the microorganism that inhibit the growth of *Staphylococcus* bacteria in culture plate.

Ans. *Penicillium notatum*

(iv) Why antibiotics cannot be used to cure viral disease?

Ans. Antibiotics cannot cure viral disease because virus do not possess cell wall like bacteria that can be attacked by antibodies, instead they are protected by a protein coat. Therefore antibiotics are helpful in treating bacterial diseases like plague, diphtheria and whooping cough.

(v) What would happen if antibiotics were not discovered?

Ans. The mortality rate would have increased due to no antibiotic availability for curing disease caused by microorganisms.

3. Observe the diagram given below and answer the questions that follows.

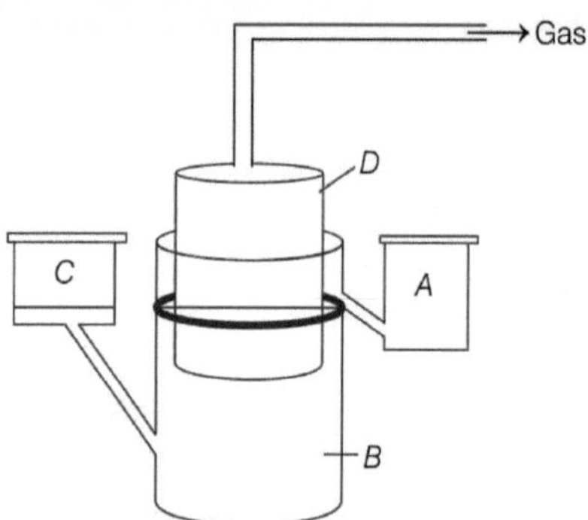

(i) What is the label *B* represent in the figure?

Ans. *B* represents digester. It is used to anaerobically decompose biodegradable materials to produce biogas.

(ii) What is biogas?

Ans. Biogas is methane rich fuel gas produced by anaerobic breakdown of waste biomass by methanogenic bacteria.

(iii) Which is the main raw material used in biogas production?

Ans. Cattle (cow) dung has been recognised as the main raw material for biogas plants.

Other materials like night soil, poultry litter and agricultural wastes are also used.

(iv) Which source of energy is biogas?

Ans. Biogas is a renewable and non-conventional resource as its production and usage cycle is continuous and generates no CO_2.

(v) Which group of microbes observed in a biogas plant?

Ans. The group of microbes observed in a biogas plants are called methanogens. These bacteria grow anaerobically on cellulosic material and produce large amounts of methane along with carbon dioxide and hydrogen gas.

Chapter Test

Multiple Choice Questions

1. Name an example of a rod-shaped virus.
   (a) Ebola virus
   (b) Tobacco mosaic virus
   (c) Influenza virus
   (d) Both (a) and (c)

2. The technology of biogas production from cow dung was developed in India largely due to the efforts of
   (a) Gas Authority of India
   (b) Oil and Natural Gas Commission
   (c) Indian Agricultural Research Institute, Khadi and Village Industries Commission
   (d) All of the above

3. A fungus which is used as a method of biocontrol is
   (a) *Glomus*
   (b) *Trichoderma*
   (c) *Penicillium*
   (d) *Aspergillus*

4. Match the following columns.

	Column I		Column II
A.	Symbiotic nitrogen-fixing bacteria	1.	Mosquitoes
B.	Dragonflies	2.	*Rhizobium*
C.	*Bacillus thuringiensis*	3.	*Azotobacter*
D.	Free-living N_2-fixing bacteria	4.	Butterfly caterpillars

   Codes

	A	B	C	D
(a)	1	4	3	2
(b)	4	3	2	1
(c)	2	1	4	3
(d)	2	1	3	4

5. Which of the following is not used as a biopesticide?
   (a) *Bacillus thuringiensis*
   (b) *Trichoderma harzianum*
   (c) *Nuclear Polyhedrosis Virus (NPV)*
   (d) *Xanthomonas campestris*

Assertion-Reasoning MCQs

Direction (Q. Nos. 1-3) *Each of these questions contains two statements, Assertion (A) and Reason (R). Each of these questions also has four alternative choices, any one of which is the correct answer. You have to select one of the codes (a), (b), (c) and (d) given below.*

   (a) Both A and R are true and R is the correct explanation of A
   (b) Both A and R are true, but R is not the correct explanation of A
   (c) A is true, but R is false
   (d) A is false, but R is true

1. **Assertion** (A) Primary treatment is also known as physical treatment.

   Reason (R) It involves physical removal of small and large, floating and suspended solids from sewage through filtration and sedimentation.

2. **Assertion** (A) The type of gas produced by microbes during their growth depends upon the microbes.

   Reason (R) These bacteria are methanogens.

3. **Assertion** (A) Chemical fertilisers are used in increasing amounts.

   Reason (R) This results in an increased agricultural output.

Short Answer Type Questions

1. What is toddy? Which plant sap is used in making toddy?

2. (i) Why bottled fruit juices appear clearer?
   (ii) Name any two species of fungus, which are used in manufacturing of antibiotics. **(NCERT)**

3. Explain the consequence if the oxygen availability to activated sludge flocs is reduced.

4. Give reasons, why?
   (i) Cow dung is preferred for biogas production.
   (ii) *Saccharomyces cerevisiae* is commonly known as baker's yeast.

5. How has the bacterium *Bacillus thuringiensis* helped us in controlling caterpillars of insect-pests?

Long Answer Type Questions

1. Observe the diagram given below and answer the questions that follows.

   (i) Identify the above shown figure related to sewage water treatment.
   (ii) Is secondary treatment enough for sewage water treatment? If not, what treatment is followed prior to/post this treatment?
   (iii) What does BOD test measure?

2. What is biogas? Explain its production with the help of a diagram.

Answers

Multiple Choice Questions

1. (b)   *2. (c)*   *3. (b)*   *4. (c)*   *5. (d)*

Assertion-Reasoning MCQs

1. (a)   *2. (b)*   *3. (a)*

For Detailed Solutions
Scan the code

CHAPTER 03

Biotechnology: Principles and Processes

In this Chapter...

- Principles of Biotechnology
- Tools of Recombinant DNA Technology
- Processes of Recombinant DNA Technology

Biotechnology is the technique of using living organisms or enzymes from organisms to produce products and processes useful to humans. The term was coined by **Karl Ereky** in 1917.

Biotechnology deals with the large scale production and marketing of products such as enzymes, insulin or antibiotics, etc., that are of importance to mankind.

The European Federation of Biotechnology (EFB) has given a definition of biotechnology as the integration of natural science and organisms, cells, parts thereof and molecular analogues for products and services'.

Principles of Biotechnology

Following two core techniques gave birth to modern biotechnology

1. **Genetic engineering** It is the alteration of the chemistry of genetic material (DNA/RNA) and the introduction of these into host organisms to consequently change in the phenotype of the host organism. **Paul Berg** is known as the **Father of Genetic Engineering**.

2. **Bioprocess engineering** It is the maintenance of sterile conditions in order to enable the growth of only desired microbes or eukaryotic cells in large quantities for the production of antibiotics, enzymes, hormones, vaccines, etc.

Genetic Engineering

- It is the deliberate modification of an organism's DNA, using various techniques. This altered DNA (recombinant DNA) is then introduced into host organisms to change their phenotype.

- This is followed by growing this genetically modified cell in large quantities, by maintaining sterile environment, for the manufacture of biotechnological products like antibiotics, vaccines, enzymes, etc.

- Techniques of genetic engineering include construction of **recombinant DNA**, **gene cloning** and **gene transfer**. These techniques allow the isolation and introduction of a set of desirable genes without introducing undesirable genes into the target organism.

- **Origin of replication** (*ori*) is a specific DNA sequence in the chromosome which can initiate DNA replication. The foreign DNA introduced into the host genome has to be linked with the origin of replication in the host chromosome for the gene to be able to multiply. This is also known as **cloning** which involves making multiple identical copies of any template DNA. If the foreign gene is not linked to the *ori* sequence, it may not be able to multiply.

- In 1972, the first recombinant DNA was constructed by **Stanley Cohen** and **Herbert Boyer**. They isolated the antibiotic resistance gene by cutting out a piece of DNA from a **plasmid** (autonomously replicating circular extrachromosomal DNA) of *Salmonella typhimurium*. The cutting of DNA at specific locations became possible with the help of **restriction enzymes** (molecular scissors).

- The cut pieces of DNA were then linked with the plasmid DNA using DNA ligase enzyme. These plasmids act as **vectors** to transfer the piece of DNA attached to it into the host organism. This makes a new circular autonomously replicating DNA created *in vitro* and is known as the **recombinant DNA**.

- The recombinant DNA is transferred into *Escherichia coli*, a bacterium closely related to *Salmonella*, where it replicates using the new host's DNA polymerase enzyme and makes multiple copies of itself. It also produces multiple copies of the antibiotic resistance gene in the new host (*E. coli*). This process is called as **cloning** of antibiotic resistance gene in *E. coli*.

- There are three basic steps involved in genetically modifying an organism
  - Identification of DNA with desirable genes.
  - Introduction of the identified DNA into the host.
  - Maintenance of introduced DNA in the host and transfer of the DNA to its progeny.

Tools of Recombinant DNA Technology

Genetic engineering or recombinant DNA technology can be accomplished only with the usage of key tools like

  (i) Enzymes
  (ii) Cloning vectors
  (iii) Competent host organisms

These tools of *r*DNA technology are discussed in details below

Enzymes

There are various enzymes involved in genetic engineering which simplifies this complex process.

The enzymes involved are

1. Restriction Enzymes (Molecular scissors)

- These are enzymes which are used for cutting of DNA at specific locations during *r*DNA technology. These enzymes belong to a larger class of **nucleases,** which are of two types

  (i) **Exonucleases** remove nucleotides from the ends of the DNA (either $5'$ or $3'$) in one strand of duplex.

  (ii) **Endonucleases** make cuts at specific position within DNA.

- The first restriction endonuclease named *Hind* II was isolated by **Smith Wilcox** and **Kelley** in 1968. It was found that it always cuts DNA molecule at a particular point recognising a specific sequence of the six base pairs known as the **recognition sequence** for *Hind* II.

- More than 900 restriction enzymes are known today that have been isolated from over 230 bacterial strains and each of which recognises different recognition sequences.

Restriction endonucleases are not present in eukaryotic cells.

Differences between Exonucleases and Endonucleases

Exonucleases	Endonucleases
They cleave base pairs of DNA at their terminal ends.	They cleave DNA at specific point except the terminal ends.
They act on single strand of DNA or gaps in double-stranded DNA.	They cleave one strand (figure below) or both strands (figure below) of double-stranded DNA.
They do not cut RNA.	They may cut RNA.

Naming of Restriction Enzymes

- The convention for naming these enzymes proceeds in a way that the first letter of the name comes from the **genus** and the second two letters come from the **species** of prokaryotic cell from which they were isolated, e.g. *Eco*RI comes from *E. coli* RY13.

- The letter 'R' is derived from the name of **strain**. Roman numbers following the names, indicate the order in which the enzymes were isolated from that strain of bacteria.

Mechanism of Action of Restriction Endonuclease

- Each restriction endonuclease functions by 'inspecting' the length of a DNA sequence.

- Once it finds specific recognition sequence, it will bind to DNA and cut each of the two strands of double helix at specific points in their sugar-phosphate backbones.

- Each restriction endonuclease recognises a specific **palindromic nucleotide sequences** in the DNA. **Palindromes** are group of letters that form the same words when read both from forward and backward, e.g. 'MALAYALAM'. Therefore, the palindrome in DNA is a base pair sequence that is same when read forward or background, e.g. the following sequences read the same on the two strands in $5' \longrightarrow 3'$ direction as well as $3' \longrightarrow 5'$ direction.

$$5' \longrightarrow \text{GAATTC} \longrightarrow 3'$$
$$3' \longrightarrow \text{CTTAAG} \longrightarrow 5'$$

- Restriction enzymes cut the strand of DNA a little away from the centre of the palindrome sites, but between the same two bases on the opposite strands.

- This leaves single-stranded portion at the ends. These are overhanging stretches called **sticky ends** present on each strand.

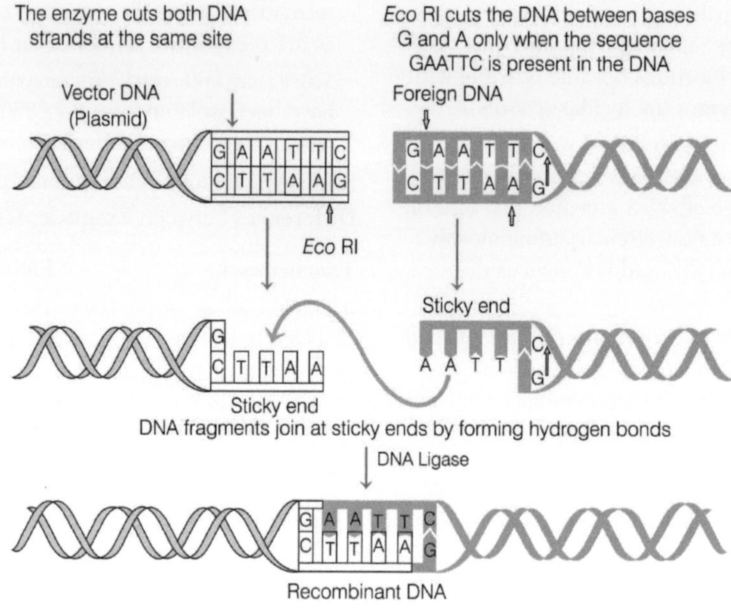

Steps in the formation of recombinant DNA by action of restriction endonuclease enzyme *Eco* RI

- These are named so because they form hydrogen bonds with their complementary cut counter parts. This stickiness of the ends facilitates the action of the enzyme DNA ligase.

- In genetic engineering, restriction endonucleases are used to form recombinant molecules of DNA, which are composed of DNA from different sources or genomes.

- In order to create a recombinant vector molecule, it is necessary that the vector and the source DNA are cut with the same restriction enzyme, so that the resultant DNA fragments have the same sticky ends, which are complementary to each other and can be joined together (end-to-end) using DNA ligases.

2. DNA Ligases (Molecular glue)

These enzymes repair broken DNA by joining two nucleotides. They are used in genetic engineering to reverse the action of restriction enzymes, i.e. to join complementary DNA strands/ends together, e.g. T_4 DNA ligase.

3. Alkaline Phosphatase (AP)

This enzyme removes the phosphate group from the 5´ end of a DNA molecule, leaving a free 5´ hydroxyl group, it prevents unwanted self-ligation of vector DNA molecules during the formation of recombinant DNA.

4. DNA Polymerases

This enzyme helps in *in vitro* synthesis of complementary DNA (*c*DNA) strand on DNA templates.

Cloning Vectors

The DNA molecule that can carry a foreign DNA segment and replicate inside the host cell is called as a **vector**.

- Plasmids and bacteriophages are used as **cloning vector**s. This is because plasmids and bacteriophages have the ability to replicate within the bacterial cell independent of chromosomal DNA.

- Bacteriophages have very high copy numbers of their genome within the bacterial cells. But in case of plasmids, some may have only one or two copies per cell whereas others may have 15-100 copies per cell.

- Cloning vectors use the machinery of bacterial cell to replicate and thereby, increase the copy number (make clones) of the DNA inserted into them.

- These help easy linking of foreign DNA and allow the selection of recombinants (bacterial cells that have picked up recombinant plasmid) from non-recombinants (those who have not).

Features of Cloning Vector

All vectors have four special features that are required to facilitate cloning into a vector.

1. **Origin of replication** (*ori*) is the sequence from where replication starts and any piece of DNA when linked to this sequence can be made to replicate within the host cells. This sequence also controls the copy number of the linked DNA.

2. **Selectable marker** helps in identifying and eliminating non-transformants and selectively permitting the growth of the transformants.

   Transformation is the procedure through which a piece of DNA is introduced into a host bacterium. Normally, antibiotics such as ampicillin, chloramphenicol, tetracycline or kanamycin, etc., are considered useful selectable markers.

3. **Cloning** (recognition) **sites** These are generally required to link the foreign or alien DNA with the vector. For this, the vector requires very few or single recognition sites for commonly used restriction enzymes. If more than one recognition site is present within the vector, it will generate several fragments that will lead to more complication in gene cloning.

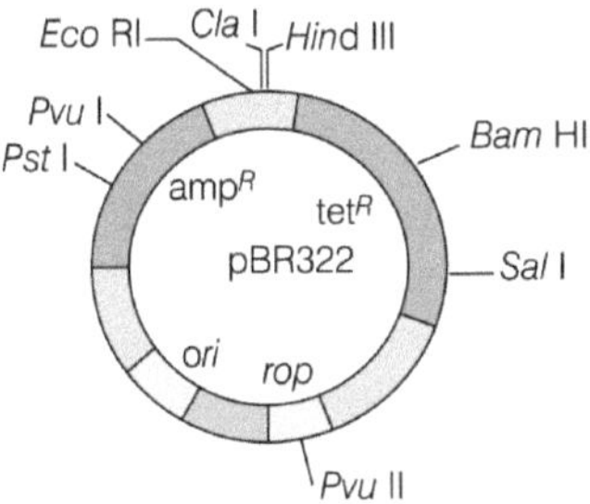

E. coli cloning vector pBR322 showing restriction sites (Hind III, EcoRI, BamHI, Sal I, Pvu II, Pst I, Cla I), ori and antibiotic resistance genes (amp^R and tet^R). rop codes for the proteins involved in the replication of the plasmid

The **ligation** of the foreign DNA is carried out at a restriction site present in one of the two **antibiotic resistance genes**. Selection of recombinants formed can be done by one of the following methods, given below

(i) **Inactivation of antibiotic resistance gene** If a foreign DNA is ligated at the *Bam*HI site of tetracycline-resistance gene in the vector pBR322, the recombinant plasmid will loose tetracycline resistance.

But, it can still be selected out from non-recombinant ones by plating transformants on ampicillin containing medium. The transformants growing on medium containing ampicillin are then transferred on a medium containing tetracycline.

The **recombinants** will grow on ampicillin containing medium, but not on that containing tetracycline. On the other side, **non-recombinants** will grow on both media and thus, recombinants are selected.

In this example, one antibiotic resistance gene helps in selecting the transformants, whereas the other antibiotic resistance gene gets inactivated due to insertion of alien DNA and helps in selection of recombinants.

(ii) **Insertional inactivation** The selection of recombinants due to inactivation of antibiotic gene is a cumbersome procedure, because it requires simultaneous plating on two plates having different antibiotics. Therefore, the alternative selectable markers have been developed, which differentiate recombinants from non-recombinants. It is based on their ability to produce colour in the presence of **chromogenic substrate**.

In this process, a recombinant DNA is inserted within the coding sequence of an enzyme β-**galactosidase**. This results into inactivation of the enzyme, which is referred to as **insertional inactivation**. Therefore, the bacterial colonies having inserted plasmid, shows **no colouration** (recombinant colonies), while those without plasmid will show **blue colour**. Here, β-galactosidase works as a **reporter enzyme** (produced by reporter gene) whose inactivity helps to identify transformed and non-transformed bacterial colonies.

4. **Vectors for cloning genes in plants and animals** A pathogen of several dicot plants is able to deliver a piece of DNA, i.e. 'T-DNA' to transform normal plant cells into a tumour cells and disect these tumour cells to produce the chemicals required by the pathogen. Similarly, retrovirus in animals have the ability to transform normal cells into **cancerous cells**.

   - The tumour inducing (Ti) plasmid of *Agrobacterium tumefaciens* has now been modified into a cloning vector which is able to use the mechanisms to deliver genes of our interest into a variety of plants.
   - Similarly, retroviruses can be disarmed and used to deliver desirable genes into animal cells.

Competent Host Organisms

DNA is a hydrophilic molecule, so it cannot pass through cell membranes. In order to force bacteria to take up the plasmid, the bacterial cells must first be made **competent**. The competency is the ability of a cell to take up foreign DNA.

The cells can be made competent by following methods

1. **Chemical method** ($CaCl_2$ method) In this, the cells are treated with a specific concentration of a divalent cation such as calcium which increases the efficiency with which DNA enters the bacterium through the pores in its cell wall. The cells are incubated with recombinant DNA on ice, followed by placing them briefly at 42°C and then putting them back on ice. This treatment that enables the bacteria to take up the recombinant DNA is known as **heat shock method**.

2. **Physical method** The **microinjection** is the physical method used to introduce foreign DNA into host cell. In this method, recombinant DNA is directly injected into the nucleus of an animal cell.

Biolistics or **Gene gun** is another method suitable for introduction of DNA into plants, in which cells are bombarded with high velocity microparticles of gold or tungsten coated with DNA.

3. **Disarmed pathogen vectors** In this method, vectors that can cause infection are used to infect the cell to transfer the recombinant DNA into the host, e.g. retrovirus, papilloma virus and adenovirus in case of animals and *Agrobacterium* in case of plants.

Processes of Recombinant DNA Technology

Recombinant DNA technology involves various steps in a specific sequence such as isolation of the desired genetic material (DNA), cutting of DNA at specific locations, isolation of desired DNA fragment, amplification of gene of interest by PCR, ligation of DNA fragments into a vector, insertion of recombinant DNA into host cell, culturing the host cells in a medium at large scale and extraction of the desired product.

Isolation of the Genetic Material (DNA)

Nucleic acid is the genetic material, which is present in all living organisms. In majority of organisms, this is present in the form of **Deoxyribonucleic Acid** (DNA), which must be present in pure form, i.e. free from other macromolecules in order to cut with restriction enzymes.

This is done in the following sequence

(i) Since DNA is enclosed within membranes, so in order to release DNA along with other macromolecules such as proteins, polysaccharides and lipids, bacterial cells, plant or animal tissues are treated with the enzyme such as lysozyme (bacteria), cellulase (plant cells), chitinase (fungus), respectively.

(ii) RNA can be removed by treating it with **ribonuclease**, whereas proteins can be removed by its treatment with **protease**.

(iii) Other molecules can be removed by appropriate treatments and ultimately purified DNA will precipitate out, after the addition of chilled **ethanol**. This can be seen as collection of fine threads in the suspension which can be removed by **spooling.**

Cutting of DNA at Specific Locations

Restriction enzyme digestions are performed by incubating purified DNA molecules with the restriction enzyme. This is done at the optimal conditions for that specific enzyme.

Separation and Isolation of DNA Fragments

- The cutting of DNA by restriction endonucleases results in the fragments of DNA which are separated by a technique known as **gel electrophoresis.**

- Since, the DNA fragments are negatively charged molecules, so they can be separated by applying an electric field which

makes DNA molecules move towards the anode (+), under an electric field through an appropriate medium or matrix.

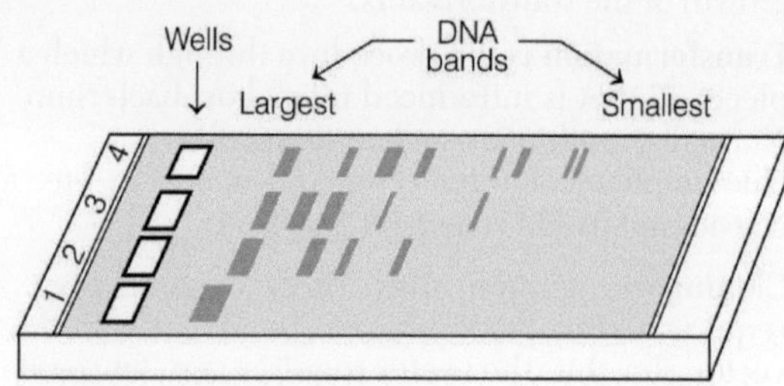

A typical agarose gel electrophoresis showing migration of undigested (lane 1) and digested set of DNA fragments (lane 2-4)

- The most commonly used matrix is **agarose**, a natural polymer extracted from sea weeds. DNA fragments resolve (separate) according to their size through sieving effect provided by the agarose gel.

- Hence the smaller the fragment size, farther it moves. The separated DNA fragments can be visualised only after staining the DNA with **Ethidium Bromide** (EtBr) followed by exposure to UV radiation. The bright orange coloured bands of DNA, are seen when exposed to UV light.

- These separate stained bands of DNA are cut out from the agarose gel and extracted from the gel piece, by a process known as **elution**. Thus, the DNA fragments (containing gene of interest) are purified and used for the construction of recombinant DNA by joining them with cloning vectors in the presence of DNA ligase.

Amplification of Gene of Interest Using PCR

PCR stands for **Polymerase Chain Reaction**, a method of amplifying the fragments of DNA. This method can make multiple copies of even a single DNA fragment or the gene of interest in a test tube. The reaction mixture requires

(i) **DNA template** The double-stranded DNA that needs to be amplified.

(ii) **Primers** These are chemically synthesised oligonucleotides (short segment of DNA) that are complementary to the regions of DNA template.

(iii) **Enzymes** Two commonly used enzymes in PCR reaction are

- *Taq* **polymerase** It is isolated from a thermophilic bacterium, i.e. *Thermus aquaticus* and has a property to remain active during the high temperature induced denaturation of double-stranded DNA. It also helps in the amplification of a segment of DNA.

- *Vent* **polymerase** It is isolated from *Thermococcus litoralis.*

(iv) **Nucleotide bases** These are added by DNA polymerase to the growing chain.

- Three main steps involved in the PCR technique are

  Step I **Denaturation** The double-stranded DNA is denatured by using high temperature of 95° C for 15 seconds. Now each separated single strand acts as a template for DNA synthesis.

  Step II **Annealing** Two sets of oligonucleotide primers are annealed (hybridised) to the separated single-strands. This step is carried out at a slightly lower temperature (40-60° C).

  Step III **Extension** The thermostable enzyme *Taq* DNA polymerase is used in this reaction, extends the primers by adding *d*NTPs (deoxynucleoside triphosphates) complementary to those of the template DNA. Mg^{2+} is required as a cofactor for thermostable DNA polymerase.

- These steps are repeated many times in order to obtain several copies of desired DNA.

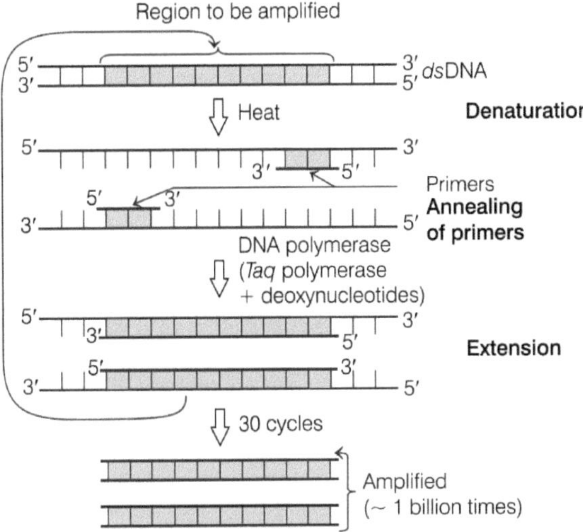

Polymerase Chain Reaction (PCR) : Each cycle has three steps, i.e. (i) Denaturation, (ii) Annealing, (iii) Extension

- Applications of PCR are in *r*DNA technology, DNA sequencing, DNA fingerprinting, early diagnosis of infections, disease, etc.

Ligation of DNA Fragment into a Vector

This process requires a vector DNA and a source DNA. In order to obtain sticky ends, both of these should cut with the same endonuclease, after which, both are ligated by mixing vector DNA, gene of interest and enzyme, **DNA ligase** to form the **recombinant DNA/hybrid DNA.**

Insertion of Recombinant DNA into the Host Cell/Organism

This can occur by several methods, before which the recipient cells are made competent to receive the DNA. If a recombinant DNA bearing gene for resistance to an antibiotic (e.g. ampicillin) is transferred into *E. coli* cells, the host cells become transformed into ampicillin resistant cells. The ampicillin resistance gene in this case is called a **selectable marker**. When transformed cells are grown on agar plates containing ampicillin, only **transformants** will grow and others will die.

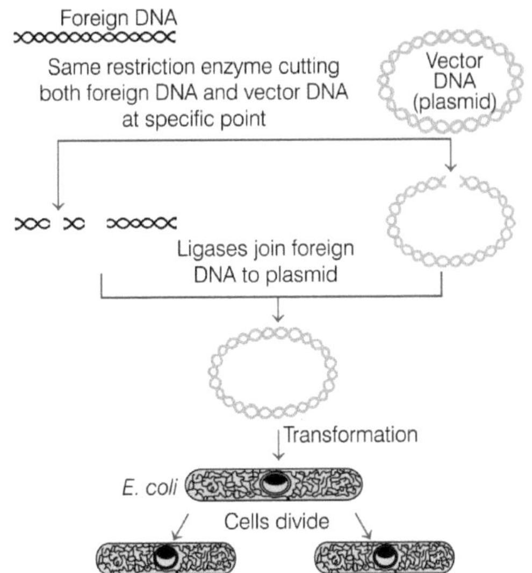

Diagrammatic representation of recombinant DNA technology

Obtaining or Culturing the Foreign Gene Product

Any protein encoding gene expressed in a heterologous host, it is called **recombinant protein**. The cells harbouring cloned genes of interest are grown on a small scale in the laboratory (i.e. appropriate nutrient medium at optimal conditions). These cell cultures are used for extracting the desired protein using various separation techniques.

Bioreactors

These are the large volume vessels approximately (100-1000 L) in which raw materials are biologically converted into specific products, individual enzymes, etc., using microbial, plant, animal or human cells.

A bioreactor provides the optimal conditions for achieving the desired product by providing optimum growth conditions like temperature, pH, substrate, salts, vitamins and oxygen.

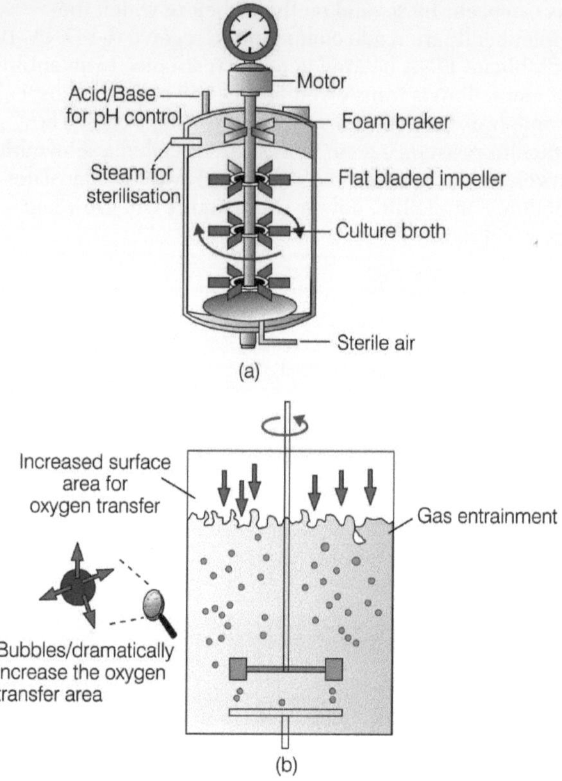

(a) Simple stirred-tank bioreactor, (b) Sparged stirred-tank bioreactor through which sterile air bubbles are sparged

The cells can also be multiplied in a **continuous culture** system. In this, the used medium is drained out from one side while fresh medium is added from the other side to maintain the cells in their physiologically most active log/exponential phase. This type of culturing method produces a larger biomass leading to higher yields of desired protein.

The components of a bioreactor are

  (i) An agitator system

 (ii) An oxygen delivery system

(iii) A foam control system

(iv) A temperature control system

 (v) pH control system

(vi) A sampling port to withdraw culture periodically

The most commonly used bioreactors are of stirring type. **Stirring type bioreactors** are further of two types, i.e. simple and sparged.

- **A simple stirred-tank bioreactor** is usually cylindrical or with a curved base to facilitate even mixing of reactor contents.

- The **sparged-stirred-tank bioreactor** also facilitates the mixing of components and ensures oxygen availability throughout the bioreactor. Alternatively, air is bubbled through the reactor. Which sterile air bubbles are sparged.

Downstream Processing

After completion of the biosynthetic phase, the product has to be subjected through a series of processes before it is ready for marketing as a finished product. The processes include (i) separation and (ii) purification of products, which are collectively called the **downstream processing**.

The product is then subjected to quality control testing and formulated with addition of kept in suitable preservatives. Downstream processing and quality control test generally differ from product to product.

Chapter Practice

Objective Questions

• Multiple Choice Questions

1. The techniques of genetic engineering include
(a) gene transfer
(b) creation of recombinant DNA
(c) gene cloning
(d) All of the above

Ans. (*d*) The technique of genetic engineering includes gene transfer, creation of recombinant DNA and gene cloning. Thus, option (d) is correct.

2. Autonomously replicating circular extrachromosomal DNA is
(a) vector
(b) capsid
(c) plasmid
(d) bacteriophages

Ans. (*c*) Autonomously replicating circular extrachromosomal DNA is plasmid.

3. Restriction enzymes belong to which class of enzymes?
(a) Ligases
(b) Exonucleases
(c) Nucleases
(d) Proteases

Ans. (*c*) Restriction enzymes belong to large classes of enzymes called nucleases, which are of two kinds, exonucleases and endonucleases.

4. Match the Column I with Column II with respect to the nomenclature of enzyme *Eco* RI and select the correct option from the codes given below.

	Column I		Column II
A.	*E*	1.	Ist in order of identification
B.	*co*	2.	Genus
C.	R	3.	Species
D.	I	4.	Strain

Codes

	A	B	C	D			A	B	C	D
(a)	3	4	1	2		(b)	2	3	4	1
(c)	2	1	4	3		(d)	2	3	1	4

Ans. (*b*) A–2, B–3, C–4, D–1

5. Which of the following statements does not hold true for restriction enzyme? **(NCERT Exemplar)**
(a) It recognises a palindromic nucleotide sequence
(b) It is an endonuclease
(c) It is isolated from viruses
(d) It can produce the same kind of sticky ends in different DNA molecules

Ans. (*c*) The statement in option (c) is not true for restriction enzymes. It can be corrected as
Restriction enzymes are isolated from bacteria and not from viruses.

6. Match the following columns.

	Column I		Column II
A.	Plasmids	1.	Virus infecting bacteria
B.	Bacteriophages	2.	Natural polymer of D-galactose
C.	Cosmids	3.	Hybrid vector derived from plasmids
D.	Agarose	4.	Circular extrachromosomal DNA

Codes

	A	B	C	D			A	B	C	D
(a)	2	1	3	4		(b)	4	1	3	2
(c)	3	2	1	4		(d)	1	4	3	2

Ans. (*b*) A–4, B–1, C–3, D–2

7. The given figure is the diagrammatic representation of the vector pBR322. Which one of the given options correctly identifies its certain component(s)?

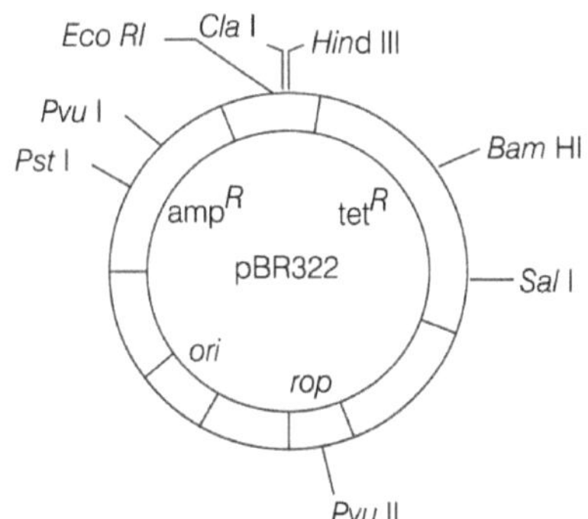

(a) *ori*–original restriction enzymes

(b) *rop*–reduced osmotic pressure

(c) *Hind* III, *Eco* RI–selectable markers

(d) amp^R, tet^R–antibiotic resistance genes

Ans. (*d*) Option (d) correctly identifies its certain component, i.e. amp^R, tet^R as antibiotic resistance gene. Others are incorrect and can be corrected as

Ori-origin of replication, *rop*-replication of the plasmid and *Hind* III, *Eco*RI–Restriction sites.

8. The presence of more than one recognition site within vector will lead to the

(a) generation of several fragments

(b) generation of one fragment

(c) generation of half fragment

(d) None of the above

Ans. (*a*) The presence of more than one recognition within the vector will generate several fragments which will complicate the gene cloning process.

9. What is the source of the Ti (Tumour inducing) plasmid which is modified and used as a cloning vector to deliver the desirable genes into plant cells?

(a) *Agrobacterium tumefaciens*

(b) *Thermophilus aquaticus*

(c) *Pyrococcus furiosus*

(d) *Aedes aegypti*

Ans. (*a*) *Agrobacterium tumefaciens* is the source of Ti plamid which is modified and used as a cloning vector to deliver the desirable genes into plant cells.

10. Gel electrophoresis is used for the

(a) separation and isolation of DNA fragments

(b) construction of recombinant DNA by joining with cloning vectors

(c) culturing the host cells in a medium at a large scale

(d) replication of DNA for many times

Ans. (*a*) Gel electrophoresis is used to separate and isolate macromolecules like DNA, RNA and proteins according to their size and charge.

11. The treatment of host cell with divalent cation leads to the

(a) change in permeability of DNA

(b) increased efficiency with which DNA enters the bacterium

(c) decreased efficiency with which DNA enters the bacterium

(d) change in permeability of host

Ans. (*b*) Host is made competent by treating them with specific concentration of a divalent cation such as calcium, which increases the efficiency with which DNA enters the bacterium through the creation of pores in its cell wall or cell membrane.

12. The given figure refers to

 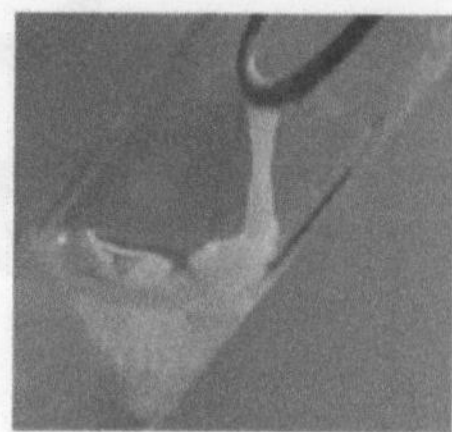

(a) DNA spooling

(b) DNA digestion

(c) DNA recognition

(d) DNA bands

Ans. (*a*) The given figure refers to DNA spooling.

13. Polymerase chain reaction is a technique used for

(a) *in vivo* replication of DNA

(b) *in vivo* synthesis of *m*RNA

(c) *in vitro* synthesis of *m*RNA

(d) *in vitro* replication of specific DNA sequence using thermostable DNA polymerase

Ans. (*d*) The polymerase chain reaction is a technique that is used for *in vitro* replication of specific DNA sequence using thermostable DNA polymerase.

14. Stirred-tank bioreactors are advantageous over shake flasks because they

(a) provide high temperature and pH

(b) provide better aeration and mixing properties

(c) do not allow the entry of CO_2

(d) are easy to operate

Ans. (*b*) A stirred-tank bioreactor is more advantageous than shake flasks as these provide better aeration and mixing properties. It has an agitator system to mix the contents properly and also an oxygen delivery and also system to ensure better availability of oxygen.

15. Downstream process includes

I. Formation of the product with suitable preservatives.

II. Purification of the product.

III. Quality control testing and clinical trials in case of drugs.

IV. Separation of the product from the reactor.

Which of the statements given above are correct?

(a) I, II and III

(b) I, II and IV

(c) II, III and IV

(d) I, II, III and IV

Ans. (*d*) All the given statements are correct.

• Assertion-Reasoning MCQs

Direction (Q. Nos. 1-5) *Each of these questions contains two statements, Assertion (A) and Reason (R). Each of these questions also has four alternative choices, any one of which is the correct answer. You have to select one of the codes (a), (b), (c) and (d) given below.*

(a) Both A and R are true and R is the correct explanation of A

(b) Both A and R are true, but R is not the correct explanation of A

(c) A is true, but R is false

(d) A is false, but R is true

1. **Assertion** (A) Biotechnology deals with techniques that use living organisms to produce products useful for humans.

Reason (R) It uses only a unicellular organism.

Ans. (*c*) A is true, but R is false. R can be corrected as Biotechnology uses unicellular as well as multicellular organisms for producing useful products *via* different techniques.

2. **Assertion** (A) Origin of replication is an essential part of a vector.

Reason (R) *Ori* is responsible for initiating replication.

Ans. (*a*) Both A and R are true and R is the correct explanation of A.

Origin of replication (*ori*) is the sequence from where replication starts and any piece of DNA when linked to this sequence can be made to replicate within the host cell. Thus, it is an essential part of a vector.

3. **Assertion** (A) In gel electrophoresis, DNA fragments are separated.

Reason (R) DNA is negatively charged, so it moves towards anode under electric field.

Ans. (*a*) Both A and R are true and R is the correct explanation of A.

DNA fragments can be isolated with the help of gel electrophoresis. In which negatively charged, DNA moves towards the anode (positively charged) under an electric field through a matrix.

4. **Assertion** (A) In recombinant DNA technology, human genes are often transferred into bacteria or yeast.

Reason (R) Both bacteria and yeast multiply very fast to form huge population which express the desired gene.

Ans. (*a*) Both A and R are true and R is the correct explanation of A.

5. **Assertion** (A) The tumour inducing plasmid (Ti plasmid) of *Agrobacterium tumefaciens* acts as a cloning vector in recombinant DNA technology.

Reason (R) The Ti plasmid which is used in the mechanisms of delivering genes to a cell remains pathogenic.

Ans. (*c*) A is true, but R is false. R can be corrected as

The tumour inducing, (Ti plasmid) of *Agrobacterium tumefaciens* has been modified into a cloning vector which is not pathogenic to the plants. However, it can still be used to deliver genes of interest into target plant cells.

• Case Based MCQ

1. **Direction** *Read the following passage and answer the questions that follows.*

Selectable marker is a gene, which helps in selecting transformed host cells and eliminating non-transformants. The process of the selection of recombinants from non-recombinants occurs as the transformants containing tetracycline resistant gene are plated on an ampicillin containing medium. The mixture is then transferred on a medium containing antibiotic tetracycline. The recombinants will form colonies in ampicillin medium, but will not form colonies in tetracycline medium. The non-recombinants will grow on both the mediums thus separating out recombinants from non-recombinants. An alternative method used for the selection of transformed cell is known as insertional inactivation.

(i) When an alien DNA is ligated in tetracycline resistant gene, the recombinant

(a) become tetracycline resistant

(b) will loose tetracycline resistant

(c) will remain same

(d) None of the above

Ans. (*b*) When an alien DNA is ligated in tetracycline resistant gene, the recombinant will loose tetracycline resistant gene.

(ii) In insertional inactivation, the recombinant DNA is inserted within the coding sequence of

(a) β-galactosidase

(b) tetracycline resistant gene

(c) restriction enzyme

(d) ampicillin resistant gene

Ans. (*a*) In insertional inactivation, the recombinant DNA is inserted within the coding sequence of the enzyme, β-galactosidase. This results into inactivation of the gene synthesising this enzyme.

(iii) Recombinant colonies in insertional inactivation are differentiated on the basis of
(a) production of blue colour
(b) production of no colour
(c) production of red colour
(d) production of green colour

Ans. (*b*) Recombinant colonies in insertional inactivation are differentiated on the basis of production of no colour. As recombinant produces no colour and non-recombinant gives blue colour in the presence of chromogenic substrate.

(iv) Which of the following is/are function(s) of a selectable marker?
(a) Provides resistance against a substrate
(b) Inhibits the growth of normal cell in a culture
(c) Helps to create a chromosome map
(d) Both (a) and (b)

Ans. (*d*) A selectable marker provides resistance against a substrate and inhibits the growth of normal cell in a culture. Thus, option (d) is correct.

(v) **Assertion** (A) Selection of recombinants due to inactivation of antibiotics is cumbersome procedure.

Reason (R) It requires simultaneous plating on two plates having different antibiotics.
(a) Both A and R are true and R is the correct explanation of A
(b) Both A and R are true, but R is not the correct explanation of A
(c) A is true, but R is false
(d) Both A and R are false

Ans. (*a*) Both A and R are true and R is the correct explanation of A.

Selection of recombinants due to inactivation of antibiotics is a cumbersome procedure, because it requires simultaneous plating on two plates having different antibiotics. So, alternative selectable markers are developed which differentiate recombinants from non-recombinants on the basis of their ability to produce colour in the presence of a chromogenic substrate.

PART 2

Subjective Questions

• Short Answer (SA) Type Questions

1. Explain the work carried out by Cohen and Boyer that contributed immensely in biotechnology.

Ans. **Stanley Cohen** and **Herbert Boyer** in 1972 constructed the first recombinant DNA that emerged from linking of a gene encoding antibiotic resistance with a native **plasmid**. They isolated the antibiotic resistance gene by cutting out a piece of DNA from a plasmid of *Salmonella typhimurium*.

The cut piece of DNA was then linked with plasmid DNA with the help of **DNA ligase**. The plasmid DNA acted as a vector to transfer the piece of DNA attached to it which made a new combination of circular self-replicating DNA, created *in vitro* known as **recombinant DNA**. When this DNA was transferred into *Escherichia coli*, it could replicate using new host's DNA polymerase enzyme and will produce multiple copies or clones.

This work by Cohen and Boyer was very helpful in producing clones and also inserting desired DNA for specific proteins.

2. (i) Why was a bacterium used in the first instance of the construction of an artificial recombinant DNA molecule?
(ii) Name the scientists who accomplished this and how. **(Delhi 2016C)**

Ans. (i) *Salmonella tymphimurium* was used in the first instance of the construction of artificial recombinant DNA molecule because it has a plasmid which has an autonomously replicating circular extrachromosomal DNA. It also has an antibiotic resistance gene.

(ii) **Stanley Cohen** and **Herbert Boyer** accomplished this in 1972. Antibiotic resistant gene was isolated using restriction enzymes and introduced into the plasmid of the bacterium, i.e. *Salmonella tymphimurium.*

Later the recombinant plasmid was introduced into the bacterium, *E. coli,* so that it could make copies of gene.

3. Do eukaryotic cells have restriction endonucleases? Justify your answer. **(NCERT)**

Ans. No, eukaryotic cells do not have restriction endonucleases because the DNA of eukaryotes is highly methylated due to the presence of enzymes methylase which protects the DNA from the activity of restriction enzymes.

But prokaryotes/ bacteria have this enzyme as a defence mechanism to destroy the foreign DNA or to restrict the growth of bacteriophages. Hence, all the restriction endonucleases have been isolated from various strains of bacteria.

4. A recombinant DNA molecule was created by ligating a gene to a plasmid vector. By mistake, an exonuclease was added to the tube containing the recombinant DNA. How does this affect the next step in the experiment, i.e. bacterial transformation?

Ans. The experiment will not likely to be affected as recombinant DNA molecule is circular and closed, with no free ends. Hence, it will not be a substrate for exonuclease enzyme which removes nucleotides from the free ends of DNA.

5. Restriction enzymes that are used in the construction of recombinant DNA are endonucleases which cut the DNA at 'specific'-recognition sequence? What would be the disadvantage if they do not cut the DNA at specific-recognition sequence?

Ans. If the restriction enzymes would cut DNA at random sites instead of at specific sites, then the DNA fragments obtained will not have 'sticky ends'. In the absence of sticky ends, construction of recombinant DNA molecule would not be possible.

6. What does 'Hind' and 'III' refer to in the enzyme *Hind* III?

Ans. The first letter 'H' indicates the genus of the organism, from which the enzyme was isolated, i.e. H-genus, *Haemophilus*.
The roman number (III) denotes the sequence in which the restriction endonuclease from that particular genus, species and strain of bacteria have been isolated, i.e. third restriction endonuclease to be isolated from this species.

7. Explain with the help of a suitable example the naming of a restriction endonuclease. **(Delhi 2014)**

Or Write the basis of naming the restriction endonuclease *Eco* RI. **(Delhi 2020)**

Ans. The convention for naming of restriction endonuclease proceeds in a way that the first letter of the name comes from the **genus** and the second two letters come from the **species** of prokaryotic cell from which they were isolated.

For example, in restriction endonuclease, *Eco*RI comes from *E. coli* RY13, where the letter 'R' is derived from the name of **strain**. Roman numbers following the names, indicate the order in which the enzymes were isolated from that strain of bacteria.

8. (i) Mention the difference in the mode of action of exonuclease and endonuclease.
   (ii) How does restriction endonuclease *Eco* RI function? **(Delhi 2013)**

Ans. (i) **Exonucleases** cleave base pairs of DNA at their terminal ends (either 5′ or 3′), while the **endonucleases** cleave DNA at any point within the DNA segment at specific position except terminal ends.

(ii) Restriction endonuclease *Eco*RI cuts the DNA strands a little away from the palindromic sequences, but between the same two bases on the two strands

<pre>
        Eco RI
    5′–G↓A–A–T–T–C–3′
    3′–C–T–T–A–A↑G–5′
        Eco RI
</pre>

9. Collect five examples of palindromic DNA sequences by consulting your teacher. Better try to create a palindromic sequences by following base pair rules. **(NCERT)**

Ans. Five examples of palindromic DNA sequences are
   (i) 5′–A A G C T T–3′
       3′–T T C G A A–5′
   (ii) 5′–G G A T C C–3′
       3′–C C T A G G–5′
   (iii) 5′–A G G C C T–3′
       3′–T C C G G A–5′
   (iv) 5′–G A A T T C–3′
       3′–C T T A A G–5′
   (v) 5′–A C T A G T–3′
       3′–T G A T C A–5′

10. How are 'sticky ends' formed on a DNA strand? Why are they so called? **(Delhi 2014, 2010)**

Ans. Restriction enzymes cut the strands of the DNA, a little away from the centre of the palindromic sites, but between the same two bases on opposite strands. This leaves sticky single-stranded position at the ends. These overhanging stretches are called 'sticky ends'.
These are named so because they form hydrogen bonds with their complementary cut counter parts which facilitates the action of the enzyme DNA ligase.

11. The following illustrates the linking of DNA fragments.

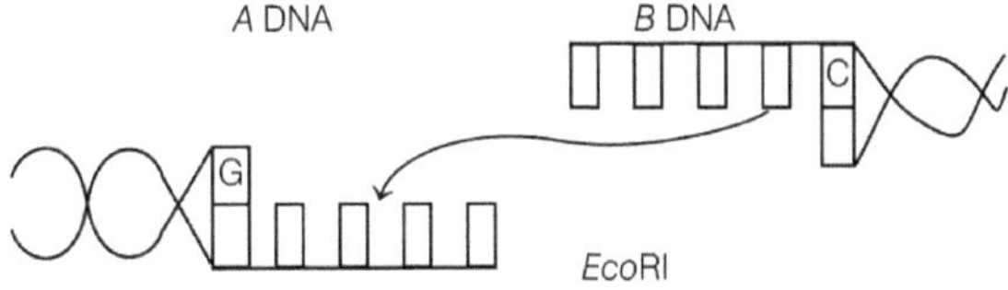

(i) Write the name of A and B.
(ii) Complete the palindrome, which is recognised by *Eco*RI.
(iii) Write the name of the enzyme that can link the two DNA fragments.

Ans. (i) A–Vector DNA/Plasmid DNA, B–Foreign DNA
(ii) 5′ –GAATTC–3′;
    3′–CTTAAG–5′
(iii) DNA ligase.

12. What is called molecular glue and why?

Ans. DNA ligases are called molecular glue because they repair broken DNA by joining two nucleotides. These are used in genetic engineering to reverse the action of restriction enzymes, i.e. to join complementary DNA strands/ends together.

13. A plasmid without a selectable marker was choosen as vector for cloning a gene. How does this affect the experiment?

Ans. In a gene cloning experiment, first a recombinant DNA molecule is constructed, where the gene of interest is ligated to the vector (the step would not be affected) and introduced inside the host cell (transformation).

Since, not all the cells get transformed with the recombinant/plasmid DNA, in the absence of selectable marker, it will be difficult to distinguish between transformants and non-transformant, because role of selectable marker is in the selection of transformants.

14. All cloning vectors do have a selectable marker. Describe its role in recombinant DNA technology. **(All India 2020)**

Ans. All cloning vectors have a selectable marker. Selectable marker helps in identifying or selecting transformants and eliminating non-transformants by selectively permitting the growth of the transformants.

15. From what have you learnt, can you tell whether enzymes are bigger or DNA is bigger in molecular size? How did you know? **(NCERT)**

Ans. DNA molecules are bigger in molecular size as compared to the enzymes. Small segments of the DNA called genes, control the synthesis of proteins and enzymes. DNA is made up of sugar, phosphate and nitrogen, while enzymes are made up of only protein molecules.

16. Explain the roles of the following with the help of an example each in recombinant DNA technology

(a) Restriction enzymes　　(b) Plasmids
(All India 2018)

Ans. (a) The restriction enzymes are known as molecular scissors.

These are used to cut plasmid DNA as well as foreign DNA at desired sites. The foreign DNA is then inserted into plasmid DNA. Then the plasmid takes the foreign DNA into the desired host organism.

Example Restriction enzyme *Hind* II. It was isolated from *Haemophilus influenzae*.
It produces DNA segments with blunt ends.

(b) **Plasmids** These are extrachromosomal, self-replicating, double-stranded, closed and circular DNA molecules, found only in bacteria and few yeast cells. These are used as vectors to carry the desired gene (foreign genes) into the desired organisms.

Example pBR322 is widely used plasmid vector. This plasmid has genes for resistance against ampicillin and tatracycline.

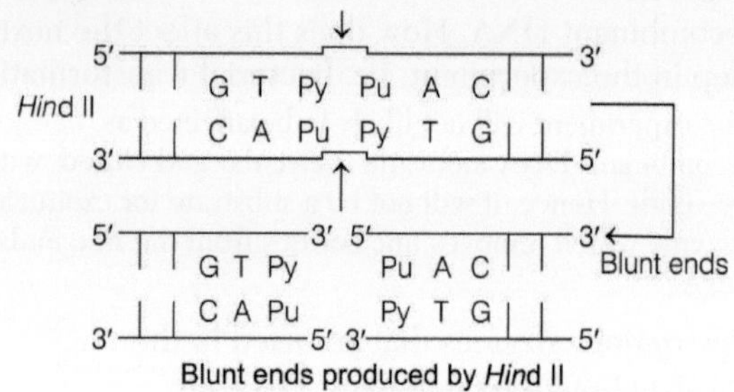

Blunt ends produced by *Hind* II

17. (i) How are recombinant vectors created?
(ii) For creating one recombinant vector only one type of restriction endonuclease is required. Give reason.

Ans. (i) The vector DNA is cut at a particular restriction site using a restriction enzyme (to cut the desired DNA segment). The alien DNA is then linked with the plasmid DNA using an enzyme called ligase to form the recombinant vector.

(ii) A restriction enzyme recognises and cuts the DNA at a particular sequence, called recognition site. If more than one restriction enzymes are present, they will generate several segments and will complicate gene cloning.

18. How is copy number of the plasmid vector related to yield of recombinant protein? **(NCERT Exemplar)**

Ans. The recombinant DNA can multiply as many times as the copy number of the plasmid vector, thereby determining the yield of recombinant protein. So, higher the copy number of the plasmid vector, higher will be the yield of recombinant protein.

19. Explain briefly.

(i) Restriction enzymes and DNA　(ii) Chitinase
(NCERT)

Ans. (i) **Restriction enzymes and DNA** These enzymes cut the helix of DNA on a specific site. So, these are also known as molecular scissors. DNA is a genetic material which is responsible to transfer genetic characters from one generation to the other.

(ii) **Chitinase** It is an enzyme used to break the cell wall of fungi to release its cellular parts. Certain plants and fungus consist of a cell wall composed of chitin, which provides strength to the cell. Chitinase is used when there is a need to break this wall and allows entry of foreign DNA in plant cells.

20. 'β-galactosidase enzyme is considered a better selectable marker'. Justify the statement. **(Delhi 2019)**

Ans. Coding sequence of β-galactosidase is a better selectable marker, as the recombinants and non-recombinants are differentiated on the basis of their ability to produce colour in the presence of a chromogenic substrate, while the selection of recombinants due to inactivation of antibiotic resistant gene is a tedious and time taking process to grow them simultaneously on two antibiotics.

21. (i) Identify *A* and *B* illustrations in the following.
(ii) Write the term given to *C* and *D* and why?

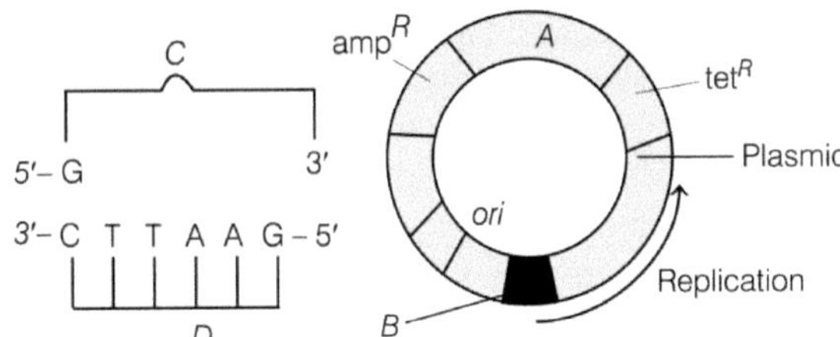

Ans. (i) *A*–Recognition site of the restriction endonuclease.
B–*rop* gene that codes for the protein involved in replication of plasmid.
(ii) *C* and *D* are palindromic sequences, as the sequence of base pairs reads the same on the two strands when the orientation of reading is kept same.

22. *A* and *B* are two different cloning vectors in two different bacterial colonies cultured in chromogenic substrate. Bacterial colonies with cloning vector *A* were colourless, whereas those with *B* were blue coloured. Explain by giving reasons for the difference in colour that appeared.

Ans. On the basis of colour production in the presence of chromogenic substrate, the recombinants and non-recombinants can be differentiated. In this, a recombinant DNA is inserted within the coding sequence of an enzyme β-galactosidase, which results in the inactivation of enzyme.

In plate *A*, the bacterial colonies having inserted plasmid, show no colouration. While in plate *B*, insertion of plasmid does not occur, therefore it shows blue colour.

23. (i) Explain how to find whether an *E. coli* bacterium has transformed or not, when a recombinant DNA bearing ampicillin-resistance gene is transferred into it.
(ii) What does the ampicillin-resistant gene act as, in the above case?　**(Delhi 2013)**

Ans. (i) The recombinant/transformant can be selected out from the non-recombinants/ non-transformants by plating the transformants on ampicillin-containing medium. The transformants will grow in it, while the non-transformants will not grow.
(ii) It acts as a selectable marker.

24. What modification is done on the Ti plasmid of *Agrobacterium tumefaciens* to convert it into a cloning vector?　**(NCERT Exemplar)**
Or State how has *Agrobacterium tumefaciens* been made a useful cloning vector to transfer DNA to plant cells.　**(Delhi 2014)**

Ans. Tumour inducing (Ti) plasmid of *Agrobacterium tumefaciens* is modified into a cloning vector by removing/altering the gene responsible for its pathogenic property. This is so, that it does not cause harm, but can act as a delivery system for the genes of interest into a variety of plants.

25. Describe the role of $CaCl_2$ in the preparation of competent cells.　**(NCERT Exemplar)**

Ans. $CaCl_2$ is known to increase the efficiency of DNA uptake to produce transformed bacterial cells. The divalent Ca^{2+} ions create transient pores on the bacterial cell wall by which the entry of foreign DNA is facilitated into the bacterial cells.

26. List the steps involved in *r*DNA technology.

Ans. Steps of *r*DNA technology are
(i) Isolation of DNA
(ii) Fragmentation of DNA by restriction endonucleases
(iii) Isolation of the desired DNA fragments
(iv) Amplification of the gene of interest
(v) Ligation of the DNA fragment into the vector using DNA ligase
(vi) Transfer of the recombinant DNA into the host
(vii) Culturing the host cell on a suitable medium on a large scale
(viii) Extraction of the desired product
(ix) Downstream processing of the products as finished products.

27. (i) Mention the importance of gel electrophoresis in biotechnology.
(ii) Explain the process of this technique.
　(All India 2019)

Ans. (i) DNA fragments formed by the use of restriction endonucleases are separated by gel electrophoresis.
(ii) Since, the DNA fragments are negatively charged molecules, so they can be separated by applying an electric field which makes DNA molecules move towards the anode (+), under an electric field through an appropriate medium or matrix.
The most commonly used matrix is **agarose**. DNA fragments resolve (separate) according to their size through sieving effect provided by the agarose gel.

Hence, the smaller the fragment size, farther it moves. The separated DNA fragments can be visualised only after staining the DNA with **Ethidium Bromide** (EtBr) followed by exposure to UV radiation.

These separate stained bands of DNA are cut out from the agarose gel and extracted from the gel piece, by a process known as **elution**.

28. A mixture of fragmented DNA was electrophoresed in an agarose gel. After staining the gel with ethidium bromide, no DNA bands were observed. What could be the reason?

Ans. The reasons are as follows
(i) DNA sample that was loaded on the gel may have got contaminated with nuclease (exo or endo both) and completely degraded.
(ii) Electrodes were put in opposite orientation in the gel assembly that is anode towards the wells (where DNA sample is loaded). Since, DNA molecules are

negatively charged, they move toward anode and hence, move out of the gel instead of moving into the matrix of gel.

(iii) Ethidium bromide was not added at all or was not added in sufficient concentration and so DNA was not visible.

29. A plasmid DNA and a linear DNA (both of the same size) have one site for a restriction endonuclease. When cut and separated on agarose gel electrophoresis, plasmid shows one DNA band, while linear DNA shows two fragments. Explain.
(NCERT Exemplar)

Ans. Plasmid DNA when cut and separated on agarose gel electrophoresis, shows one DNA band because plasmid is a circular DNA molecule and when it is cut with enzyme, it becomes linear, but does not get fragmented.

Whereas, a linear DNA molecule gets cut into two fragments. Hence, a single DNA band is observed for plasmid, while two DNA bands are observed for linear DNA in agarose gel.

30. Describe the process of amplification of 'gene of interest' using PCR technique. **(Delhi 2019)**

Ans. Amplification of gene is done using Polymerase Chain Reaction (PCR). It is carried out in the following steps

(i) **Denaturation** The double-stranded DNA is denatured by applying high temperature of 95°C for 15 seconds. Each separated strand acts as a template.

(ii) **Annealing** Two sets of primers are added, which anneal to the 3' end of each separated strand. This step is carried out at a slightly lower temperature (40°-60°C).

(iii) **Extension** DNA polymerase extends the primers by adding nucleotides complementary to the template provided in the reaction. *Taq* polymerase is used in the reaction, which can tolerate heat. All these steps are repeated many times to get several copies of the desired DNA.

31. How and why is the bacterium *Thermus aquaticus* employed in DNA technology? Explain.
(All India 2009)

Or Name the source of the DNA polymerase used in PCR technique. Mention why is it used ?
(All India 2013)

Or Give the name of the organism from where the thermostable DNA polymerase is isolated. State its role in genetic engineering. **(Foreign 2011)**

Ans. Bacterium, *Thermus aquaticus* is a source of enzyme *Taq* polymerase. As it is a thermostable enzyme and works at high temperature, it is used to amplify DNA *in vitro* by PCR. The amplified fragment of desired DNA can be used to ligate with the vector for further cloning.

32. While doing a PCR, denaturation step is missed. What will be its effect on the process?
(NCERT Exemplar)

Ans. If denaturation of double-stranded DNA does not take place, then primers will not be able to anneal to the template. Amplification will not occur and no extension will take place.

33. Describe the roles of (i) high temperature, (ii) primers and (iii) bacterium, *Thermus aquaticus* in carrying the process of polymerase chain reaction. **(All india 2019)**

Ans. (i) **Role of heat** In PCR (*in vitro*), the DNA strands are separated by heating at 95°C for 15 seconds. Heating causes the H-bonds between bases of two strands to get broken leading to unwinding.

(ii) **Role of primers** Primers are short lengths of DNA about 20 bp long that are required to start DNA polymerisation in PCR. The primers hybridise to their complementary sequence on the DNA strands at 40-60°C temperature and help in DNA polymerisation.

(iii) **Role of *Thermus aquaticus*** An enzyme called *Taq* polymerase is isolated from *Thermus aquaticus*. Since, this bacterium thrives in temperature as high as 95°C, without undergoing denaturation. Therefore, this enzyme is used in PCR instead of normal DNA polymerase.

34. Mention three uses of PCR. **(Delhi 2009)**

Ans. Three uses of PCR are

(i) It is used during *r*DNA for the production of newer and desired DNA.

(ii) It is used for DNA sequencing.

(iii) It is used in DNA fingerprinting.

35. What would happen when one grows a recombinant bacterium in the bioreactor but forget to add antibiotic to the medium in which the recombinant is growing?

Ans. In the absence of antibiotic, there will be no pressure on recombinants to retain the plasmid (containing the gene of our interest). Since, maintaining a high copy number of plasmids is a metabolic burden to the microbial cells, it will thus tend to loose the plasmid.

36. Besides better aeration and mixing properties, what other advantages do stirred-tank bioreactors have over shake flasks? **(NCERT)**

Ans. Besides better aeration and mixing properties stirred-tank bioreactors also facilitate mixing and oxygen availability throughout the bioreactor. It has an oxygen delivery system, a foam control system and a temperature controller. Small volumes of cultures are periodically withdrawn from the reactor for sampling.

37. How is a continuous culture system maintained in bioreactors and why ? **(Delhi 2019)**

Ans. The cells can be multiplied in a continuous culture system. In this, the used medium is drained out from one side, while fresh medium is added from the other side to maintain the cells in their physiologically most active (log/exponential) phase. This type of culturing method produces a larger biomass leading to higher yields of desired products.

• Long Answer (LA) Type Questions

1. Discuss with your teacher and find out how to distinguish between

   (i) Plasmid DNA and chromosomal DNA

   (ii) DNA and RNA

   (iii) Exonucleases and endonucleases **(NCERT)**

Ans. (i) Differences between plasmid and chromosomal DNA are as follows

Plasmid DNA	Chromosomal DNA
A circular, extrachromosomal DNA.	Generally linear.
Not associated with histone proteins.	Associated with histone proteins.
Contains very few genes, but may not be necessary for the cell.	Consists of complete genome vital for the cellular functions.
Replicates independently.	Replicates with genome.

(ii) Differences between DNA and RNA are as follows

DNA	RNA
It is a double-stranded nucleic acid molecule.	It is a single-stranded nucleic acid molecule.
It has deoxyribose sugar component.	It has ribose sugar component.
It has four nucleotides that act as its building blocks, adenine, guanine, cytosine and thymine.	It has uracil instead of thymine along with adenine, guanine and cytosine.
Function It has genetic information encoded in its base sequence.	**Function** It has information coded for building proteins.

(iii) Differences between exonucleases and endonucleases are as follows

Exonucleases	Endonucleases
They cleave base pairs of DNA at their terminal ends.	They cleave DNA at specific point except the terminal ends.
They act on single strand of DNA or gaps in double-stranded DNA.	They cleave one strand or both strands of double-stranded DNA.
They do not cut RNA.	They may cut RNA.

2. Which methods are used to selection of recombinants formed?

Ans. Selection of recombinants formed can be done by one of the following methods, given below

   (i) **Inactivation of antibiotic resistance gene** If a foreign DNA is ligated at the *Bam*HI site of tetracycline-resistance gene in the vector pBR322, the recombinant plasmid will loose tetracycline resistance.

   But, it can still be selected out from non-recombinant ones by plating transformants on ampicillin containing medium. The transformants growing on medium containing ampicillin are then transferred on a medium containing tetracycline.

   The **recombinants** will grow on ampicillin containing medium, but not on that containing tetracycline. On the other side, **non-recombinants** will grow on both media and thus, recombinants are selected.

   In this example, one antibiotic resistance gene helps in selecting the transformants, whereas the other antibiotic resistance gene gets inactivated due to insertion of alien DNA and helps in selection of recombinants.

   (ii) **Insertional inactivation** The selection of recombinants due to inactivation of antibiotic gene is a cumbersome procedure, because it requires simultaneous plating on two plates having different antibiotics. Therefore, the alternative selectable markers have been developed, which differentiate recombinants from non-recombinants. It is based on their ability to produce colour in the presence of **chromogenic substrate**.

   In this process, a recombinant DNA is inserted within the coding sequence of an enzyme β-galactosidase. This results into inactivation of the enzyme, which is referred to as **insertional inactivation**. Therefore, the bacterial colonies having inserted plasmid, shows **no colouration** (recombinant colonies), while those without plasmid will show **blue colour**. Here β-galactosidase works as a **reporter enzyme** (produced by reporter gene) whose inactivity helps to identify transformed and non-transformed bacterial colonies.

3. Describe the role of *Agrobacterium tumefaciens* in transforming a plant cell.

Ans. A soil-inhabiting, plant pathogenic bacterium, *Agrobacterium tumefaciens*, infects broad-leaved crops including tomato, soyabean, sunflower and cotton, but not the cereals. It causes tumours called **crown galls**.

Tumour formation is induced by its plasmid, which is, therefore called **Ti-plasmid** (Ti for tumour inducing). The Ti-plasmid integrates a segment of its DNA, termed T-DNA, into the chromosomal DNA of its host plant cells. The T-DNA causes tumours. As gene transfer occurs without human effort, the bacterium is known as **natural genetic engineer** of plants.

Plant molecular biologists have started using Ti-plasmids as vectors to transfer foreign genes of interest into the target plant cells. They use a version of the plasmid from which tumour forming gene has been eliminated. The transformed bacteria do not cause disease, but still deliver genes of interest into a variety of plants.

4. How bacterial cells are made competent to take up DNA?

Ans. DNA is a hydrophilic molecule, so it cannot pass through cell membranes. In order to force bacteria to take up the plasmid, the bacterial cells must first be made **competent**. The competency is the ability of a cell to take up foreign DNA.

The cells can be made competent by following methods

1. **Chemical method** ($CaCl_2$ method) In this, the cells are treated with a specific concentration of a divalent cation such as calcium which increases the efficiency with which DNA enters the bacterium through the pores in its cell wall. The cells are incubated with recombinant DNA on ice, followed by placing them briefly at 42°C and then putting them back on ice.

    This treatment that enables the bacteria to take up the recombinant DNA is known as **heat shock method**.

2. **Physical method** The **microinjection** is the physical method used to introduce foreign DNA into host cell. In this method, recombinant DNA is directly injected into the nucleus of an animal cell.
    Biolistics or **Gene gun** It is another method suitable for the introduction of DNA into plants, in which cells are bombarded with high velocity microparticles of gold or tungsten coated with DNA.

3. **Disarmed pathogen vectors** In this method, vectors that can cause infection are used to infect the cell to transfer the recombinant DNA into the host, e.g. retrovirus, papilloma virus and adenovirus in case of animals and *Agrobacterium* in case of plants.

5. If a desired gene is identified in an organism for some experiments, explain the process of the following. **(All India 2011)**
    (i) Cutting this desired gene at specific location.
    (ii) Synthesis of multiple copies of this desired gene.

Ans. (i) The desired gene is cut by using the enzymes restriction endonucleases. Firstly, the restriction endonucleases that recognise the palindromic nucleotide sequence of the desired gene is identified.
    The endonuclease inspects the entire DNA sequences to find and recognise the site. It cut each of the double helix at a specific point, which is a little away from the centre of the palindromic site. The cutting site is between the same two bases on the opposite strands. This results in overhanging of single-stranded stretches, which act as sticky ends.

It can be represented by the following diagram.

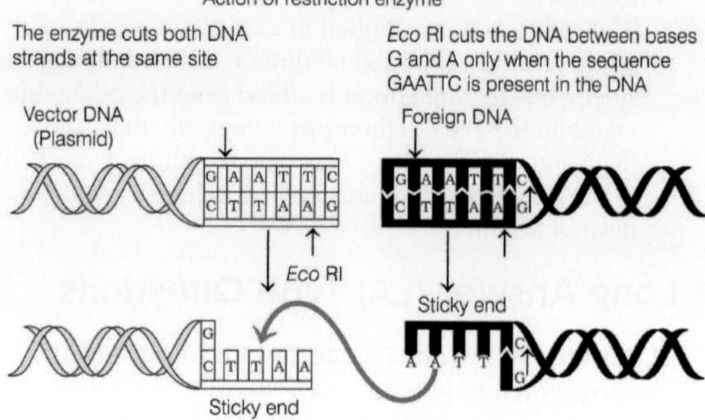

Steps in the formation of recombinant DNA by action of restriction endonuclease enzyme *Eco* RI

(ii) Multiple copies of the desired gene are synthesised by Polymerase Chain Reaction (PCR) method.

In this method, the desired gene is synthesised *in vitro*. The double-stranded DNA is denatured using high temperature of 95° C and the strands are separated. Each separated strand acts as a template.

Two sets of oligonucleotide primers are annealed to the denatured DNA strands. The thermostable *Taq* polymerase extends the primers using nucleotides provided in the reaction mixture. Finally, the amplified fragments are ligated into recipient cells.

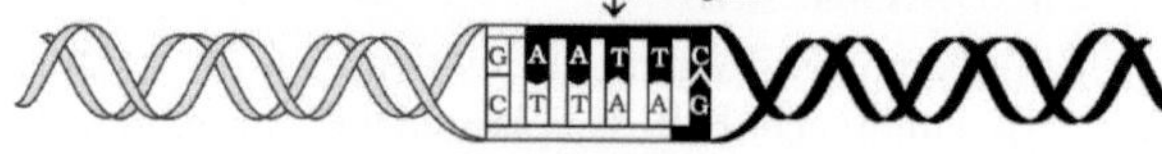

Polymerase Chain Reaction (PCR)

6. (i) How has the development of bioreactor helped in biotechnology?

   (ii) Name the most commonly used bioreactor and describe its working. **(All India 2018)**

Ans. (i) **Bioreactors** are the large volume vessels approximately (100-1000 L) in which raw materials are biologically converted into specific products, individual enzymes, etc., using microbial, plant, animal or human cells.

A bioreactor provides the optimal conditions for achieving the desired product by providing optimum growth conditions like temperature, pH, substrate, salts, vitamins and oxygen.

The cells can also be multiplied in a **continuous culture** system. In this, the used medium is drained out from one side while fresh medium is added from the other side to maintain the cells in their physiologically most active log/exponential phase. This type of culturing method produces a larger biomass leading to higher yields of desired protein. Thus, it plays a very important role particularly in traditional biotechnology.

   (ii) The most commonly used bioreactor is **simple stirred tank bioreactor**. It is usually cylindrical or with a curved base to facilitate the mixing of the reactor contents. The stirrer activity facilitates even mixing and availability of O_2 throughout the bioreactor.

Alternatively air can also be bubbled into the medium. As shown in the figure below, it has an agitator system, a temperature control system, a pH control system and sample ports so that small samples can be withdrawn periodically.

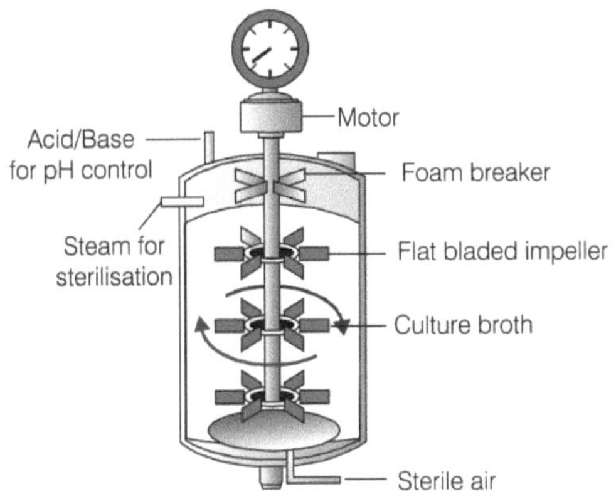

Simple stirred-tank bioreactor

• Case Based Questions

1. Observe the diagram given below and answer the questions that follows.

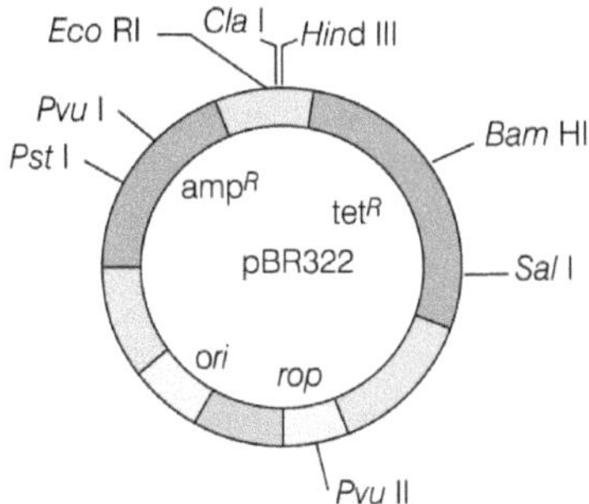

  (i) What is pBR322?

Ans. pBR322 is an *E. coli* cloning vector. It is small, autonomously replicating circular, extrachromosomal and double-stranded DNA molecule.

  (ii) What is the function of *rop*?

Ans. *rop* in pBR322 encodes for protein involved in replication of plasmid.

  (iii) What significance do amp^R and tet^R hold?

Ans. amp^R and tet^R are called selectable marker and are resistant to ampicillin and tetracycline, respectively. Their use makes differentiation of recombinants from non-recombinants easily.

  (iv) What is *ori*?

Ans. *Ori* stands for origin of replication. It is a sequence from where replication starts and any piece of DNA, when linked to the sequence, can be made to replicate within the host cell.

  (v) What do the letters 'pBR' of pBR322 indicate?

Ans. In pBR322, 'P' indicates that it is a plasmid and BR stands for Boliver and Rodriguez who constructed this plasmid.

2. Observe the given diagram and answer the questions that follows.

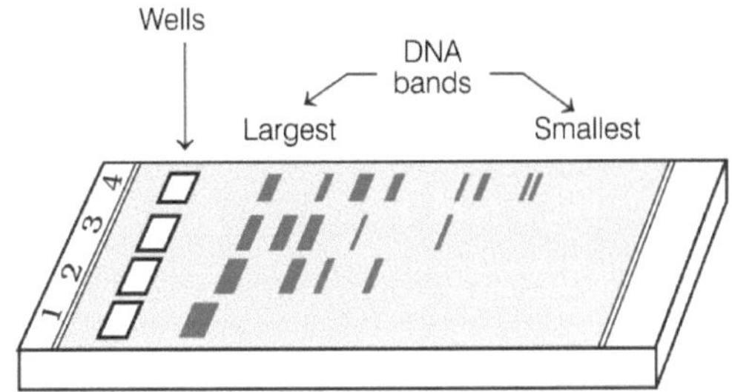

(i) Which process/technique is being shown in above diagram?

Ans. The above diagram shows agarose gel electrophoresis technique that is used in the field of biochemistry, genetics, etc., to separate mixture of macromolecules like DNA.

(ii) What will be the direction of movement of the DNA fragments in this technique?

Ans. DNA being negatively charged when placed in gel electrophoresis, will always move toward the positive electrode or anode.

(iii) 'Smaller the size of DNA fragment, the lesser it moves'. Is this statement true or false?

Ans. The given statement is false and can be corrected as Separation of DNA fragments takes place according to their sizes. The smallest the size of DNA fragment, farher it will move.

(iv) Which stain is generally used to visualise separated DNA fragments?

Ans. Ethidium bromide is used to visualise separated DNA fragments.

(v) Which macromolecules are separate by this technique?

Ans. This technique is used to separate macromolecules like RNA, DNA and proteins.

3. Direction *Read the following passage and answer the questions that follows.*

In recombinant technology, the desired genes for administraton is/are selected, followed by selecting a perfect vector into which the desired gene is to be integrated and *r*DNA formed.

The recombinant cells can be multiplied in large scale using a continuous culture system and can be achieved by using a bioreaction.

These are large vessels, 100-1000L in which raw materials are biologically converted into specific products, individual enzymes, etc., using microbial plant, animal or human cells.

A bioreaction provides optimum conditions for the growth of the desired product. These conditions include temperature, pH, substrate, etc.

(i) Which conditions apart from the temperature, pH and substrate are provided by the bioreactor.?

Ans. Apart from temperature, pH and substrate, a bioreaction provides oxygen, salts and vitamins also.

(ii) What happens in a continuous culture system?

Ans. In a continuous culture system, the used medium is drained cut from one side and fresh medium is added from the either side to maintain the cells in their physiologically active state.

(iii) Name the components of a bioreaction.

Ans. Components of a bioreaction included the following

    (a) an agitator system

    (b) an oxygen delivery system

    (c) foam control system

    (d) temperature control system

    (e) pH control system

    (f) Sampling parts to withdraw the culture.

(iv) Write the name of two bioreactors?

Ans. The most commonly used bioreactors are of stirring type which are of two types, i.e.

    (a) simple stirred-tank bioreactor

    (b) sparged stirred-tank bioreactor

(v) What is the purpose of sparged stirred tank bioreactor?

Ans. It facilitates mixing of components and ensures oxygen availability throughout the bioreactor.

Chapter Test

Multiple Choice Questions

1. Restriction endonucleases are enzymes, which
(a) make cuts at specific positions within the DNA molecule
(b) recognise a specific nucleotide sequence for binding and then cleave both the strands of DNA
(c) restrict the action of the enzyme DNA polymerase
(d) remove nucleotides from the ends of the DNA molecule

2. The function of DNA ligase in recombinant technology is
(a) fragmentation of DNA
(b) transfer DNA into host cell
(c) link newly formed DNA fragments
(d) separate DNA fragments by their charge and size

3. In recombinant DNA technique, the term vector refers to a
(a) donor DNA, it is identified and picked up through electrophoresis
(b) plasmid, transfers DNA into living cell
(c) collection of entire genome in the form of plasmid
(d) enzyme that cuts the DNA at specific sites

4. Identify A, B, C and D in the given diagram of *E. coli* cloning vector pBR322.

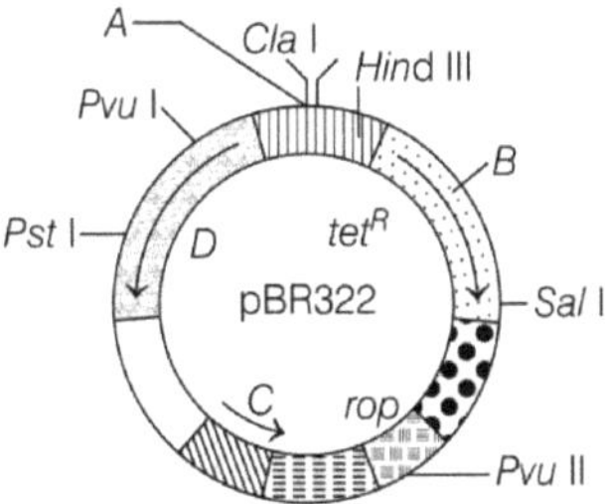

(a) A–Eco RI, B–Bam HI, C–ori, D–amp^R
(b) A–amp^R, B–ori, C–Bam HI, D–Eco RI
(c) A–ori, B–Bam HI, C–Eco RI, D–amp^R
(d) A–Bam HI, B–Eco RI, C–amp^R, D–ori

5. The process of recombinant DNA technology has following steps

I. Amplification of gene

II. Insertion of recombinant DNA into the host cell

III. Cutting of DNA at specific location using restriction enzyme

IV. Isolation of genetic material (DNA)

Pick out the option for the correct sequence of step for the process of recombinant DNA technology.
(a) II, III, IV and I
(b) IV, II, III and I
(c) I, II, III and IV
(d) IV, III, I and II

Assertion-Reasoning MCQs

Direction (Q. Nos. 1-3) *Each of these questions contains two statements, Assertion (A) and Reason (R). Each of these questions also has four alternative choices, any one of which is the correct answer. You have to select one of the codes (a), (b), (c) and (d) given below.*

(a) Both A and R are true and R is the correct explanation of A
(b) Both A and R are true, but R is not the correct explanation of A
(c) A is true, but R is false
(d) A is false, but R is true

1. Assertion (A) Maintenance of sterile environment is essential for manufacture of biotechnological products.

Reason (R) This is to enable growth of desired prokaryotic or eukaryotic cells.

2. Assertion (A) Foreign DNA and vector DNA are cut with the help of ligase.

Reason (R) Ligase acts by forming phosphodiester bonds.

3. Assertion (A) Use of chitinase enzyme is necessary for isolation of DNA from fungal cells.

Reason (R) Fungal cell wall is made up of chitin and chitinase is able to digest it.

Short Answer Type Questions

1. Write any four ways used to introduce a desired DNA segment into a bacterial cell in recombinant DNA technology experiments. **(All India 2013)**

2. Consider the following statements.
(i) Origin of replication or *ori* site is a specific sequence of DNA from where replication initiates.
(ii) Selectable markers are genes which impart unique features to a vector, e.g. antibiotic resistance.

Reconcile the above statements and explain why these features are considered essential to facilitate cloning into a vector during RDT.

3. Outline how restriction enzymes are used for removing sections of DNA from a chromosome.

4. What essential features must be present in a cloning vehicle/cloning vector?

Long Answer Type Questions

1. Any recombinant DNA with desired gene is required in billion copies for commercial use. How is this amplification done? Explain.

2. What is bioreactor? What are its types?

Answers

Multiple Choice Questions

1. (b)　*2.* (c)　*3.* (b)　*4.* (a)　*5.* (d)

Assertion-Reasoning MCQs

1. (a)　*2.* (d)　*3.* (a)

For Detailed Solutions
Scan the code

CHAPTER 04

Biotechnology and its Applications

In this Chapter...

- Biotechnological Applications in Agriculture
- Biotechnological Applications in Medicine
- Transgenic Animals
- Ethical Issues

- Biotechnology is useful to humans in producing various products by using microbes, plants, animals and their metabolic machinery. This became possible due to Recombinant DNA Technology, in which valuable and useful manipulation of genes in various living species is done to obtain desirable products at large scale.

- The applications of biotechnology include therapeutics, diagnostics, **Genetically Modified** (GM) crops for agriculture, processed food, bioremediation, waste treatment and energy production. Three critical research areas of biotechnology are

  (i) To provide the best catalyst in the form of improved organism usually a microbe or a pure enzyme.

  (ii) To create optimal conditions through engineering for a catalyst to act.

  (iii) Downstream processing technologies to purify the organic compounds or proteins.

Biotechnological Applications in Agriculture

- To feed the increasing population of the world, we need to enhance our food production. This can be done by applying following options

  (i) Agrochemical based agriculture

  (ii) Organic agriculture

  (iii) Genetically engineered crops based agriculture

- The **green revolution** has succeeded in enhancing the food supply to three folds but yet it was not enough to feed the rapidly growing human population. It has increased the yield of crops mainly due to the use of improved varieties of crops, agrochemicals (fertilisers and pesticides) and better management practices.

- But most of the agrochemicals have harmful effects on the environment and they are expensive for farmers in developing countries. It is also difficult to further increase the yield with existing varieties using conventional breeding. Therefore, the best solution to overcome all these issues is to develop and use Genetically Modified (GM) crops.

Genetically Modified Organisms (GMOs)

- The plants, bacteria, fungi and animals whose genes have been altered by manipulation are called Genetically Modified Organisms (GMO). These are also called **transgenic organisms**, as they contain and express one or more foreign genes called **transgenes**. GM plants are useful in many ways.

- Genetic modification has done the following changes to the phenotypic expression of the plants

  (i) Crops became more tolerant to abiotic stresses like cold, drought, salt and heat.

  (ii) Dependence on chemical pesticides has reduced, i.e. pest-resistant crops.

  (iii) It helped to reduce post-harvest losses.

(iv) Efficiency of mineral usage increased in plants, preventing early exhaustion of fertility of soil.

(v) Enhanced nutritional value of food, e.g. vitamin-A enriched rice (golden rice).

Other than the above mentioned uses, genetic modifications have been used to create tailor-made plants to supply alternative resources to the industries in the form of starches, fuels and pharmaceuticals.

Biopesticides

An application of biotechnology in agriculture is the production of pest-resistant plants which could decrease the amount of pesticides being used. *Bt* toxin is produced by a bacterium called *Bacillus thuringiensis.*

Bt toxin gene has been cloned from the bacteria and been expressed in plants to provide resistance to the insects without the need for insecticides and so named as biopesticide, e.g. *Bt* cotton, *Bt* corn, rice, tomato, potato and soybean, etc.

Bt Cotton

- *Bt* cotton is created by using some strains of bacterium, *Bacillus thuringiensis* (*Bt* is a short form). This bacterium produces a protein that kills certain insects such as lepidopterans (tobacco budworm, armyworm), coleopterans (beetles) and dipterans (flies, mosquitoes).

- *Bacillus thuringiensis* forms protein crystals (Cry) during a particular phase of their growth. These crystals contain a toxic **insecticidal protein**. But this toxin does not kill the *Bacillus* (bacterium), because *Bt* toxin protein exists as inactive protoxins but once an insect ingests the inactive toxin, it is converted into its active form due to the **alkaline pH** of the gut which solubilises the crystals.

- The activated toxin binds to the surface of midgut epithelial cells and creates pores that cause cell swelling and lysis leading to the death of an insect. *Bt* tobacco was first cultured to kill hornworm (*Manduca sexta*). The toxin is encoded by the *cry* genes, which are insect group specific.

- For example,

  (i) *cry* IAc and *cry* IIAb control cotton bollworms.

  (ii) *cry* IAb controls corn borer.

  (iii) *cry* IIIAb controls colorado potato beetle.

  (iv) *cry* IIIBb controls corn rot worm.

Biotechnological Applications in Medicine

- The recombinant DNA technological processes have made immense impact in the area of healthcare by enabling mass production of safe and more effective **therapeutic** drugs.

- The recombinant therapeutics do not induce unwanted immunological responses as in common case of similar products isolated from non-human sources.

- At present, about 30 recombinant therapeutics have been approved for human use all over the world. Out of these, 12 are marketed in India.

Genetically Engineered Insulin

- It has lead to sufficient availability of insulin for the management of adult onset diabetes. Insulin used for diabetes was earlier extracted from the pancreas of slaughtered cattle and pigs. This insulin developed allergy or other types of reactions due to the foreign protein.

- Insulin consists of two short polypeptide chains, i.e. chain 'A' and chain 'B' that are linked together by disulphide bridges.

- In mammals, including humans, insulin is synthesised as a **pro-hormone** (needs to be processed before it becomes a fully mature and functional hormone) which contains an extra stretch called the **C-peptide**.

- This C-peptide is not present in the mature insulin and is removed during maturation into insulin. Therefore, the main challenge for the production of insulin using *r*DNA techniques was getting insulin assembled into a mature form.

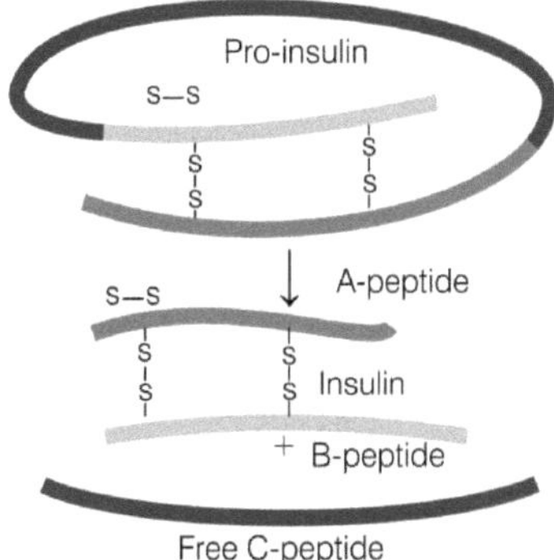

Maturation of pro-insulin into insulin after removal of C-peptide (simplified)

- In 1983, **Eli Lilly**, an American company prepared two DNA sequences corresponding to A and B-chains of human insulin and introduced them in plasmids of *E. coli* to produce insulin chains. These chains (A and B) were produced separately, extracted and combined by creating disulphide bonds to form human insulin called **humulin**.

Recombinant Vaccine

- Vaccines produced through genetic engineering methods are called recombinant vaccines or **second generation vaccines.**
- They have gene inserts for the surface proteins of a pathogen which enhance immunity but do not result in infection.
- These plasmids are inserted in bacteria or yeast cells that express the viral proteins which are then injected into the human host as vaccine. There they are recognised as foreign and an immune response is elicited.
- Recombinant hepatitis-B vaccine and polio vaccine are the examples of *r*DNA vaccine.

Stem Cell Technology

- It is now known to be the most rapidly developing field that combines the efforts of cell biologists and geneticists for the treatment of a variety of malignant and non-malignant diseases by using stem cells.
- Stem cells are undifferentiated biological cells that can differentiate into specialised cells and can divide (through mitosis) to produce more stem cells. These cells are found in multicellular organisms.
- They are mainly of two types, i.e. **embryonic stem cells,** which are isolated from the inner cell mass of blastocysts and **adult stem cells**, which exist throughout the body after embryonic development and are found inside different types of tissues such as brain.
- The potential applications of stem cell include organ and tissue regeneration, bone marrow transplantation, brain disease treatment, cell deficiency therapy, cardiovascular disease treatment, blood disease treatment, etc.

Gene Therapy

- It is a collection of methods which allow correction of gene defects, diagnosed in a child or an embryo. It involves replacing a defective mutant gene with a **functional gene.** It works effectively against single gene disorders, enzymatic disorders and immunodeficiency disorders.
- The **first gene therapy** was performed in a 4 years old girl in 1990, who had **Adenosine Deaminase** (ADA) deficiency. The enzyme, adenosine deaminase is crucial for the immune system to function.

- The disorder is caused due to the deletion of the gene for adenosine deaminase.
- In some children, ADA deficiency can be cured by bone marrow transplantation and in, others by enzyme replacement therapy. But, the problem with both of these approaches is that they are not completely curative. This is why gene therapy was introduced to cure this ailment.
- Steps followed in enzyme replacement gene therapy are given below
  - In first step of gene therapy, lymphocytes from the blood of the patient are grown in a culture outside the body.
  - A functional ADA *c*DNA (using a retroviral vector) is then introduced into these lymphocytes which are subsequently returned to the patient.
  - As these cells are not immortal, the patient requires periodic infusion of such genetically engineered lymphocytes. But if the gene isolated from marrow cells producing ADA is introduced into cells at early embryonic stages, it could be a permanent cure.
- Some other diseases that can be treated by gene therapy are haemophilia, cystic fibrosis, Parkinson's disease, etc.

Transgenic Animals

These are the animals which have their DNA manipulated to possess and express an extra (foreign) gene. Examples are transgenic rats, rabbits, pigs, sheep, etc. Out of all the existing transgenic animals, 95% are mice.

Several benefits and uses of transgenic animals are

1. **Normal physiology and development** Transgenic animals can be specifically designed to allow the study of how genes are regulated and how they affect the normal functioning of the body and its development. For example, the study of complex factors involved in growth such as insulin like growth factors.

2. **Study of disease** Many transgenic animals are designed to increase the understanding of how genes contribute to the development of diseases such as cancer, cystic fibrosis, rheumatoid arthritis and Alzheimer's. These are specially made to serve as models for human diseases, so that investigation of new treatments for diseases is made possible.

3. **Biological products** Human diseases can be treated by medicines that contain biological products.

   (i) Transgenic animals that produce useful biological products can be created by the introduction of the portion of the DNA or genes that code for a particular product such as human protein (α-1-antitrypsin) which is used to treat emphysema. Similar attempts are being made for the treatment of Phenylketonuria (PKU) and cystic fibrosis.

(ii) In 1997, the first transgenic cow, **Rosie** produced human protein enriched milk (2.4 g/L).
The milk contained the human **alpha lactalbumin** and was nutritionally a more balanced product for human babies than natural cow's milk.

4. **Vaccine safety** Transgenic mice are being used for testing the safety of vaccines before they are used on humans, e.g. polio vaccine. If found reliable and successful they could replace the use of monkeys in order to test the safety of batches of the vaccine.

5. **Chemical safety testing** It is also known as toxicity or safety testing. It is similar to the procedure used for testing toxicity of drugs.

Transgenic animals are made that carry the genes, which make them more sensitive to toxic substances than the non-transgenic animals. They are then exposed to toxic substances and effects are studied. This allows us to obtain result in less time.

Ethical Issues

- Manipulation of living organisms by human race can be unethical and should not go unregulated. The genetic modification of organisms can have unpredictable results, when such organisms are introduced into the ecosystem.

- The modification or usage of living organisms for public services has also created problems with patents granted for the same.

- Therefore, there is a need for some ethical standards to evaluate our actions. These sets of standards that are used to regulate our activities in relation to biological world are called **bioethics**.

- Public is very much concerned that certain companies are being granted patents for the products and technologies that make use of the genetic materials, plants and other biological resources that have long been developed by the farmers and indigenous people of a specific region/country.

- In order to control these issues, Indian Government has setup an organisation **Genetic Engineering Approval Committee** (GEAC) which makes all decisions regarding the validity of GM research and the safety of introducing GMOs for public services.

Patent

It is a set of exclusive rights granted by a government to the inventors or their assignee to prevent others from commercial use of their invention. And when patent is granted for biological entities and for products derived from them, they are called **biopatents**. Primarily USA, Japan and members of European Union are awarding biopatents.

Biopiracy

- It refers to use of bioresources by multinational companies and other organisations without proper authorisation from the countries or people concerned without any payment.

- Some nations are developing laws to prevent such unauthorised exploitation of their bioresources and traditional knowledge.

- The Indian Parliament has recently cleared the second amendment of the **Indian Patents Bill** that takes such issues of biopiracies into consideration including patent terms, emergency provisions and research and development initiative.

Controversies in India Regarding Biopatent and Biopiracy

When a patent is taken on plants and seeds derived from Indian biological resources, biopiracy occurs. Challenging and stopping such biopiracy is the duty of government. Following are the plants on which controversies occurred in India

Basmati Rice

- Rice is being used since thousands of years in Asia's agricultural history, of which 2,00,000 varieties are in India alone.

- **Basmati** is unique for its aroma and flavour, whose 27 varieties are cultivated in India. An American company **Rice Tec** won a patent on Basmati Rice Lines and Grains in 1997 through the US Patent and Trademark Office and was allowed to sell a 'new variety' in US and Abroad.

- This new variety of Basmati was actually derived from the Indian farmer's varieties.

- Indian Basmati was crossed with semi-dwarf varieties and claimed as an invention or a novelty by the American company. The patent extends to functional equivalents implying that other people selling Basmati rice could be restricted by the patent.

Turmeric and Neem

- In May 1995, the US Patent Office granted to the University of Mississippi Medical Center a patent for 'Use of Turmeric in Wound Healing'.

- In 1996, another patent was granted to the firm of WR Grace and Co., by the European Patent Office, Munich for 'fungicidal uses of neem oil'.

- Thus, if we do not pay attention or counter these patent applications, our rich legacy will be encashed by other countries and individuals.

Chapter Practice

Objective Questions

• Multiple Choice Questions

1. Biotechnology mainly deals with
  (a) industrial scale production of pharmaceutical
  (b) biological use of genetically modified microbes, fungi, plants and animals
  (c) Both (a) and (b)
  (d) None of the above

Ans. (*c*) Biotechnology deals with a large scale production of pharmaceuticals and biological use of genetically modified microbes, fungi, plants and animals in various applications like agriculture, medicine, etc.

2. Plants, bacteria, fungi and animals whose genes have been altered by manipulation are called
  (a) genetically modified organisms
  (b) hybrid organisms
  (c) pest resistant organisms
  (d) insect resistant organisms

Ans. (*a*) Genes of plants, bacteria, fungi and animals have been altered by genetic manipulations. Therefore, these organisms are called Genetically Modified Organisms (GMOs). These are used in research, medicine, food production, etc.

3. *Bt* toxin is
  (a) intracellular crystalline protein
  (b) extracellular crystalline protein
  (c) intracellular monosaccharide
  (d) extracellular polysaccharide

Ans. (*a*) *Bt* toxin is an intracellular crystalline protein that exists as inactive protoxin which once ingested by an insect, gets activated, binds to the surface of midgut epithelial cells and creates pores which cause cell swelling and lysis, leading to death of an insect.

4. Insect resistant transgenic cotton has been produced by inserting a piece of DNA from
  (a) an insect
  (b) a bacterium
  (c) a wild relative of cotton
  (d) a virus

Ans. (*b*) Insect resistant transgenic cotton has been produced by inserting a piece of DNA from a bacterium, *Bacillus thuringiensis* into the genome of cotton.

5. Match the following columns.

	Column I		Column II
A.	*Bt* tobacco	1.	Vitamin-A
B.	Lepidopterans	2.	High yield and pest resistant
C.	*Bt* cotton	3.	*Manduca sexta*
D.	Golden rice	4.	Tobacco budworm

Codes

```
    A  B  C  D
(a) 3  4  2  1
(b) 1  2  4  3
(c) 4  2  3  1
(d) 3  1  2  4
```

Ans. (*a*) A–3, B–4, C–2, D–1

6. Which bacterium was the first to be used as biopesticide on the commercial scale in the world?
  (a) *Bacillus thuringiensis*
  (b) *E. coli*
  (c) *Pseudomonas aeruginosa*
  (d) *Agrobacterium tumefaciens*

Ans. (*a*) *Bacillus thringiensis*, is a natural spore forming bacterium was the first to be used as a biopesticide on a commercial scale in the world.

7. Which of the following statements is/are correct ?
  I. The proinsulin has an extra peptide called C-peptide.
  II. The functional insulin has A and B chains linked together by hydrogen bonds.
  III. Genetically engineered insulin is produced in *E. coli*.
  IV. In man, insulin is synthesised as a proinsulin.
  Codes
  (a) I and II   (b) I and III
  (c) III and IV   (d) I, III and IV

Ans. (*d*) Statements I, III and IV are correct, while statement II is incorrect. Incorrect statement can be corrected as
Insulin is composed of two peptide chains referred to as the A chain and B chain. A and B chains are linked together by two disulphide bonds.

8. The first clinical gene therapy was done for the treatment of   **(NCERT Exemplar)**
  (a) AIDS
  (b) cancer
  (c) cystic fibrosis
  (d) SCID (Severe Combined Immuno Deficiency) resulting from the deficiency of ADA

Ans. (*d*) The first clinical gene therapy was done for the treatment of SCID (Severe Combined Immuno Deficiency) on a 4 years old girl in 1990.

9. A patient has a defective gene for the enzyme Adenosine Deaminase (ADA). He/She lacks functional cells and therefore, fails to fight the infecting pathogens. The cells are
  (a) B-lymphocytes   (b) Phagocytes
  (c) T-lymphocytes   (d) Both (a) and (c)

Ans. (*d*) The patient has a defective gene for the enzyme Adenosine Deaminase (ADA). This enzyme is involved in maturation of B and T-lymphocytes and is crucial for the functioning of immune system due to this, he/she lacks functional lymphocytes and therefore, fails to fight the infecting pathogens.

10. Transgenic animals are produced
  I. To study the normal physiology and development.
  II. To study diseases.
  III. To obtain useful biological products.
  IV. To test the vaccine safety.
  V. To test the chemical safety.

  Which of the above statements are correct?
  (a) I, II and III   (b) II, III and IV
  (c) I, II, III and V   (d) I, II, III, IV and V

Ans. (*d*) All the given statements are correct.

11. Which property of transgenic animals is used in chemical safety testing?
  (a) Insensitivity to toxic substances
  (b) Sensitivity to toxic substances
  (c) Resistance to toxic substances
  (d) Both (a) and (c)

Ans. (*b*) The property of sensitivity to toxic substance is used in chemical safety testing. Transgenic animals are useful as disease models and producers of substances for human welfare.

12. Which gene was introduced in the first transgenic cow?
  (a) Human α-lactalbumin
  (b) β-1-antitrypsin
  (c) α-1-antitrypsin
  (d) *cry* l Ac

Ans. (*a*) Gene for human alpha (α) lactalbumin was introduced into the genes of the first transgenic cow, which made the milk nutritionally richer.

13. Which of the following is related to bioethics?
  (a) Process of discovery and commercialisation of new products
  (b) Use of bioresources without proper authorisation
  (c) Both (a) and (b)
  (d) Standards used to regulate human activities in relation to biological world

Ans. (*d*) The set of standards used to relate human activities in relation to biological world is called bioethics.

14. Which of the following statements about biopatents is/are correct?
  I. Biopatents protect intellectual property right of an inventor.
  II. Biopatents of all products are subjected to commercialisation.
  III. Biopatents should be granted carefully and impartially.
  IV. Biopatenting requires examination of legal, ethical and social issues.

  Choose the correct option.
  (a) Only II   (b) I, III and IV
  (c) II and IV   (d) I, II, III and IV

Ans. (*b*) All given statements are correct about biopatents except II. Incorrect statement can be corrected as

  Biopatent is a patent granted by the government to the inventor for biological entities and for products obtained from them. These are not always for commercialisation, but some are for scientific research benefits.

15. Match the following columns.

	Column I		Column II
A.	Rosie	1.	Emphysema
B.	Biopiracy	2.	Right granted for biological entities
C.	Biopatent	3.	Illegal removal of biological material
D.	α-1 antitrypsin	4.	Transgenic cow

Codes

	A	B	C	D		A	B	C	D
(a)	4	3	2	1	(b)	3	2	1	4
(c)	2	1	4	3	(d)	4	1	3	2

Ans. (*a*) A–4, B–3, C–2, D–1

• Assertion-Reasoning MCQs

Direction (Q. Nos. 1-5) *Each of the following questions contains two statements, Assertion (A) and Reason (R). Each of these questions also has four alternative choices, any one of which is the correct answer. You have to select one of the codes (a), (b), (c) and (d) given below.*

  (a) Both A and R are true and R is the correct explanation of A
  (b) Both A and R are true, but R is not the correct explanation of A
  (c) A is true, but R is false
  (d) A is false, but R is true

1. Assertion (A) Many crops are incorporated with foreign genes to make them tolerant to abiotic stresses.

   Reason (R) Genomes of many plants are manipulated or altered by combining them with other genes to get desired traits.

Ans. (*a*) Both A and R are true and R is the correct explanation of A.

2. Assertion (A) *Agrobacterium tumefaciens* is popular in genetic engineering because this bacterium is associated with the stems of all cereal and pulse crops.

   Reason (R) Using *Agrobacterium* as vector, the genes can be transferred in biotechnological techniques.

Ans. (*d*) A is false, but R is true. A can be corrected as

   Agrobacterium tumefaciens is popular in genetic engineering. As it contains a large Ti-plasmid (tumour inducing plasmid) and it can transfer a part of its plasmid DNA to the host plant. Therefore, the bacterium can be used as the vector and helps in the transfer of genes in biotechnological techniques.

3. Assertion (A) Humulin is better than conventional insulin.

   Reason (R) Conventional insulin produces many side effects.

Ans. (*a*) Both A and R are true and R is the correct explanation of A.

4. Assertion (A) Recombinant therapeutics do not induce unwanted immunological responses.

   Reason (R) The human body does not recognise them as foreign elements.

Ans. (*a*) Both A and R are true and R is the correct explanation of A.

   Since, recombinant therapeutics are identical to human proteins, the human body does not recognise them as foreign elements.

   Thus, they do not induce unwanted immunological responses and are free from risk of infection.

5. Assertion (A) ADA deficiency disorder is caused due to the excessive synthesis of gene for adenosine deaminase.

   Reason (R) It affects the human immune system.

Ans. (*d*) A is false, but R is true. A can be corrected as

   ADA deficiency disorder is caused due to the lack of gene which codes for adenosine deaminase. This enzyme is crucial for the immune system to function. Thus, ADA deficiency affects the immune system of the human.

• Case Based MCQ

Direction *Read the following passage and answer the questions that follows.*

Biotechnology deals with techniques of using live organisms to produce products useful to humans. But this manipulation of living organisms is going without regulation. Therefore, some ethical standards are required to evaluate the morality of human activities. In India, Government has setup organisation such as GEAC, which make decisions regarding the validity of GM research and patent issues.

(i) Biopatent means

   (a) right to use an invention
   (b) right to use biological resources
   (c) right to use applications or processes
   (d) All of the above

Ans. (*d*) A biopatent means a government protection granted for biological entities and their products. It gives right to use an invention, biological resources or use of application or processes. Thus, option (d) is correct.

(ii) Rules of conduct that are used to regulate activities with respect to biological world is called

   (a) bioethics   (b) biowar
   (c) biopiracy   (d) biopatent

Ans. (*a*) Rules of conduct that are used to regulate activities with respect to biological world is called bioethics.

(iii) Biopiracy is related to

   (a) traditional knowledge exploitation
   (b) biomolecules and regarding bioresources exploitation
   (c) stealing of bioresources
   (d) All of the above

Ans. (*d*) Biopiracy is related to traditional knowledge exploitations, biomolecules and regarding bioresources exploitation and stealing of bioresources.

   Thus, option (d) is correct.

(iv) Which Indian plants have either been patented or attempts have been made to patent them by Western nations for their use?

   (a) Basmati rice
   (b) Turmeric
   (c) Neem
   (d) All of the above

Ans. (*d*) In the past patent attempts have been made on Basmati rice, turmeric and neem by Western nations.

   Thus, option (d) is correct.

(v) **Assertion** (A) *Bacillus anthracis* exemplifies how biotechnology can be used for destructive purposes.

Reason (R) The spores of anthrax bacterium were spread *via* letters in the form of powder.

(a) Both A and R are true and R is the correct explanation of A

(b) Both A and R are true, but R is not the correct explanation of A

(c) A is true, but R is false

(d) Both A and R are false

Ans. (*b*) Both A and R are true, but R is not the correct explanation of A.

Biotechnology is very useful to mankind but *Bacillus anthracis* examplifies how biotechnology can be used for destructive purposes, i.e. as bioweapons. For example, in 2001 powdered anthrax spores were deliberately put into letter which was mailed through US portal because of which many people were affected by the bacteria.

PART 2
Subjective Questions

• Short Answer (SA) Type Questions

1. In view of the current food crisis, it is said that we need another green revolution. Highlight the major limitations of the earlier green revolution.

Ans. Major limitations of the earlier green revolution are as follows

(i) Generally undesired characters also breed along with desired ones.

(ii) Regular use of fertilisers affected both soil fertility and quality.

(iii) Extensive use of pesticides/insecticides/weedicides resulted in harmful effects on the natural components of the ecosystem.

So, another green revolution that can curb these problems and enhance the quality of food production in limited land resources is certainly required.

2. Expand GMO. How is it different from a hybrid?
(NCERT Exemplar)

Ans. GMO stands for Genetically Modified Organism.

It differs from a hybrid because in a hybrid, cross is done between total genomes of two species or strains, whereas in a GMO, foreign genes from an entirely different species are introduced in the organism and are usually maintained as extrachromosomal entity or are integrated into the genome of the organism.

3. What is GMO? List any five possible advantages of a GMO to a farmer. **(All India 2016)**

Or List any four ways by which GMOs have been useful for enhanced crop output. **(Delhi 2019)**

Or Why GMOs are so called ? List the different ways in which GMO plants have benefitted and have become useful to humans. **(All India 2020)**

Ans. The plants, bacteria, fungi and animals whose genes have been altered by manipulation are called Genetically Modified Organisms (GMOs).

Advantages of GMOs to a Farmer

(i) Crops become more tolerant to abiotic stresses like cold, drought, salt and heat.

(ii) Dependence on chemical pesticides has reduced, i.e. pest-resistant crops.

(iii) Helped to reduce post-harvest losses.

(iv) Efficiency of mineral usage increased in plants, preventing early exhaustion of fertility of soil.

(v) Enhanced nutritional value of food, e.g. vitamin-A enriched rice.

4. Find out from the internet what is golden rice.
(NCERT)

Ans. Golden rice is a genetically modified rice with high levels of β-carotene and other carotenoids. This rice is modified in order to enhance the quantity of vitamin-A in it. It is called golden due to the gold like colour it gets from β-carotene.

5. What are transgenic bacteria? Illustrate with an example. **(NCERT)**

Ans. Bacteria that have had their DNA manipulated to possess and express an extra (foreign) gene are known as transgenic bacteria, e.g. DNA sequences introduced in plasmid of *E. coli* to produce insulin chains.

6. How has the study of biotechnology helped in developing pest resistant cotton crop? Explain.
(Delhi 2016C)

Or

One of the major contribution of biotechnology is to develop pest resistant varieties of cotton plants. Explain how it has been made possible.
(Foreign 2015)

Ans. The pests that destroy the cotton balls are cotton bollworms and cotton borer. *Bt* cotton is created by using some strains of a bacterium, *Bacillus thuringiensis* (*Bt* is short form).

This bacterium produces protein that kills certain insects such as lepidopterans (tobacco budworm and armyworm), coleopterans (beetles) and dipterans (flies and mosquitoes).

Bacillus thuringiensis forms protein crystals during a particular phase of their growth. These crystals contain a toxic insecticidal protein. *Bt* toxin protein exists as inactive protoxins in bacteria, but once an insect ingests this inactive toxin, it is converted into an active form due to the alkaline pH of the gut, which solubilises the crystals.

The activated toxin binds to the surface of midgut epithelial cells and creates pores that cause cell swelling and lysis leading to death of insect.

7. Why certain cotton plants are called *Bt* cotton?

(All India 2011)

Ans. Certain cotton plants are called *Bt* cotton because they bear specific *Bt* toxin genes which were isolated from *Bacillus thuringiensis* and incorporated into certain cotton plants.

8. Why does *Bt* toxin not kill the bacterium that produces it, but kills the insect that ingests it?

(Delhi 2014)

Ans. *Bt* toxin is produced by a soil bacterium called *Bacillus thuringiensis*. This toxin does not kill the bacterium which produces it, because it is present in an inactive and crystalline form. It becomes active and toxic only when it is consumed by insects such as lepidopterans, etc., due to the alkaline pH of their gut.

9. Many proteins are secreted in their inactive form. This is also true to many toxic proteins produced by microorganisms. Explain how the mechanism is useful for the organism producing the toxin?

Ans. Many proteins including certain toxins are secreted in their inactive form. They get activated only when exposed to a specific trigger (pH, temperature, etc.). This mechanism is advantageous to the organism (e.g. bacteria) producing the toxins, as the bacteria does not get killed by the action of proteins present in the toxin.

10. *Bt* cotton is resistant to pests, such as lepidopterans, dipterans and coleopterans. Is *Bt* cotton resistant to other pests as well?

Ans. *Bt* cotton is made resistant to only certain specific taxa of pests. It is quite likely that in future some other pests may infest this *Bt* cotton.

11. Why do lepidopterans die when they feed on *Bt* cotton plant? Explain how does it happen.

(Delhi 2017)

Ans. *Bt* cotton plants are the transgenic plants that express a *Bacillus thuringiensis* gene called *cry* gene.

This gene, encodes for protein crystals having insecticidal properties against insects of group Lepidoptera, Diptera and Coleoptera. Inside the bacterium, these proteins

remain inactive and do not harm the bacteria. However, these inactive crystals can get activated in the alkaline pH of the gut of insects upon ingestion.

After activation, these crystals can bind to the receptors present on the membranes of gut epithelial cells. Due to this binding, the membrane swells and pores are created on them. These pores lead to bursting of cell. Hence, the lepidopteran dies.

12. Differentiate the terms 'Cry' and '*cry*'.

Ans. 'Cry' refers to protein symbol and its first letter is always capital. It is written in Roman letters. Whereas '*cry*' refers to the gene which is usually written in small letters and is invariably in italics.

13. What are Cry proteins? Name an organism that produces it. How has man exploited this protein to his benefit?

(NCERT)

Ans. The proteins encoded by the gene named *cry* are called Cry proteins. Organism that produces Cry proteins is *Bacillus thuringiensis*.

Man has exploited this protein for his benefits by incorporating *cry* genes in several crops such as potato, cotton, corn, etc., due to which they become resistant to pest which can damage the crop, e.g. *cry*IAc and *cry*IIAb control the cotton bollworms and *cry* IAb controls corn borer. They help in high yield of healthy crops.

14. Write the functions of

(i) *cry* IAc gene

(ii) RNA interference (RNAi)　　**(Outside Delhi 2015C)**

Ans.　(i) *cry* IAc codes for toxic insecticidal protein as inactive protoxins in *Bacillus thurginesis*. This toxin may kill the cotton bollworm.

(ii) RNA interference is associated with silencing of specific *m*RNA and is a method of cellular defence in eukaryotes.

15. State the consequence when *Meloidogyne incognita* consumes cells with RNAi gene.　**(Delhi 2011C)**

Ans. If *Meloidogyne incognita* consumes cells with RNAi, gene silencing of the specific *m*RNA occurs due to complementary *ds*RNA molecule formation that binds and prevents translation of *m*RNA, thus causing death of the nematode.

16. How has RNA*i* technique helped to prevent the infestation of roots in tobacco plants by a nematode, *Meloidogyne incognita*?　**(Delhi 2016)**

Or How has the use of *Agrobacterium* as vectors helped in controlling *Meloidogyne incognita*, infestation in tobacco plants? Explain in correct sequence.　**(All India 2018)**

Ans. RNA interference is a gene-silencing process that blocks the expression of genes in the parasite when it enters the host's body. RNAi takes place in all eukaryotic organisms as a method of cellular defence.

RNAi method involves silencing of a specific *m*RNA due to complementary *ds*RNA molecule that binds and prevents translation of the *m*RNA (gene silencing).

The technique is helpful in preventing the infestation of roots in tobacco plants by a nematode, *Meloidogyne incognita*. This can be done by introducing nematode specific genes using *Agrobacterium* vectors into the host plant such that both sense and antisense RNA get produced into the host cells.

These two RNAs are complementary to each other and form *ds*RNA which initiates RNAi and hence, silence the specific *m*RNA of the nematode a consequence of which, the parasite cannot survive in transgenic host. Hence, the transgenic plant gets protected from the parasite by itself.

17. Write the difference between the proinsulin and mature insulin. **(Delhi 2020)**

Ans. Insulin is a hormone secreted by pancreas. It consists of two short polypeptide chains, i.e. chains A and B, linked together by disulphide bridges. Chain-A contains 21 amino acids, while chain-B contains 30 amino acids.

In mammals, insulin is synthesised as a prohormone, i.e. it needs to be processed before it becomes fully mature and functional hormone. This prohormone contains an extra stretch called the C-peptide of 33 amino acids. This is known as proinsulin.

The insulin that lack C-peptide is called mature insulin.

18. How did an American Company, Eli Lilly use the knowledge of *r*DNA technology to produce human insulin? **(All India 2015)**

Or

How did Eli Lilly synthesise the human insulin? Mention one difference between this insulin and the one produced by the human pancreas. **(All India 2010)**

Or

How did American company Eli Lilly produce human insulin using *r*DNA technique? **(Delhi 2020)**

Ans. In 1983, Eli Lilly, an American company prepared two DNA sequences corresponding to A and B-chains of human insulin and introduced them in plasmids of *E. coli* to produce insulin chains. These chains (A and B) were produced separately, extracted and combined by creating disulphide bonds to form human insulin called humulin.

The insulin in human pancreas is synthesised as a prohormone containing the C-peptide which is removed in mature hormone. But the insulin synthesised by recombinant DNA technology did not contain C-peptide and was prepared in the mature form.

19. List the disadvantages of insulin obtained from the pancreas of slaughtered cows and pigs.

Ans. The disadvantages of insulin obtained from the pancreas of slaughtered cows and pigs are

(i) Insulin being a hormone is produced in very little amounts in the body. Hence, a large number of animals need to be sacrificed for obtaining small quantities of insulin. This makes the cost of insulin very high (demand being many fold higher than supply).

(ii) Slaughtering of animals is not ethical.

(iii) There is a potential of immune response in humans against the administered insulin which is derived from animals.

(iv) There is possibility of slaughtered animals being infested with some infectious microorganism which may contaminate insulin.

20. Recombinant DNA technology is of great importance in the field of medicine. With the help of a flow chart, show how this techonolgy has been used in preparing genetically engineered human insulins. **(Delhi 2015)**

Ans. An American company Eli Lilly produced insulin *via* recombinant DNA technology in 1983. Insulin production by using recombinant DNA technology is shown in flow chart below

DNA sequences corresponding to the two polypeptides, i.e. A and B-chains of insulin are synthesised *in vitro*

↓

They are introduced into plasmid DNA of *E. coli*

↓

This bacterium is cloned under suitable conditions

↓

The transgene is expressed in the form of polypeptides, i.e. A and B-chains secreted into the medium

↓

They are extracted and combined by creating disulphide bridge to form human insulin.

21. List the advantages of recombinant insulin.

Ans. The advantages of recombinant insulin are

(i) There is no need of animals to be sacrificed for the production of recombinant insulin.

(ii) Recombinant insulin was not found allergic to patients, while the insulin from an animal source caused some patients to develop allergy or other types of reactions to the foreign protein.

(iii) The cost of recombinant insulin is not very high (supply being many fold higher than demand).

22. Name the source used to produce hepatitis-B vaccine using *r*DNA technology. **(Delhi 2015C)**

Ans. Recombinant DNA technology has allowed the production of antigenic polypeptides of pathogen in bacteria or yeast. Vaccines produced using this approach allow large scale production and hence, greater availability for immunisation, e.g. source of hepatitis-B vaccine is yeast.

23. Diagrammatically represent the experimental steps in cloning and expressing a human gene (say the gene for growth hormone) into a bacterium like *E. coli*. **(NCERT)**

Ans. The multiple identical copies of specific template DNA can be produced by DNA cloning. It can be carried out by the use of a vector to carry specific foreign DNA fragment into the host cell. The mechanism of cloning and transfer of a gene for human growth hormone into *E. coli* is diagrammatically represented below

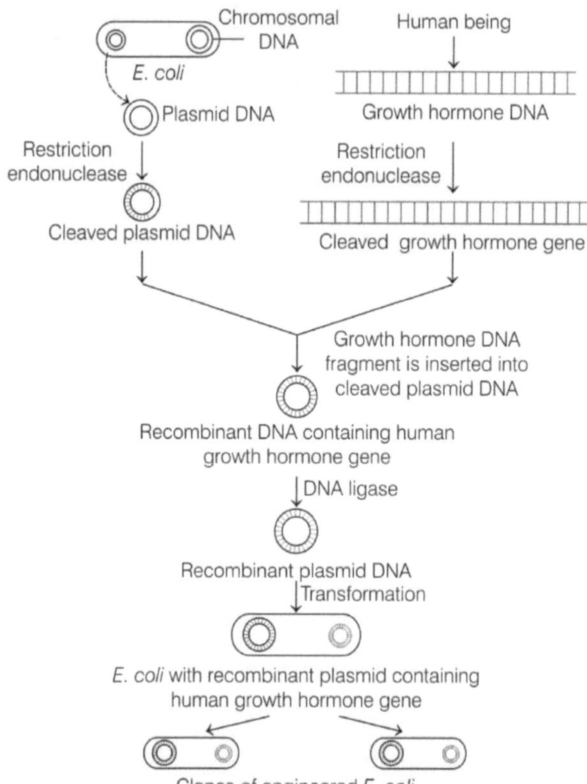

Representation of cloning and expression of human gene into *E. coli*

24. What is stem cell technology? What are its applications?

Ans. It is now known to be the most rapidly developing field that combines the efforts of cell biologists and geneticists for the treatment of a variety of malignant and non-malignant diseases by using stem cells. Stem cells are undifferentiated biological cells that can differentiate into specialised cells and can divide (through mitosis) to produce more stem cells. These cells are found in multicellular organisms. They are mainly of two types, i.e. **embryonic stem cells,** which are isolated from the inner cell mass of blastocysts and **adult stem cells**, which exist throughout the body after embryonic development and are found inside different type of tissues such as brain.

The potential applications of stem cell include organ and tissue regeneration, bone marrow transplantation, brain disease treatment, cell deficiency therapy, cardiovascular disease treatment, blood disease treatment, etc.

25. What is gene therapy? Name the first clinical case in which it was used. **(Delhi 2014)**

Or What is gene therapy? Illustrate using the example of Adenosine Deaminase (ADA) deficiency? **(NCERT)**

Ans. Gene therapy is a collection of methods which allow the correction of a genetic defect diagnosed in a child or embryo.

The first clinical case in which gene therapy was used in 1990 on a 4 years old girl with ADA deficiency.

ADA is an autosomal recessive inherited disorder which occurs due to a defective ADA enzyme that causes Severe Combined Immunodeficiency or SCID Syndrome. It can be cured by bone marrow transplantation and by enzyme replacement therapy. For this process, an engineered retrovirus having a functional ADA gene is made use of for transferring functional ADA gene into the patients stem cells and the modified cells with good ADA gene are then reintroduced into the patients body.

26. Write the function of adenosine deaminase enzyme. State the cause of ADA deficiency in humans. Mention a possible permanent cure for an ADA deficiency patient. **(Delhi 2013)**

Ans. Adenosine Deaminase or ADA enzyme is important for the proper functioning of the immune system of a person.

The disorder is caused due to the deletion of the gene for adenosine deaminase. ADA deficiency can be cured by bone marrow transplantation and in, others by enzyme replacement therapy.

However, both of these curative. Gene therapy is a permanent cure if the gene isolated from marrow cells producing ADA is introduced into cells at early embryonic stage.

27. Gene therapy is an attempt to correct a genetic defect by providing a normal gene into the individual. By this the normal function can be restored. An alternate method would be to provide the gene product (protein/enzyme) known as enzyme replacement therapy, which would also restore the function. Which in your opinion is a better option? Give reason for your answer.

Ans. Gene therapy would be a better option because it has the potential to completely cure the patient. It is because the correct gene once introduced in the patient, can continue to produce the correct protein enzyme. Enzyme therapy does not offer permanent cure as it needs to be given to the patient on regular basis. It is also more expensive.

28. Two girls, A and B aged 4 and 5 years respectively visited a hospital with a similar genetic disorder. The girl A was provided enzyme-replacement therapy and was advised to revisit periodically for further treatment. The girl B was, however, given a therapy that did not require revisit for further treatment.

   (i) Name the ailments the two girls were suffering from?

   (ii) Why did the treatment provided to girl A require repeated visits?

   (iii) How was the girl B cured permanently?

(Delhi 2019)

Ans. (i) Both girls were suffering from Adenosine Deaminase (ADA) deficiency due to probable deletion of gene that codes for ADA production.

   (ii) Girl A was treated with injections of functional ADA or bone marrow transplant. These techniques are not completely curative as these lymphocytes are not immortal and require repeated treatment.

   (iii) Girl B was treated using gene therapy where the gene isolated from marrow cells producing ADA was introduced into cells at an early embryonic stage for a possible permanent cure. Hence, she did not require revisit for further treatment.

29. Explain enzyme replacement therapy to treat adenosine deaminase deficiency. Mention two disadvantages of this procedure. **(All India 2016)**

Ans. In enzyme replacement therapy, the patient is given functional ADA (Adenosine Deaminase) by injection.

Steps involved in ADA gene therapy are

   (i) The lymphocytes from the blood of the patient are grown in a culture outside the body.

   (ii) A functional ADA *c*DNA (using a retroviral vector) is then introduced into these lymphocytes which are subsequently returned to the patient.

Disadvantages

   (i) The patient does not completely recover from the disease.

   (ii) It needs periodic injections of the enzyme to the patients.

30. Why are certain animals called 'transgenic'? Give an example of such an animal that is being used for testing the vaccine safety for a specific human disease. Name the disease. **(Delhi 2020)**

Ans. Certain animals are called transgenic because their DNA is manipulated to possess and express an useful and extra (foreign) gene. Transgenic mice are being used for testing the vaccine safety for the polio disease, before being used in humans. It can replace the use of monkeys to test the safety of the batches of the vaccine.

31. With respect to understanding diseases, discuss the importance of transgenic animal models.

(NCERT Exemplar)

Ans. Transgenic animals are important in the following fields

   (i) They are being used in basic science research to elucidate the role of genes in the development of diseases like cancer, cystic fibrosis, rheumatoid arthritis and Alzheimer's.

   (ii) They are valuable tools in the drug development process itself.

   (iii) Milk producing transgenics can produce medicines or human proteins (insulin, growth hormone, etc.) in large quantities.

   (iv) Transgenics can be a source of transplant organs as well.

32. How are transgenic animals used in chemical safety testing?

Ans. Transgenic animals are employed for testing the safety of various chemicals (drugs, etc.) before being released for public use. It is also called as toxicity or safety testing. Transgenic animals are developed carrying the genes which make them more susceptible to the chemical substances than others. These animals are then exposed to the chemicals under test and effects generated are studied.

These studies help in identifying the desirable and harmful effects of the chemical substances and their further improvement.

33. Transgenic animals are the animals in which a foreign gene is expressed. Such animals can be used to study the fundamental biological process, phenomenon as well as for producing products useful for mankind. Give one example for each type.

Ans. Transgenic animals are the animals in which a foreign genes are expressed. Such animals can be used to study the fundamental biological process/phenomenon, e.g. by using model organisms like mouse we can determine how genes are regulated (gene regulation), how they affect the normal functions of the body and its development, etc.

Transgenic animals are also used for producing products useful for mankind, e.g. transgenic cow (Rosie), which produced human protein enriched milk (2.4 g/L). The milk contained the human alpha lactalbumin and was nutritionally a more balanced product for human babies than natural cow milk.

34. Explain alpha lactalbumin. Where is it produced in human body? **(All India 2010)**

Ans. Alpha lactalbumin is a human milk protein which helps to increase the production of lactose in the body. It is produced in human milk.

35. Describe how biotechnology has helped in producing more nutritionally balanced milk. **(Delhi 2012)**

Ans. Biotechnology leads to production of transgenic cow, Rosie that produced around 2.4 g/L human protein enriched milk. This milk contained the human alpha lactalbumin and was nutritionally more balanced than a natural cow's milk.

36. Highlight five areas where biotechnology has influenced our lives.

Ans. Biotechnology has influenced our lives in the following ways

  (i) It has provided us with genetically modified crops of better quality and high nutritive value.

  (ii) It has made better and safer recombinant vaccines available to the human.

  (iii) It has helped to develop transgenic animals that can produce human proteins.

  (iv) It has enabled the cure of genetic diseases using gene therapy.

  (v) Environment pollution has also been taken care of with the help of genetically engineered microbes.

37. While creating genetically modified organisms, genetic barriers are not respected. How can this be dangerous in the long run? **(NCERT Exemplar)**

Ans. Genetic modification of organisms can have unpredictable results when such organisms are introduced into the ecosystem. Because the real effects of gene manipulation are visible only when such organisms react with other components and organisms of the ecosystem.

38. Write the full forms of the following

  (i) GEAC (ii) PKU

Ans. (i) Genetic Engineering Approval Committee
  (ii) Phenylketonuria

39. Differentiate between bioethics and biopatent.

Ans. The sets of standards which are used to regulate our activities in relation to biological world are called bioethics. Patent is a set of exclusive rights granted by the government to the inventors or their assignee to prevent others from commercial use of their invention. It is known as biopatent.

40. Write a short note on biopiracy highlighting the exploitation of developing countries by the developed countries. **(NCERT Exemplar)**

Ans. Biopiracy refers to the use of bioresources by multinational companies and other organisations without proper authorisation from the countries and people concerned without compensatory payment.

The majority of industrialised nations are financially rich but poor in biodiversity and traditional knowledge, in comparison to developing and underdeveloped countries hence exploit them both morally and financially.

Some examples of biopiracy are

  (i) In 1995, US patent office granted patent for medicinal use of turmeric to University of Mississippi Medical Center.

  (ii) In 1996, WR Grace and Co. got patent for fungicidal uses of neem by European Patent Office Munich.

41. Describe the responsibility of GEAC setup by the Indian Government. **(All India 2009)**

Ans. Genetic Engineering Approval Committee (GEAC) makes decision regarding the validity of GM research and the safety of introducing GM organisms for public services.

42. What is biopiracy? State the initiative taken by the Indian Parliament against it. **(Delhi 2014)**

Ans. Biopiracy is the unauthorised use of biological resources by multinationals or other organisations, i.e. without proper permissions from relevant authorities or people concerned with it.

Indian parliament has recently passed the 2nd amendment of Indian patents bill, which considers various issues related with biopiracy. For example, terms of patent, emergency provisions, research and development initiative.

• Long Answer (LA) Type Questions

1. Compare and contrast the advantages and disadvantages of the production of genetically modified crops. **(NCERT)**

Ans. Advantages of GM crops are

  (i) More tolerance to abiotic stresses (cold, drought, salt and heat).

  (ii) Reduced reliance on chemical pesticides (pest-resistant crops).

  (iii) Increased efficiency of mineral usage prevents early exhaustion of fertility of soil.

Disadvantages of GM crops are

  (i) Transgenic genes in genetically modified crops endanger native species.

  (ii) They cause damage to the natural environment by reducing biodiversity.

  (iii) They may also cause human health problems due to altered genes and transferred antibiotic resistance.

2. Explain with the help of one example how genetically modified plants can

  (i) reduce usage of chemical pesticides.

  (ii) Enhance nutritional value of food crops.

Ans. (i) Genetically modified plants can reduce the usage of chemical pesticides by introducing pest resistant plants.
  For example, there are several nematodes that parasitic, a wide variety of plants and animals including human beings. A nematode, *Meloidogyne incognita* infects the roots of tobacco plants and

causes a great reduction in yield. A novel strategy was adopted to prevent this infestation which was based on the process of **RNA interference** (RNAi).

Using *Agrobacterium* vectors, nematode, specific genes were introduced into the host plant. The introduction of DNA was such that it produced both sense and antisense RNA in the host cells.

These two RNA's being complementary to each other formed a double-stranded RNA that initiated RNAi and thus, silenced the specific *m*RNA of the nematode. The consequence was that the parasite could not survive in a transgenic host expressing specific interfering RNA.

(ii) Genetically modified plants can enhance the nutritional value of food crops.

For example, 'Golden rice' developed at Swiss Federal Institute of technology is an example of nutritionally modified crop. It is rich in vitamin-A (β-carotene). The rice grains are golden-yellow in colour. It contains 'beta-carotene' gene from daffodil plant and also from some bacteria. Golden rice can prevent child blindness which is caused due to the deficiency of vitamin-A.

3. What is meant by the term biopesticide? Name and explain the mode of action of a popular biopesticide.

Ans. Biopesticides are certain types of pesticides which are derived from natural materials like plants, animals and microbes. A popular biopesticide, named *Bacillus thuringiensis* or *Bt* toxin is used to prevent various plants from a variety of pests and insects.

Plants introduced with *Bt* toxin include *Bt* cotton, *Bt* soyabean, *Bt* rice, etc.

Bacillus thuringiensis is a bacterium that gives *Bt* toxin protein. It forms protein crystals (Cry) during a particular phase in their growth. The crystals contain a toxin insecticidal protein that does not harm the bacterium as it is inactivated.

The protein gets activated once it is ingested by the insect due to its solubility in the alkaline pH of the gut of the insect. The activated toxin binds to the surface of the midgut epithelial cells and creates pores which cause cell swelling and lysis, leading to insect death.

4. (i) Name the insect that attacks cotton crops and causes lot of damage to the crop. How has *Bt* cotton plant overcome this problem and saved the crop ? Explain.

(ii) Write the role of gene *cry* IAb.　　**(All India 2020)**

Ans. (i) The insect that attacks cotton crops is cotton bollworms.

Bt cotton is made by using a bacterium called as *Bacillus thuringiensis*. This bacterium produces a protein that kills certain insects. *B. thuringiensis* forms protein crystals (Cry) during a phase of its

growth. These crystals contain a toxic insecticidal protein. Specific *Bt* toxin genes were isolated from *Bacillus thuringiensis* and incorporated into cotton.

This *Bt* toxin does not kill the *Bacillus* because it exists as inactive protoxins in its body. However, when an insect ingests the inactive toxin, it gets exposed to the alkaline pH of the gut, which solubilises the crystals and converts it into active form. The activated toxin binds to the surface of midgut epithelial cells and create pores that cause cell swelling and lysis and eventually causes death of the insect. In this manner, the crop is saved from insects and a large yield is obtained.

(ii) Gene *cry* IAb secretes a protein that inhibits the growth of corn borer insects.

5. Discuss transgenic animals. Explain any four ways in which such animals can be beneficial for humans.
　　　　　　　　　　　　　　　　　(Foreign 2008)

Ans. Animals that have had their DNA manipulated to possess and express an extra (foreign) gene are known as **transgenic animals**, e.g. transgenic rats, rabbits, pigs, sheep, cows and fishes.

There are several benefits of transgenic animals

1. **Normal physiology and development** Transgenic animals can be specifically designed to allow the study of how genes are regulated and how they affect the normal functioning of the body and its development. For example, the study of complex factors involved in growth such as insulin like growth factors.

2. **Study of disease** Many transgenic animals are specially made to serve as models for human diseases, so that the investigation of new treatments for diseases is made possible.

3. **Biological products** Human diseases can be treated by medicines that contain biological products.

(i) Transgenic animals that produce useful biological products can be created by the introduction of the portion of the DNA or genes that code for a particular product such as human protein (α-1-antitrypsin) which is used to treat emphysema. Similar attempts are being made for the treatment of Phenylketonuria (PKU) and cystic fibrosis.

(ii) The first transgenic cow, **Rosie** produced human protein enriched milk (2.4 g/L) in 1997. The milk contained the human **alpha lactalbumin** and was nutritionally a more balanced product for human babies than natural cow's milk.

4. **Vaccine safety** Transgenic mice are being used for testing the safety of vaccines before they are used on humans, e.g. polio vaccine. If found reliable and successful they could replace the use of monkeys in order to test the safety of batches of the vaccine.

6. Write a self-explanatory note on biopatent.

Ans. Patent is a set of exclusive rights granted by a government to the inventors or their assignee to prevent others from commercial use of their invention. And when patent is granted for biological entities and for products derived from them, they are called biopatents.

Biopatents may be granted for

(i) Strains of microorganisms

(ii) DNA sequences

(iii) Cell lines

(iv) Various biotechnological procedures, etc.

Biopatents are necessary because if they are not claimed then it can cause the cases of biopiracy, i.e. there are chances of commercial exploitation or monopolisation of biological products or genetically related products. India has faced many cases of biopiracy over its biological resources. For example,

(i) In May 1995, US Patent Office granted a patent for use of turmeric in wound healing, to the University of Mississippi Medical Center, but in India from ancient times peoples are using turmeric as wound healing, its medicinal properties are written in our vedas.

(ii) Another example is of Basmati rice. Rice is being used for many years in India, their is about 2,00,000 varieties of rice is present in India and out of which 27 varieties are of Basmati rice but in 1997 US Patent Office granted patent to an American based company.

Through both the patents were cancelled after India government took action against it but biopatents should be claimed to protect the rich legacy of our country.

7. Ignoring our traditional knowledge can be prove costly in the area of biological patenting. Justify.

Ans. Human communities have always generated, refined and passed on the knowledge from generation to generation. Such knowledge is called traditional knowledge and is often an important part of the cultural identities. A number of cases relating to traditional knowledge have attracted international attention.

As a result, the issue of traditional knowledge has been brought to the general debate surrounding intellectual property. These cases involve, what is often referred to as 'biopiracy'.

The examples of turmeric and neem (Indian traditional herbal medicine) illustrates the issues that can arise when patent protection is granted to inventions relating to traditional knowledge which is already in the public domain. In these cases, invalid patents were issued because the patent examiners were not aware or the relevant traditional knowledge.

For example, India is one of the country possessing the richest diversity of rice (2000 varieties). Basmati rice is distinct for its unique aroma and flavour and 27 documented varieties of Basmati are grown in India.

There is reference to Basmati in ancient texts, folklore and poetry, as it has been grown for centuries.

In 1997, an American company Rice Tec. Got Patent rights on Basmati rice through the US Patent and Trademark Office. This allowed the company to sell a 'new' variety of Basmati, in the US and Abroad.

This 'new' variety of Basmati had actually been derived from Indian farmers' varieties. Indian Basmati was crossed with semi-dwarf varieties and claimed as an invention or a novelty. The patent extends to functional equivalents, implying that other people selling Basmati rice could be restricted by the patent.

If we are not vigilant and we do not immediately counter these patent applications, other countries/individuals may encash on our rich legacy and we may not be able to do anything about it.

• Case Based Questions

1. Direction *Read the following passage and answer the questions that follows.*

Introduced by Eli Lily and company in 1982, humulin U-100 insulins are affordable choices that celebrate over 30 years of helping people manage type 1 and type 2 diabetes. Prior to its development, diabetics used insulin isolated from pig and cow pancreas.

Humulin is created through rDNA technology. Its licensing by the FDA in 1982 also made it the first recombinant pharmaceutical approved for the use in the United States. Recombinant pharmaceuticals are created by inserting genes from one species into a host species, often yeast or bacteria, where they do not occur naturally. The genes code for a desired product and therefore the GMOs can be grown and used as a kind of living factory to produce the product.

In this case, genes coding for human insulin are inserted into the bacteria. Bacteria produce insulin, which is harvested and used as active ingredient in humulin.

(i) How is genetically engineered human insulin prepared?

Ans. Genetically engineered human insulin is prepared by using *E. coli*. With the help of rDNA technology, insulin producing gene from human is transferred into *E. coli* bacteria which produce human insulin or humulin for clinical use.

(ii) Which method is used to prepare cDNA in insulin preparation?

Ans. Reverse transcription is used to prepare cDNA in insulin preparation. The enzyme used here, Reverse transcriptase is used to create cDNA libraries from mRNA.

(iii) Why is the insulin obtained from genetically engineered organism more useful?

Ans. Insulin obtained from genetically engineered organism is more useful because it provides unlimited quantity of insulin at a time without the risk of transmission of animal diseases through insulin.

(iv) How would you differentiate between a mature and an immature insulin?

Ans. In mammals, including humans, insulin is synthesised as a prohormone which contains an extra stretch called the C-peptide. This C-peptide is present in immature insulin and absent in mature insulin.

(v) What will be the main challenge for the production of insulin using recombinant DNA technology?

Ans. The main challenge for the production of insulin using recombinant DNA technology is getting insulin assembled into a mature form.

2. Direction *Read the following passage and answer the questions that follows.*

A GM or transgenic crop is a plant that has a novel combination of genetic material obtained through the use of modern biotechnology. For example, a GM crop can contain a gene that has been artificially inserted instead of the plant acquiring it through pollination. The resulting plant is said to be genetically modified although in reality all crops have been 'genetically modified' from their original wild state by domestication, selection and controlled breeding over long periods of times. In 1994, Calgene's delayed-ripening tomato (*Flavr Savr*) became the first genetically modified food crop to be produced and consumed in an industrialised country. Since, the recorded commercialisation of GM crops in 1996 to 2018, several countries have contributed to ~ 113-fold increase in the global area of transgenic crops.

(i) What effect do eating genetically modified foods have on your genes?

Ans. There is no effects have been found related to Genetically Modified (GM) foods currently in the market.

(ii) Why should foods derived from genetically modified crops be tested for possible reactions in people?

Ans. Genetically modified crops should be tested for possible reactions in people, because these crops are prepared by the insertion of gene of the other species into their DNA. So, there is a possibility that they can cause some health issues, i.e. allergies due to release of new kind of proteins. Hence, GM crops should be tested.

(iii) Are foods derived from genetically modified crops nutritionally superior?

Ans. Most of the genetically modified crops currently available are designed to reduce farmers' production costs. They are neither better nor worse than foods from conventional crops.

(iv) GM crops are designed to develop natural resistance from insects and pests. Which crops are modified using *Bacillus thuringiensis*?

Ans. Crops modified using *Bacillus thuringiensis* are corn, cotton, tomato, rice, potato and soybean.

3. Observe the diagram shown below for the process of humulin production and answer the questions that follows.

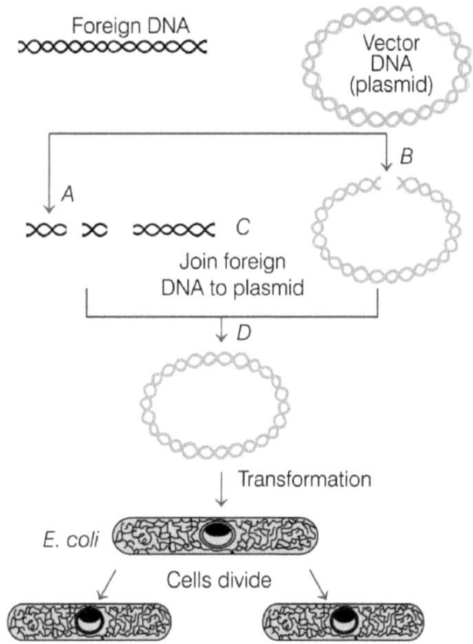

(i) What does the label *C* represent and what is its role?

Ans. Label *C* represents DNA ligase which is an enzyme that is used to join together two different types of DNA molecules.

(ii) Which of the labels represents an enzyme that is utilised for cutting the molecule of DNA?

Ans. Label *A* depicting restriction endonuclease which is utilised for cutting the molecule of DNA.

(iii) 'Humulin' is a term used for?

Ans. Humulin is a term used for human insulin made from recombinant DNA that is identical to insulin present in humans and is used to treat diabetes.

(iv) Through which bond chains A and B of humulin are bonded?

Ans. Both chains A and B are produced separately and combined by creating disulphide bonds to form humulin.

(v) Which DNA sequences will be introduced in label *B* to produce humulin?

Ans. DNA sequences corresponding to the two polypeptides that is A and B chains of insulin are synthesised *in vitro* and introduced into label *B*.

Chapter Test

Multiple Choice Questions

1. The decisions regarding the validity of GMOs (Genetically Modified Organisms) research and the safety of introducing GM organisms and their product for the public services in India is taken by
(a) Genetic Engineering Approval Committee
(b) Department of Recombinant DNA Technology
(c) Department of Science and Biotechnology
(d) National Biotechnology Board

2. Silencing of a gene could be achieved through the use of
(a) short interfering RNA (RNAi) only
(b) antisense RNA only
(c) Both RNAi and antisense RNA
(d) None of the above

3. The first human hormone produced by recombinant DNA technology is
(a) insulin
(b) oestrogen
(c) thyroxine
(d) progesterone

4. Consider the following statements.
I. *Bt* toxin gene has been cloned from the bacteria.
II. Genetic engineering works only on animals and has not yet been successfully used on plants.
III. Strains of *Bacillus thuringiensis* are used in producing bioinsecticidal plants.

Which of the above statements are correct?
(a) I and II
(b) I and III
(c) II and III
(d) I, II and III

5. In 1997, the first transgenic cow, Rosie produced
(a) human protein enriched milk (2.4 g/L)
(b) human protein enriched milk (2.8 g/L)
(c) human calcium enriched milk (2.4 g/L)
(d) human calcium enriched milk (2.8 g/L)

6. Biopiracy is related to which of the following?
(a) Traditional knowledge
(b) Biomolecules and regarding bioresources
(c) Bioresources
(d) All of the above

Assertion-Reasoning MCQs

Direction (Q. Nos. 1-3) *Each of these questions contains two statements, Assertion (A) and Reason (R). Each of these questions also has four alternative choices, any one of which is the correct answer. You have to select one of the codes (a), (b), (c) and (d) given below.*

(a) Both A and R are true and R is the correct explanation of A
(b) Both A and R are true, but R is not the correct explanation of A
(c) A is true, but R is false
(d) A is false, but R is true

1. **Assertion** (A) Transgenic plant production can be achieved *via* recombinant DNA technology.
Reason (R) An organism that contains and expresses a transgene is called transgenic organism.

2. **Assertion** (A) A crop expressing a *cry* gene is usually resistant to a group of insects.
Reason (R) Cry proteins produced from *Bacillus thuringiensis* are toxic to larvae of certain insects.

3. **Assertion** (A) The ADA gene provides instruction for producing the enzyme, adenosine deaminase.
Reason (R) This enzyme is found throughout the body but is most active in lymphocytes.

Short Answer Type Questions

1. (i) Which insects are killed by *Bacillus thuringiensis*?
(ii) The *Bt* toxin binds to which cells?
(iii) In which plants, *Bt* toxin is used?

2. List the advantages of recombinant insulin.

3. What is ADA deficiency and how can it be cured?

4. Which advantages are related to transgenic cow?

5. How are the developed countries related to biopiracy cases? Explain with an example.

Long Answer Type Questions

1. Explain atleast three areas for which transgenic animals are developed.

2. Mention some therapeutical applications that are related to biotechnology.

Answers

Multiple Choice Questions

1. (a)   *2.* (c)   *3.* (a)   *4.* (b)   *5.* (a)   *6.* (d)

Assertion-Reasoning MCQs

1. (b)   *2.* (b)   *3.* (b)

For Detailed Solutions
Scan the code

CHAPTER 05

Organisms and Populations

In this Chapter...

- Organism and its Environment
- Adaptation
- Populations

A single organism cannot live alone, due to which there is always seen an inter-relationship between organisms and their surrounding. The branch of biology which deals with different principles that control this relationship is known as **ecology**.

Ecology It is the study of the interactions among organisms and between organism and its physical (abiotic) environment. It consists of two branches, **Autecology,** i.e. study of ecology at the level of species and **Synecology,** i.e. study of ecology at the level of communities.

Organisational Levels of Ecology

Ecology is basically concerned with four levels of organisation

- **Organism** It refers to the living component of the environment at individual level. It forms the basic unit of the study of ecology.
- **Population** It refers to the sum total of all organisms having similar features and potential to interbreed among themselves and produce fertile offsprings.
- **Communities** Assemblage of all the populations of different species in a specific geographical area.
- **Biome** It is a large unit which consists of a major vegetation type and associated fauna in a particular climatic zone. Tropical rainforest, deciduous forest, sea coast, deserts, etc., are the major biomes of India.

Organism and its Environment

- An environment is termed as the sum total of all external conditions (biotic and abiotic) which influence the organisms in terms of survival and reproduction.

- Ecology at the organismic level is essentially **physiological ecology**, which studies the adaptations of organisms essential for survival and reproduction in any given environment.

- We know that the rotation of our planet around the sun and the tilt of its axis cause annual variations in the intensity and duration of temperature, resulting in distinct seasons.

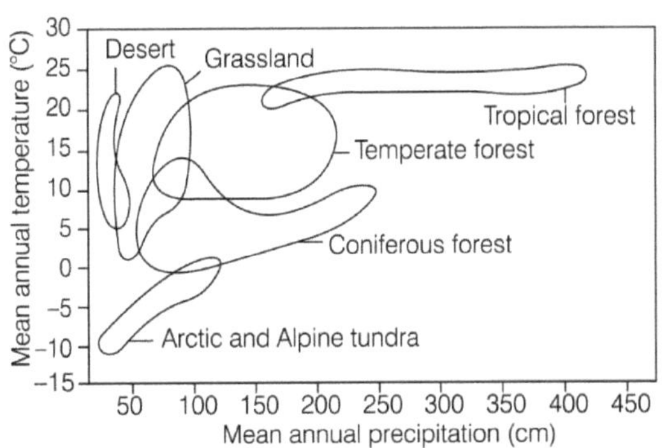

Biome distribution with respect to annual temperature and precipitation

- These variations together with annual variation in precipitation account for the formation of major biomes such as desert, rainforest and tundra.
- Regional and local variations within each biome lead to the formation of a wide variety of habitats.
- **Habitat** is a place, where an organism lives and represents a particular set of environmental conditions suitable for its successful growth.
- Each organism has an invariably defined range of conditions (evolved through natural selection) that it can tolerate, diversity in the resources it utilises and a distinct functional role in the ecological system all these together comprise its **niche.**
- **Ecological equivalents** are the organisms which occupy a part of the same niche, but have different habitats.
- Life on earth exists not just in a few favourable habitats but even in extreme and harsh habitats like scorching Rajasthan desert, rain-soaked Meghalaya forests, deep ocean trenches, torrential streams, permafrost polar regions, high mountain tops, boiling thermal springs, stinking compost pits and even our intestine is an unique habitat for hundreds of microbial species.

Note **Ramdeo Misra** *is known as the Father of Ecology in India. Due to his efforts, the Government of India established the Ministry of Environment and Forests in 1984.*

- The habitat of an organism is completely characterised by two components or factors, i.e. **abiotic** and **biotic** factors. The major abiotic physico-chemical factors include temperature, water, light and soil, biotic factors include pathogens, parasites, predators, competitors, etc., with which the organism interacts.

Adaptation

Any attribute of an organism (morphological, physiological or behavioural) that enables it to survive and reproduce in its habitat can be referred to as adaptation.

Adaptations in Plants

Different plants show different anatomical or physiological adaptations. A few examples of adaptations in plants are as follows

Adaptations in Desert Plants
(Xerophytic Plants)

- Roots grow very deep to explore any possibility of available underground water.
- Many desert plants have a thick cuticle on their leaf surfaces and have their stomata arranged in deep pits to minimise water loss through transpiration. They also have a special photosynthetic pathway known as Crassulacean Acid Metabolism (CAM) that enables their stomata to remain closed during day time so as to minimise transpiration.
- Some desert plants like *Opuntia,* have no leaves. Their leaves are reduced to spines and photosynthesis occurs in flattened stems.

Adaptations in Aquatic Habitats
(Hydrophytic Plants)

Aquatic plants or hydrophytes have evolved aerenchyma for buoyancy and floating. They have covering of wax to avoid damage through water. Roots are generally absent in plants like *Hydrilla* and *Nymphaea.*

Adaptations to Saline Environments
(Halophytic Plants)

- The plants of saline habitats which not only have the ability to tolerate high concentration of salts in their rooting medium but are also able to obtain their water supply from the same, are called **halophytes**.
- These are found in tidal marshes, coastal dunes, mangroves and saline soils. Certain green algae are also found in these areas, e.g. *Dunaliella.*
- Mangroves are the areas that not only have excess salt, but also have excess water and anaerobic conditions besides difficulty in anchoring and seed germination.
- A number of plants possess small negatively geotropic vertical roots called **pneumatophores** (have lenticels for gaseous exchange), e.g. *Avicennia, Aegialitis.*
- Another adaptation of mangrove plants is **vivipary** or seed germination while the fruit is still attached to plants, e.g. *Rhizophora, Aegiceras, Ceriops.*

Note **Oxygen release by plants** *This acts as the most significant long term adaptation of wetland species to soil anaerobiosis, e.g. Eichhornia, Pistia, etc.*

Adaptations in Animals

Animals have different physiological and behavioural adaptations to environmental stresses, etc. Some examples are given below

Adaptations in Kangaroo Rat

- The kangaroo rat in North American deserts is capable of meeting all its water requirement by internal oxidation of its body fat (water is a byproduct).
- It can also concentrate its urine, so that minimal volume of water is used to expel excretory products.

Adaptations in Desert Lizards

- They absorb heat from sun when the body temperature drops below the comfort zone and move into shade when the ambient temperature starts increasing.
- Some species burrow into the soil and escape from the above ground heat. These are behavioural responses.

Adaptations in Mammals

- Mammals from colder climates generally have shorter ears and limbs to minimise heat loss. This is called **Allen's rule**.
- In polar regions, aquatic mammals like seals have a thick layer of fat (blubber) below their skin that acts as an insulator and reduces the loss of body heat.

Adaptations at High Altitudes in Humans

- At high altitude places like Rohtang Pass near Manali (> 3500 m) and Mansarovar (in China occupied Tibet) people suffer from **altitude sickness**.
- The common symptoms include nausea, fatigue and heart palpitations. This is because at low atmospheric pressure of high altitudes, body does not get enough oxygen. The relief occurs gradually due to acclimatisation.
- The body copes up with this low oxygen stress by
  (i) increasing red blood cells production.
  (ii) decreasing the binding affinity of haemoglobin.
  (iii) increasing the breathing rate.

Note • *Tribal people living at high altitudes of Himalayas have higher RBC count than people living in plains.*

Adaptations at High and Low Temperature

- Certain bacteria (e.g. Archaebacteria) can flourish in places having temperature exceeding 100°C such as, deep sea hydrothermal vents, hot springs, etc., with the help of certain enzymes they possess. These enzymes can withstand high temperatures.
- Some invertebrates and fishes can tolerate temperatures below 0°C by extra solutes like glycerol and anti-freeze proteins that lower the freezing point of body fluids.

Populations

- Population is a set of individuals of a particular species, which are found in a particular geographical area and can interbreed.
- The population that occupies a very small area and is smaller in size, is called **local population**.
- A group of such closely related local populations is called **metapopulation**.
- **Population ecology** is an important area of ecology because it links ecology to population genetics and evolution.

Population Attributes

A population has certain attributes that an individual organism does not have. Some of them are given below

1. **Population size or density** It is the number of individuals of a species per unit area or volume.
   Population Density (PD)

$$= \frac{\text{Number of individuals in a region (N)}}{\text{Size of unit area in the region (S)}}; PD = \frac{N}{S}$$

2. **Birth rate or Natality** It is the number of births of new individuals per unit of population per unit time, e.g. if in a pond, there are 20 lotus plants last year and through reproduction, 8 new plants are added, taking the current population to 28.

   Then, birth rate $= 8/20 = 0.4$ offspring per lotus per year.

3. **Death rate or Mortality** It is the number of loss of individuals per unit of population per unit time due to death or due to the different environmental changes, competition, predation, etc.

   For example, if in a laboratory population of 40 individuals, 4 fruit flies died during a specified time interval, then the death rate $= 4/40 = 0.1$ individuals per fruit fly per week.

4. **Sex ratio** An individual is either a male or a female but a population has sex ratio. It is the number of females and males per 1000 individuals of a population in a given time.

Age Pyramid

- Population at any given time is composed of individuals of different ages. When the age distribution (per cent individuals of a given age or age group) is plotted for the population, this is called **age pyramid**.
- The age pyramids of human population generally show the age distribution of males and females in a combined diagram.
- The growth status of the population is reflected by the shape of the pyramids.
- The three types of age pyramids are as follows
  (i) Expanding   (ii) Stable   (iii) Declining

Post-reproductive

Reproductive

Pre-reproductive

Expanding   Stable   Declining

Representation of age pyramids for human populations

Population Growth

The size of a population for any species is not a static parameter, it keeps changing with time. It depends on factors such as food availability, predation pressure and adverse weather. The density of a population in a given habitat during a given period fluctuates due to the four basic processes

1. **Natality** It refers to the number of births during a given period in the population that are added to the initial density.

2. **Mortality** It is the number of deaths in the population during a given period.

3. **Immigration** It is the number of individuals of the same species that have come into the habitat from

elsewhere during the time period under consideration.

4. **Emigration** It is the number of individuals of the population who left the habitat and moved elsewhere during a given time period.

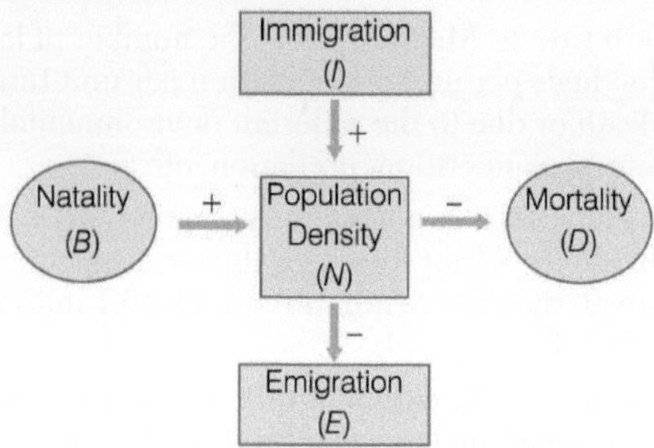

Factors influencing population density

Out of these four, natality and immigration contribute to an increase in population density, while mortality and emigration contribute to the decrease in population density.

So, if N is the population density at time t, then its density at time $t + 1$ is

$$N_{t+1} = N_t + [(B+I) - (D+E)]$$

where, N = Population density, t = Time, B = Birth rate, I = Immigration, D = Death rate and E = Emigration

From the above equation, we can see that population density will increase, if $(B + I)$ is more than $(D + E)$.

Growth Models

To study the behaviour and pattern of different populations, the following two models of population growth are used.

1. Exponential Growth

Availability of resources (food and space) is essential for the growth of population. Unlimited availability of such resources results in exponential growth of population. The increase or decrease in population density during a unit time period (t) is calculated as

$$dN/dt = (b-d)N$$

Let $(b-d) = r$, then, $dN/dt = rN$

Where, N is population size, b is birth per capita,

d is death per capita, t is time period and r is intrinsic rate of natural increase.

r is an important parameter that assesses the effects of biotic and abiotic factors on population growth. It is different for different organisms, e.g. its value is 0.015 for Norway rat and 0.12 for flour beetle.

The above equation results in a J-shaped curve as shown in graph.

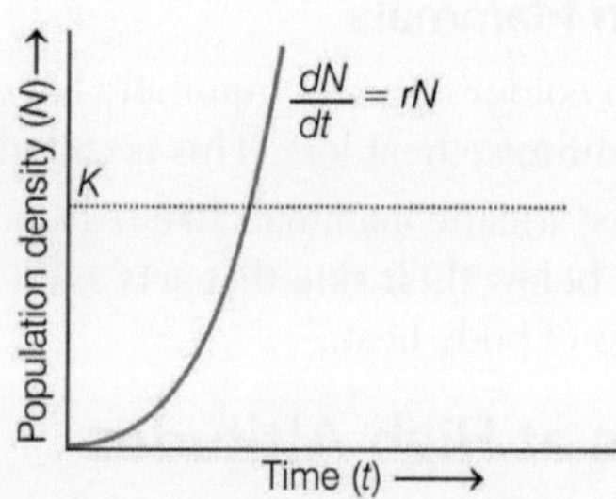

Population growth curve showing exponential growth

Integral form of exponential growth equation is

$$N_t = N_0\, e^{rt}$$

Where, N_t = Population density after time t

N_0 = Population density at time zero

r = Intrinsic rate of natural increase

e = Base of natural logarithms (2.71828).

Any species growing exponentially under unlimited resource conditions without any check, can reach enormous population densities in a short time.

2. Logistic Growth

Practically, no population of any species in nature has unlimited resources at its disposal. This leads to competition among the individuals and the survival of the 'fittest'.

Therefore, a given habitat has enough resources to support a maximum possible number, beyond which no further growth is possible. This is called the **carrying capacity** (K) for that species in that habitat.

When N is plotted in relation to time t, the logistic growth shows sigmoid curve and this type of growth is called **Verhulst-Pearl Logistic Growth**. It is calculated as

$$dN/dt = rN \left(\frac{K-N}{K} \right)$$

Where, N is population density at time t, K is carrying capacity and r is intrinsic rate of natural increase.

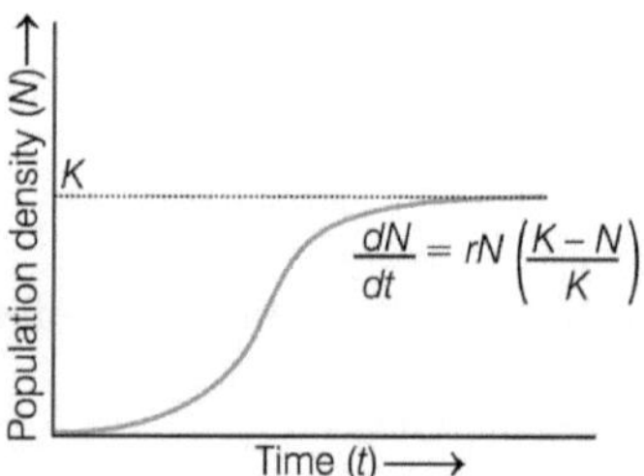

Population growth curve showing logistic growth

A population growing in a habitat with limited resources shows initially a **lag phase** followed by phases of **acceleration**, **deceleration** and finally an **asymptote phase**, when the population density reaches the carrying capacity (K).

The integral form of logistic growth equation is

$$N_t = \frac{K}{1 + \left[\dfrac{K - N_0}{N_0}\right] e^{-rt}}$$

This model is more **realistic** in nature because no population growth can sustain exponential growth indefinitely as there will be competition for the basic needs due to finite resources.

Population Interactions

In nature, living organisms such as animals, plants and microbes, cannot live in isolation and therefore, interact in various ways to form a biological community.

Interspecific interactions occur between populations of two different species. These interactions could be beneficial (+), detrimental (–) or neutral (0) as shown in given table.

Population interactions and their effects are as follows

Names of Interaction	Effects on Species A	Effects on Species B
Mutualism	+	+
Competition	–	–
Predation	+	–
Parasitism	+	–
Commensalism	+	0
Amensalism	–	0

Various population interactions are as follows

1. Predation

- It is an interspecific interaction, where an animal called **predator** kills and consumes the other weaker animal called **prey**.
- This is a biological control method. It is the nature's way of transferring energy to higher trophic levels, which is fixed by plants at the first trophic level, e.g. tiger (predator) and deer (prey).
- Important roles of predators are as follows

  (i) In the absence of predators, prey species could achieve very high population densities and cause instability. So, besides acting as 'conduits' for energy transfer across trophic levels, predators play very important role in providing population stability.

  (ii) They help in maintaining species diversity in a community, by reducing the intensity of competition among competing prey species, e.g. predator starfish *Pisaster* in the rocky intertidal communities of American Pacific Coast. In a field experiment, when all the starfish were removed from the area, more than 10 species of invertebrates became extinct within a year, because of interspecific competition.

- If a predator is too efficient and over exploits its prey, then the prey might become extinct. Following it, the predator

will also become extinct because of the lack of food. This is why predators in nature are prudent. Prey species have evolved various defence mechanisms to lessen the impact of predation. These are as follows

(a) Some species of insects and frogs are cryptically coloured (camouflaged) to avoid being detected easily by the predator.

Some are poisonous and therefore, avoided by the predators.

Monarch butterfly is highly distasteful to its predators (birds) because of a special chemical present in its body. The butterfly acquires this chemical during its caterpillar stage by feeding on a poisonous weed.

(b) Nearly 25% of all insects are known to be **phytophagous** (feeding on plant sap and other parts of plants) apart from other herbivores. So, plants have evolved various defences against them, e.g. thorns of *Acacia* and cactus are the most common morphological means of defence.

  - Some plants produce highly poisonous chemicals like cardiac glycosides, e.g. weed *Calotropis* that makes the herbivore sick, etc.
  - Chemicals like nicotine, caffeine, quinine, strychnine, opium, etc., are actually defence mechanisms against grazers and browsers.

2. Competition

- It is the interaction in which closely related species compete for the same resources which are limited. However, this is not always true.
- Some totally unrelated species could also compete for the same resources, e.g. in some shallow South American lakes, visiting flamingos and resident fishes compete for their common food, i.e. zooplanktons.
- Resources need not be limiting for competition to occur. In interference competition, the feeding efficiency of one species might be reduced due to the interfering and inhibitory presence of the other species, although the resources are plenty, e.g. when goats were introduced in Galapagos Islands, the Abingdon tortoise became extinct within a decade due to greater browsing efficiency of the goats.
- Therefore, competition can be best defined as a process in which the fitness of one species (measured in terms of its r, the intrinsic rate of increase) is significantly lower in the presence of another species.
- **Competitive release** provides another evidence of competition in nature. It is a phenomenon, in which a species whose distribution is restricted to a small geographical area because of the presence of a competitively superior species, is found to expand its distributional range dramatically, when the competing species is experimentally removed.

- **Connel's elegant field experiments** showed that on the rocky sea coasts of Scotland, the larger and competitively superior barnacle *Balanus* dominates the intertidal area and excludes the smaller barnacle *Chathamalus* from that zone.

- **Gause's competitive exclusion principle** states that two closely related species competing for the same resources cannot coexist indefinitely and the competitively inferior one will be eliminated eventually. This may hold true in case of limited resources.

- **Resource partitioning** is a mechanism evolved by competing species to ensure their co-existence. This refers to competitive co-existence.

3. Parasitism

It is the mode of interaction between two species in which one species (parasite) depends on the other species (host) for food and shelter and damages the host. In this process, one organism is benefitted (parasite), while the other is being harmed (host).

(i) Adaptation methods of a parasite are

Parasite is host-specific in a way that both host and parasite tend to co-evolve. According to its lifestyle, a parasite evolved special adaptations as

  (a) Loss of unnecessary sense organs.

  (b) Presence of adhesive organs or suckers for clinging on to host.

  (c) Loss of digestive system.

  (d) High reproductive capacity.

(ii) The life cycles of parasites are often complex, involving one or two intermediate hosts or vectors to facilitate parasitisation of its primary host. For example,

  (a) **Human liver fluke** (a trematode parasite) depends on two intermediate hosts (a snail and a fish) to complete its life cycle.

  (b) **Malarial parasite** (*Plasmodium*) needs a vector (mosquito) to spread to other hosts.

(iii) Majority of parasites harm the host. The harm is done in the following ways

- They reduce the survival, growth and reproductive ability of the host.

- They reduce its population density.

- They might render the host more vulnerable to predation by making it physically weak.

Types of Parasites

Parasites are broadly divided into following main types

1. **Ectoparasites** depend on the external surface of the host organism for food and shelter, e.g. lice on humans, ticks on dogs, copepods in marine fishes and *Cuscuta*, a parasitic plant that grows on hedge plants.

2. **Endoparasites** live inside the host's body at different sites like liver, kidney, lungs, etc., for food and shelter, e.g. tapeworm, liver fluke, *Plasmodium*, etc. The life cycles of endoparasites are more complex because of their extreme specialisation.

Brood Parasitism

It is an example of parasitism in which one organism (parasite) lays its eggs in the nest of another organism (host) for the later to incubate them. The eggs of parasitic birds have evolved to resemble the host's egg to reduce the chances of host bird from detecting and ejecting the parasitic eggs from nest, e.g. cuckoo (koel, parasite) and crow (host) during breeding season (spring to summer).

4. Mutualism

It is an interaction that confers benefits to both the interacting species.

Some examples of mutualism are

- **Lichens** represent an intimate mutualistic relationship between a fungus and photosynthesising algae or cyanobacteria. Here, the fungus helps in the absorption of nutrients and provides protection, while algae prepare the food.

- **Mycorrhizae** show close mutual association between fungi and the roots of higher plants. Fungi help the plant in absorption of nutrients, while the plant provides food for the fungus, e.g. many members of genus–*Glomus*.

- Plants need help from animals for pollination and dispersal of seeds. In return, plants provide nectar, pollens and fruits to them.

- To safeguard the mutually beneficial system, plant-animal interactions involve co-evolution of the mutualists, i.e. the evolution of the flower and its pollinator species are tightly linked with one another. For example,

  (i) Fig and its partner wasp species, the female wasp uses the fruit not only as an oviposition (egg-laying) site but uses the developing seeds within the fruit for nourishing its larvae. In return, the wasp pollinates the fig inflorescence, while searching for suitable egg-laying sites.

  (ii) Mediterranean orchid *Ophrys* employs 'sexual deceit' to get pollinated by a species of bee. One petal of its flower bears an uncanny resemblance to the female of the bee in size, colour and markings. The male bee is attracted to what it perceives as a female and 'pseudocopulates' with the flower.

  During this process, pollens are dusted from the flower on to the male bee. When the same bee pseudocopulates with another flower, it transfers pollens to it and thus, pollinates the flower.

Chapter Practice

Objective Questions

• Multiple Choice Questions

1. Formation of major biomes such as desert, rainforest takes place by
   (a) rotation of our planet around the sun
   (b) tilting of our planet to its axis
   (c) Both (a) and (b)
   (d) seasonal periodicity

Ans. (*c*) Rotation of our planet around the sun and tilt of its axis cause annual variations in the intensity and duration of temperature, resulting in formation of major biomes like deserts, rainforests and tundra.

   Thus, option (c) is correct.

2. Attribute of the organisms (morphological, physiological and behavioural) that enable organisms to survive and reproduce in its habitat are called
   (a) phenotypic plasticity   (b) adaptations
   (c) mimicry   (d) surviving abilities

Ans. (*b*) Adaptations develop due to natural selection of suitable variations appearing in living beings through mutation and recombination. These enable an organism to survive and reproduce in its habitat by undergoing behavioural, morphological and/ or physiological changes.

3. Consider the following statements.
   I. Many xerophytic plants have thick cuticle on leaf epidermis and sunken stomata.
   II. Some xerophytic plants have special photosynthetic pathway (CAM) that enables their stomata close during day.
   III. *Opuntia* has spines (modified leaves), photosynthetic phylloclade (stem).
   IV. An animal can adapt to a totally new environment by acclimatising itself to its surrounding.
   V. All adaptations are genetically not fixed.

Choose the option containing correct statements.
   (a) I, II, III and IV
   (b) II, III, IV and V
   (c) I, III, IV and V
   (d) I, II, III, IV and V

Ans. (*d*) All given statements are correct. Thus, option (d) is correct.

4. According to Allen's rule, the mammals from colder climates have
   (a) shorter ears and longer limbs
   (b) longer ears and shorter limbs
   (c) longer ears and longer limbs
   (d) shorter ears and shorter limbs

Ans. (*d*) According to Allen's rule, the mammals who live in colder climates or areas show shorter extremities like ears and limbs as compared to the mammals of warm region.

5. How seals can survive in polar climate where the temperature prevails below 0°C?
   (a) They have long hairs on their body surface
   (b) They have thick layer of fat below their skin
   (c) Both (a) and (b)
   (d) They have genetic regulation for avoiding cold climate

Ans. (*b*) In polar regions, aquatic mammals like seals have thick layer of fat below their skin that acts as an insulator and reduces the loss of body heat.

6. Population is the total number of
   (a) interbreeding individuals of a species found in a geographical area
   (b) interbreeding individuals of a species found in different geographical area
   (c) Both (a) and (b)
   (d) None of the above

Ans. (*a*) Population is the total number of interbreeding individuals of a species found in a geographical area who share and compete for similar resources.

7. 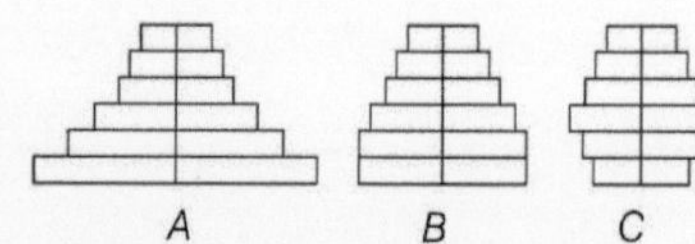

Select the correct option with respect to age pyramids.

(a) A–Expanding, B–Stable, C–Declining
(b) A–Stable, B–Expanding, C–Declining
(c) A–Stable, B–Declining, C–Expanding
(d) A–Declining, B–Stable, C–Expanding

Ans. (*a*) Option (a) is correct.

8. Match the following columns.

Column I (Attributes of population growth)	Column II (Features)
A. Mortality	1. Individuals of same species going out from population.
B. Immigration	2. Individuals of same species coming in population.
C. Emigration	3. Numbers of deaths in population during given period.

Codes

	A	B	C			A	B	C
(a)	1	3	2		(b)	2	3	1
(c)	3	2	1		(d)	2	1	3

Ans. (*c*) A–3, B–2, C–1

9. Which of the following would necessarily decrease the density of a population in a given habitat?

(a) Natality > Mortality
(b) Immigration and natality
(c) Mortality and migration
(d) Immigration > Emigration

Ans. (*c*) Mortality and migration would necessarily decrease the density of population due to loss of individual.

10. Which of the following shows Verhulst-Pearl logistic growth?

(a) $\dfrac{dN}{dt} = rN\left(\dfrac{K-N}{K}\right)$ (b) $N_t = N_o e^{rt}$

(c) $\dfrac{dN}{dt} = rN$ (d) $N\left(\dfrac{K-N}{K}\right)$

Ans. (*a*) A population growing in a habitat with limited resources shows initially a lag phase, followed by phases of increase and decrease and finally the population density reaches the carrying capacity. A plot of N in relation to time (t) results in a sigmoid curve.

This type of population growth is called Verhulst-Pearl logistic growth as explained by the following equation

$$\dfrac{dN}{dt} = rN\left(\dfrac{K-N}{K}\right)$$

11. Which option is correct for curves A and B ?

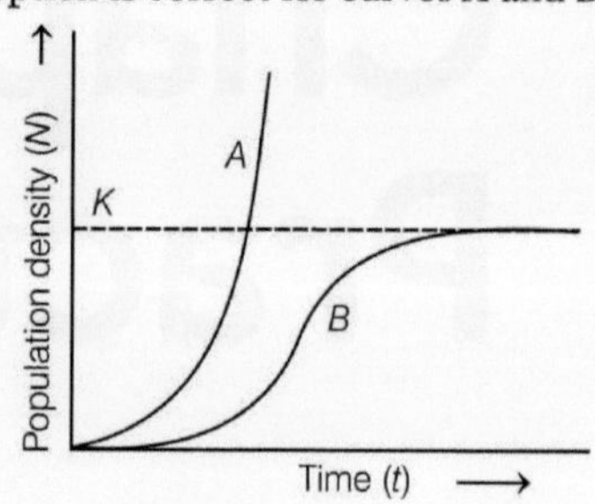

	Equation for curve A	Equation for curve B	Type of curve A	Types of curve B
(a)	$\dfrac{dN}{dt} = r - N$	$\dfrac{dN}{dt} = rN\left(\dfrac{N-K}{K}\right)$	Exponential curve	Logistic curve
(b)	$\dfrac{dN}{dt} = rN$	$\dfrac{dN}{dt} = rN\left(\dfrac{K-N}{K}\right)$	Exponential curve	Logistic curve
(c)	$\dfrac{dN}{dt} = rN$	$\dfrac{dN}{dt} = rN\left(\dfrac{K-N}{K}\right)$	S-shaped curve	J-shaped curve

(d) Both (b) and (c)

Ans. (*b*)

12. Which of the following is true regarding exponential growth?

(a) No population can grow exponentially for long
(b) Exponential growth slows down as the population nears its log phase
(c) Bacterial colonies have been observed to maintain exponential growth always
(d) Exponential growth is a commonly observed in large, slow growing species such as humans and elephants

Ans. (*a*) Option (a) is true regarding exponential growth.

13. Population interactions

Organisms I	Organisms II	Names of interaction
+	+	Mutualism
–	–	A
+	–	Predation
+	–	B
+	0	Commensalism
–	0	C

'+' sign for beneficial interaction.
'–' sign for harmful (detrimental) interaction.
'0' sign for neutral interaction.

Find out what could be A, B and C.

(a) A–Amensalism, B–Parasitism, C–Competition
(b) A–Competition, B–Parasitism, C–Amensalism
(c) A–Competition, B–Amensalism, C–Parasitism
(d) A–Amensalism, B–Competition, C–Competition

Ans. (*b*)

14. Monarch butterflies are highly distasteful to predator
(a) as it can camouflage
(b) due to a special chemical present in his body
(c) due to a poison secreted by their special glands
(d) None of the above

Ans. (*b*) Monarch butterfly is highly distasteful to its predator because of a special chemical present in their body. Interestingly, the butterfly acquires this chemical during its caterpillar stage by feeding on poisonous weeds.

15. Match the following columns.

Column I (Parasitism)		Column II (Examples)	
A.	Ectoparasite	1.	Cuckoo
B.	Endoparasite	2.	Lice
C.	Brood parasite	3.	*Ascaris*

Codes

	A	B	C			A	B	C
(a)	3	1	2		(b)	2	1	3
(c)	3	2	1		(d)	2	3	1

Ans. (*d*) A–2, B–3, C–1

• Assertion-Reasoning MCQs

Direction (Q. Nos. 1-5) *Each of these questions contains two statements, Assertion (A) and Reason (R). Each of these questions also has four alternative choices, any one of which is the correct answer. You have to select one of the codes (a), (b), (c) and (d) given below.*
(a) Both A and R are true and R is the correct explanation of A
(b) Both A and R are true, but R is not the correct explanation of A
(c) A is true, but R is false
(d) A is false, but R is true

1. **Assertion** (A) Ecological equivalents possess similar types of adaptations.
Reason (R) Ecological niche is the total interaction of a species with environment.

Ans. (*b*) Both A and R are true, but R is not the correct explanation of A.

2. **Assertion** (A) Biotic community has higher position than the population in ecological hierarchy.
Reason (R) Population of similar individuals remain isolated in the community.

Ans. (*c*) A is true, but R is false. R can be corrected as
Populations of similar individuals of a community did not remain isolate as they show interactions and interdependence.

3. **Assertion** (A) Species are groups of potentially interbreeding natural populations that are isolated from other such groups.
Reason (R) Reproductive isolation brings about distinctive morphological characters.

Ans. (*c*) A is true, but R is false. R can be corrected as
Reproductive isolation prevents members of one species to mate and produce offspring with another species. Thus, it prevents the bringing of distinctive morphological characters.
Species are groups of potentially interbreeding natural populations that are isolated (rather than being reproductively isolated) from other such groups.

4. **Assertion** (A) Predation is an interspecific interaction with a feeding strategy.
Reason (R) Predators and their prey maintain fairly stable population through time and rarely one population become abundant or scarce.

Ans. (*a*) Both A and R are true and R is the correct explanation of A.

5. **Assertion** (A) In mutualism, both the population are benefitted and neither can survive under natural condition without other.
Reason (R) Both populations are benefitted by the association, but their relationships are not obligatory.

Ans. (*c*) A is true, but R is false. R can be corrected as
In mutualism, both populations are benefitted by the association, but their relationships are obligatory, i.e. the species are in close proximity and interdependent with one another in away that one cannot survive without the other.

• Case Based MCQ

1. **Direction** *Read the following passage and answer the questions that follows.*

On earth in any natural habitat of any species, the minimal requirement is one or more species on which it can feed. Even a plant species, which makes its own food, cannot survive alone, it needs soil microbes to breakdown the organic matter in soil and return inorganic nutrients for absorption. And then how will the plant manage pollination without an animal agent. Thus, it is obvious that in nature, plants, animals and microbes do not and cannot live in isolation, but interact in various ways to form a biological community. These interactions can be interspecific and intraspecific.

(i) Interspecific interactions arise from the interactions of
(a) population of two different species
(b) population of same species
(c) two individuals of same species
(d) two individuals of different area

Ans. (*a*) Interspecific interactions arise from the interactions of population of two different species.

(ii) Interspecific interaction could be ....

(a) beneficial   (b) detrimental

(c) neutral   (d) All of these

Ans. (*d*) The interspecific interaction could be beneficial, detrimental or neutral to one of the species or both. Thus, option (d) is correct.

(iii) The population interaction in which free-living organisms that catches, kills and devours individuals of other species is called

(a) parasitism   (b) predation

(c) amensalism   (d) commensalism

Ans. (*b*) Predation is a population interaction in which free-living organisms catches, kills and devours individuals of other species.

(iv) Which interaction confers benefits to both the interacting species?

(a) Parasitism

(b) Mutualism

(c) Commensalism

(d) Amensalism

Ans. (*b*) Mutualism is an interaction that confers benefits to both the interacting species.

(v) Refer to the given table that summarises the interactions between two organisms (organism 1 and organism 2). Identify the types of interaction (*A*, *B* and *C*) and select the correct answer.

		Effects on Organism 2		
		Benefit	**Harm**	**No Effect**
Effects on Organism 1	**Benefit**	Mutualism	Predation	Commensalism
	Harm	*A*	*B*	Amensalism
	No Effect	Commensalism	Amensalism	–

  I. *A* can be either predation or parasitism.

 II. *B* can be either commensalism or amensalism.

III. *B* can be competition.

IV. *A* can be amensalism.

Codes

(a) I and II   (b) II and III

(c) III and IV   (d) I and III

Ans. (*d*) *A* can either be predation or parasitism, since one species is harmed and other is benefitted. *B* is competition, since both species harm each other.

PART 2

Subjective Questions

• Short Answer (SA) Type Questions

1. Define population and community.   (NCERT)

Ans. **Population** It refers to the sum total of all organisms having similar features and potential to interbreed among themselves and produce fertile offsprings.

Community It refers to assemblage of all the populations of different species in a specific geographical area.

2. Water is very essential for life. Write any three features each for plants and animals which enable them to survive in water scarce environment.

     (All India 2011)

Ans. Three features of plants to survive in water scarce environment are

- Roots grow very deep to explore any possibility of available underground water.
- Many desert plants have a thick cuticle on their leaf surfaces and have their stomata arranged in deep pits to minimise water loss through transpiration.
- Some desert plants like *Opuntia,* have no leaves. Their leaves are reduced to spines and photosynthesis occurs in flattened stems.

Three features of animals to survive in water scarce environment are

(i) They produce concentrated urine, so as to keep the water in their body.

(ii) Their sweat glands get closed, hence their is no water loss through sweat.

(iii) They undergo aestivation to escape harsh condition.

3. Categorise the following plants into hydrophytes, halophytes, mesophytes and xerophytes. Give reasons for your answers.

(i) *Salvinia*   (ii) *Opuntia*

(iii) *Rhizophora*   (iv) *Mangifera*

Ans. (i) *Salvinia* is hydrophyte or aquatic plants. They have aerenchyma for buoyancy and floating and have wax covering to aviod damage from water.

(ii) *Opuntia* is xerophyte plants. They have developed some modifications to survive in desert area like their leaves are reduced to spines to prevent water loss through transpiration and photosynthesis occurs in stem.

(iii) *Rhizophora* is halophyte plants. They have the ability to tolerate high concentrations of salts in their rooting medium.

(iv) *Mangifera* is a mesophyte plants. They are terrestrial plants. They require modrate amount of water. Stomata are present on the lower epidermis of plant leaves. Their closing and opening depends of weather.

4. Enumerate the adaptations that help halophytes to survive in salty conditions. **(All India 2015C)**

Ans. The adaptations that help halophytes to survive in salty conditions are

- Some halophytic plants possess small negatively geotropic vertical roots called pneumatophores (have lenticels for gaseous exchange), e.g. *Avicennia, Aegialitis*.
- Another adaptation of halophytic plants is vivipary or seed germination, while the fruit is still attached to plants, e.g. *Rhizophora, Aegiceras, Ceriops*.

5. Why the plants that inhabit a desert are not found in a mangrove? Give reasons. **(Delhi 2016C)**

Ans. The plants found in desert are not found in mangrove because desert plants have made modification in order to adapt their surrounding. For example, their leaves are reduced into spine and have sunken stomata to reduce water loss through transpiration their roots grow deeply to explore possibility of underground water.

Their stems has cuticle and are fleshy to preserve moisture. While mangrove has salty condition so to overcome this plants have specialised root which grow negatively geotropic, called pneumatophores, leaves are thin, small and green.

Stems are usually cuticularised.

6. Plants that inhabit a rainforest are not found in a wetland. Explain. **(Delhi 2016)**

Ans. The rainforest plants have a thin, smooth bark because they do not need thick bark to prevent moisture. The smoothness of the bark makes it difficult for other plants to grow on their surface. While in wetland, plants have roots in the soil under the water but they grow above the water for respiration (pneumatophores). They have adapted to growing in very wet soil. So, rainforest plants are not found in wetland.

7. How do mammals living in colder regions and seals living in polar regions able to reduce the loss of their body heat? **(Delhi 2015C)**

Ans. Mammals living in colder climates generally have shorter ears and limbs to minimise heat loss. This is called Allen's rule. In polar areas, aquatic mammals like seals have a thick layer of fat (blubber) below their skin that acts as an insulator and reduces loss of body heat.

8. Heat loss or heat gain depends upon the surface area of the organism's body. Explain with the help of a suitable example. **(All India 2016C)**

Ans. Small animals like humming bird or shrew, have a large surface area relative to their volume. So, they tend to lose body heat very fast during cold conditions. They need to spend more energy to generate body heat through metabolism. Due to this, smaller animals are rarely found in polar regions.

9. Why do people suffer from altitude sickness after reaching the high altitude regions? How does their body acclimatised after a couple of days? **(Delhi 2015C)**

Ans. People visiting high altitude regions experience altitude sickness. This is because the body does not get enough oxygen. The person shows symptoms of nausea, fatigue and heart palpitations.

After couple of days, the body responds gradually by physiological adaptation. The body compensates low O_2 availability by

(i) increasing RBCs production.

(ii) decreasing binding capacity of haemoglobin.

(iii) increased breathing rate.

10. Why do people living in high altitude have more haemoglobin and high RBC count?

Ans. In higher altitudes, the atmospheric pressure tends to decrease with the increases of height. Hence, the people living on higher altitudes have to compensate the low oxygen availability. Thus, they have higher levels of haemoglobin and RBCs count in the blood, which helps them to take in more oxygen.

11. List any three important characteristics of a population and explain. **(NCERT)**

Ans. The important characteristics of a population are as follows

1. **Population size or density** It is the number of individuals of a species per unit area or volume. Population Density

$$(PD) = \frac{\text{Number of individuals in a region (N)}}{\text{Size of unit area in the region (S)}}; PD = \frac{N}{S}$$

2. **Birth rate or Natality** It is the number of births of new individuals per unit of population per unit time, e.g. if in a pond, there are 20 lotus plants last year and through reproduction, 8 new plants are added, taking the current population to 28. Then, birth rate = 8/20 = 0.4 offspring per lotus per year.

3. **Death rate or Mortality** It is the number of loss of individuals per unit of population per unit time due to death or due to the different environmental changes, competition, predation, etc.

For example, if in a laboratory population of 40 individuals, 4 fruit flies died during a specified time interval, then the death rate = 4/40 = 0.1 individuals per fruit fly per week.

12. Draw labelled diagrams of stable and declining age pyramids of human population.   **(All India 2020C)**

Ans.

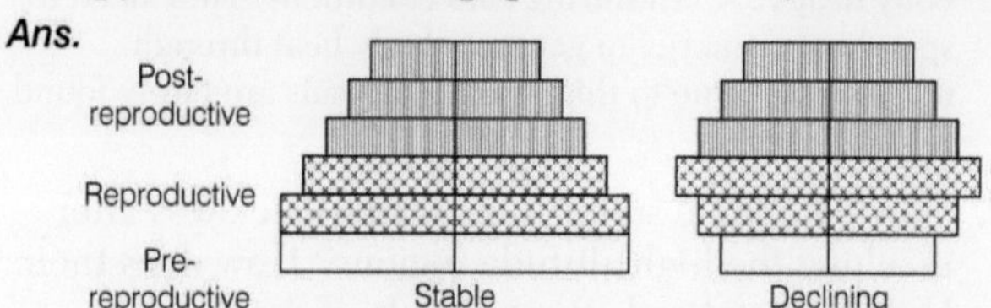

13. Define 'zero population growth rate'. Draw an age pyramid for the same.   **(NCERT Exemplar)**

Ans. When the pre-reproductive age group individuals are comparatively fewer and both reproductive and post-reproductive stages are almost in equal stage, i.e. at same level, it is zero population growth rate.

An inverted bell-shaped age pyramid is obtained for zero population growth rate.

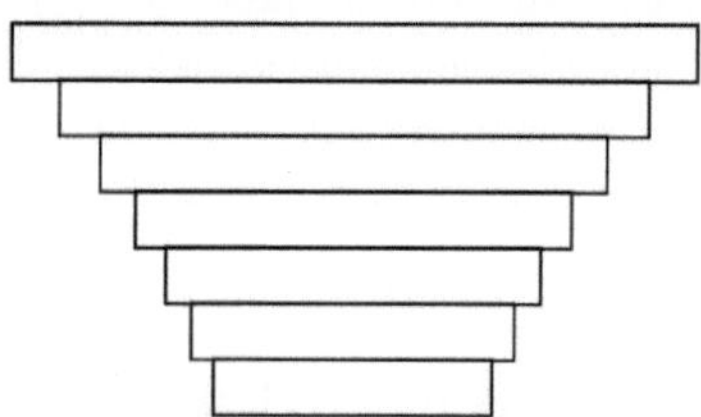

14. Write the exponential equation for J-shaped growth form.

Ans. Exponential equation for J-shaped growth form is

$$\frac{dN}{dt} = N$$

where, dN/dt is the rate of change in population size, 'r' is intrinsic rate of natural increase and 'N' is the population size.

15. A population of *Paramecium caudatum* was grown in a culture medium. After 5 days, the culture medium became overcrowded with *Paramecium* and had depleted nutrients. What will happen to the population and what type of growth curve will the population attain? Draw the growth curve.

Ans. Initially, after a lag phase, the population will grow in an exponential manner as the nutrients and space will be abundant.

When the food sources get depleted, the population density starts decreasing and ends in an asymptote phase, then the population density reaches the carrying capacity (maximum number of individuals of a population or species that a given environment can sustain indefinitely).

The population shows a pattern of logistic growth giving an S-shaped curve.

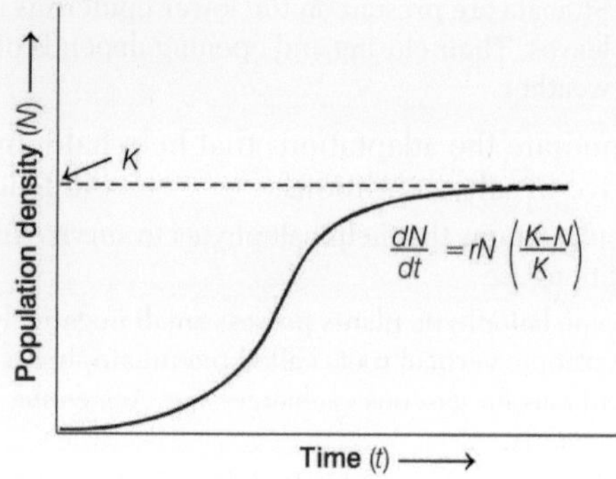

Logistic growth curve

Where, K = carrying capacity

N = population density at time 't'

r = Intrinsic rate of natural increase

16. If a population growing exponentially doubles in size in three years. What is the intrinsic rate of increase (r) of the population?   **(NCERT)**

Ans. Exponential growth of population,

$$N_t = N_0 \, e^{rt} \qquad \text{...(i)}$$

Where, N_t = Population density at time t

N_0 = Population density before time t

r = Intrinsic rate of increase

We can also write equation (i) as $\dfrac{N_t}{N_0} = e^{rt}$

Given, $\dfrac{N_t}{N_0} = 2, t = 3$ yrs $\Rightarrow 2 = e^{rt}$

Taking $\log_e$ on both sides.

$$ln\, 2 = rt \qquad [\log_e = ln;\ ln\, e^x = x]$$

$$\Rightarrow \quad r = \frac{ln\, 2}{t} = \frac{ln\, 2}{3} = \frac{0.69314}{3} = 0.23104$$

Intrinsic increase rate (r %) = $0.23104 \times 100 = 23.10\%$.

17. What is 'predation'? Explain with the help of suitable examples why is it required in a community with rich biodiversity.   **(All India 2015C)**

Ans. Predation is an interaction where one organism (predator) kills and eats the other weaker organism called prey. It is a natural way of transferring the energy fixed by plants, to higher trophic levels.

For example, snake eating a frog, tiger killing and eating a deer. Predators keep prey population under control which otherwise could achieve very high population densities and cause instability in ecosystem.

They also help in maintaining a species diversity in a community by reducing the intensity of competition among competing prey species.

18. Name important defence mechanisms in plants against herbivory. **(NCERT)**

Ans. The herbivores are predators of plants and nearly 25% insects are phytophagous (feeding on plants). So, plants show morphological as well as chemical defence against herbivores such as

  (i) Thorns of rose, *Acacia* and cactus.

  (ii) Certain plants produce chemicals, such as opium, quinine, caffeine, nicotine, etc., to protect them against being grazed by the animals.

  (iii) *Calotropis* produces highly poisonous cardiac glycosides. So, the cattle and goats do not eat this plant.

19. Explain coevolution with reference to parasites and their hosts. Mention any four special adaptive features evolved in parasites for their parasitic mode of life. **(All India 2015)**

Or Explain parasitism and coevolution with the help of one example of each. **(All India 2016)**

Ans. Coevolution is a phenomenon where many parasites have evolved to be host specific in such a way that both the host and parasite tend to coevolve, i.e. if the host develops/evolves special mechanism for rejecting or resisting, then the parasite also have to evolve mechanism to counteract and neutralise them to succeed with the same host species.

Parasites have special adaptations according to their lifestyles such as, loss of unnecessary sense organs, presence of adhesive organ or suckers, loss of digestive system and high reproductive system.

20. What are the different ways in which parasite can alter the population of hosts?

Ans. Following are the ways in which parasite can alter the population of host

  (i) They can shorten the life cycle of the host and can weaken it.

  (ii) They can drastically reduce the reproduction to the extent of causing sterility.

  (iii) They reduce its population density.

21. Name and explain the type of interaction that exists in mycorrhizae and between cattle egret and grazing cattle. **(All India 2016)**

Ans. Mycorrhiza is an association between fungi and roots of higher plants. This interaction is called mutualism. The fungi help plant in the absorption of essential nutrients from the soil, while in turn it provides the fungi with energy yielding carbohydrates. Both partners are benefitted in this relationship.

The cattle egret and grazing cattle share commensalism type of relationship. The grazing cattle flush out insects from grass while grazing. So, it becomes easier for egret to catch and feed on them. In this, one partner gets benefit, while other remains unaffected.

22. In an association of two animal species, one is a termite which feeds on wood and the other is a protozoan *Trichonympha* present in the gut of the termite. What type of association they establish?

Ans. The termite provides shelter and space for the protozoan *Trichonympha* to live. The protozoans present in gut digest the wood, which termite feeds upon. In the absence of *Trichonympha*, the termite is unable to digest wood and hence dies. Thus, the association of two given animal species represents mutualism.

23. What is mutualism? Mention any two examples where the organisms involved are commercially exploited in agriculture. **(All India 2015)**

Ans. Mutualism is an interaction that confers benefits on both the interacting species. Two examples where organisms involved are commercially exploited in agriculture are mycorrhizae and lichen.

24. Describe the mutual relationship between the fig tree and wasp and comment on the phenomenon that operates in their relationship. **(All India 2014)**

Ans. The relationship between fig tree and wasp shows mutualism. The wasp while searching for sites to lay its eggs, pollinates the fig's inflorescence.

On the other hand, the fig not only provides shelter (fruit) for oviposition but also allows wasp's larva to feed on its seeds.

25. What advantage does the sea anemone get in the sea anemone-hermit crab interaction as facultative mutualism? Give an alternative term for this kind of mutualism.

Ans. The sea anemone is transported on the back of hermit crab for reaching new food sources. Alternative term for this type of mutualism is protocooperation in which both the species are mutually benefitted but can live without each other.

26. An orchid plant is growing on the branch of mango tree. How do you describe this interaction between the orchid and mango tree? **(NCERT)**

Ans. Orchid is an epiphytic plant that grows on a mango tree branch and they together show commensalism. In this interaction, orchid is benefitted and the mango tree is neither harmed nor benefitted at all.

27. In an aquarium, two herbivorous species of fish are living together and feeding on phytoplanktons. As per the Gause's principle, one of the species is to be eliminated in due course of time, but both are surviving well in the aquarium. Give possible reasons.

Ans. Competition is a rivalry relationship between two or more organisms. A competition between individual of same species (intraspecific) is more acute than the competition between individual of different species as all the members in a intraspecific competition have same basic requirements like food, water, light, space, mating and shelter.

Gause's competitive exclusion principle states that two closely related species competing for the same resources cannot coexist indefinitely and the competitively inferior one will be eliminated eventually. This may hold true in case of limited resources.

28. Fill in the blanks. **(NCERT Exemplar)**

Species A	Species B	Types of Interaction	Examples
+	−	....	....
+	+	....	....
+	....	Commensalism	....

Ans.

Species A	Species B	Types of Interaction	Examples
+	−	Predation	Phytophagous animal and plants.
+	+	Protocooperation	Sea anemone and hermit crab.
+	0	Commensalism	An orchid growing as an epiphyte on a mango tree.

• Long Answer (LA) Type Questions

1. (i) List the defferent attributes that a population has and not an individual organism.

(ii) What is population density? Explain four different ways the population density can be measured, with the help of an example each. **(All India 2015)**

Ans. (i) Attributes that a population has but not an individual organism are birth rate, death rate, sex ratio, age pyramids or age distribution.

(ii) Population density is the number of individuals per unit area at a given time/period.

Different ways of measuring population density are as follows

(a) Biomass or percentage cover, e.g. hundred *Parthenium* plants and one huge banyan tree.

(b) By measuring relative density, e.g. the number of fish caught per trap from a lake.

(c) Numbers, e.g. human population.

(d) Indirect estimation, i.e. without seeing or actually counting population sizes, e.g. the tiger census is often based on pug marks and faecal pellets.

2. 'Analysis of age pyramids for human population can provide important inputs for long term planning strategies'. Explain. **(Delhi 2015)**

Ans. **Age pyramid** displays the age distribution (% individuals of a given age or age group) for the population. Population at any given time is composed of individuals of different ages. For human population, the age pyramids generally show age distribution of males and females in a combined diagram.

The shape of the pyramids reflects the growth status of the population that whether it is growing, stable or declining.

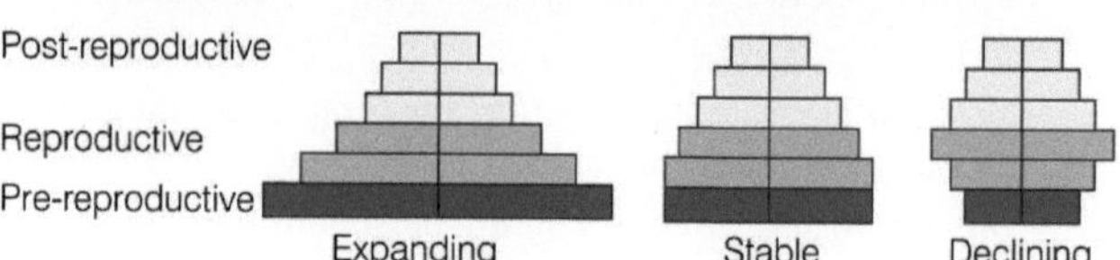

Representation of age pyramids for human population

It tells about an area's population, birth and death rates, dependants, young people and elderly people, etc. These are important inputs that can be used for long term planning strategies, e.g. to create job opportunities (if there are more young people), to focus on control of population (in case of high birth rate), to improve and invest more on medical facilities (in case of low elderly people), etc.

Hence, through in depth analysis of the age pyramids, better planning strategies, resource allocation and other planning benefits can be obtained.

3. The following diagrams are the age pyramids of different populations. Comment on the status of these populations. **(NCERT Exemplar)**

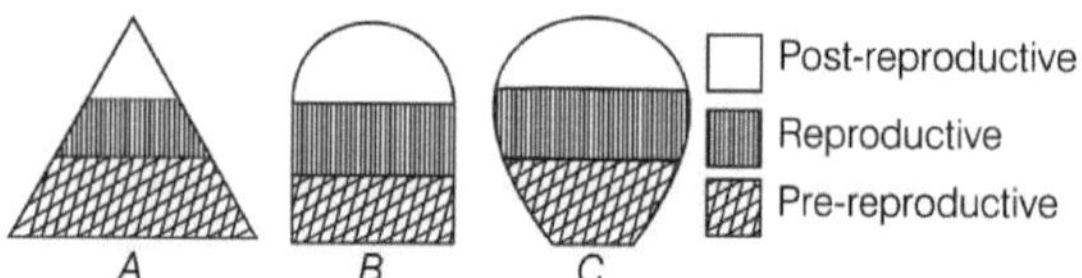

Ans. **Figure A** It is a 'pyramid'-shaped age pyramid. In this figure, the base, i.e. pre-reproductive stage is very large as compared with the reproductive and post-reproductive stages of the population. This type of age structure indicates that the population would increase rapidly.

Figure B It is an inverted bell-shaped pyramid. In this figure, the pre-reproductive and reproductive stages are same. This type of age structure indicates that the population is stable.

Figure C It is an urn-shaped pyramid. In the figure, the pre-reproductive and reproductive stages are less than the post-reproductive stages of this population. In this population, more older people are present. This type of age structure indicates that the population definitely is declining.

4. (i) Compare giving reasons, the J-shaped and S-shaped models of population growth of a species.

(ii) Explain 'Fitness of a species', as mentioned by Darwin. **(All India 2017)**

Ans. (i) Comparisons between J-shaped and S-shaped model of population growth are as follows

J-shaped Population Growth	S-shaped Population Growth
Population growth occurs in J-shaped manner when resources are unlimited in a habitat.	Population growth occurs in S-shaped manner when resources are limited in a habitat.
A stationary or steady phase is seldom achieved.	A stationary or steady phase is reached.
Population crashes ultimately due to mass mortality.	Population seldom crashes.
The growth curve is characterised by initial lag phase followed by acceleration phase.	The growth curve initially depicts a lag phase followed by acceleration phase, deceleration phase and an upper asymptote that represents the carrying capacity.

(ii) **Fitness of a species as mentioned by Darwin**
Darwinian fitness (high 'r' value) states that the population evolves to maximise its reproductive fitness in the habitat where it lives. Under a particular set of selection pressure, organisms evolve towards the most efficient reproductive strategy.

The rate of breeding varies from species to species. Some species breed only once in their lifetime (Pacific salmon fish and bamboo), while some breed many times in their lifetime (birds and mammals). Some organisms produce a large number of small-sized offsprings (oysters), whereas other produce a small number of large-sized offspring (birds and mammals).

5. Discuss the various types of positive interactions between species.

Ans. The interspecific interactions are of three types, i.e. positive or beneficial, negative or antagonistic and last neutral interaction.

Some positive interactions are scavenging, commensalism, protocooperation and mutualism.

Mutualism This interaction confers benefits on both the interacting species, e.g.

(i) Lichens represent an intimate mutualistic relationship between a fungus and photosynthesising algae or cyanobacteria.

(ii) The mycorrhizae are associations between fungi and the roots of higher plants. The fungi help the plant in the absorption of essential nutrients from the soil while the plant in turn provides the fungi with energy-yielding carbohydrates.

(iii) Plants offer nectar, juicy and nutritious fruits to animals that help to pollinate their flowers and disperse their seeds.

Commensalism This is the interaction in which one species benefits without affecting the other, e.g.

(i) An orchid growing as an epiphyte on a mango branch.

(ii) Barnacles growing on the back of a whale.

(iii) The cattle egret foraging close to the cattle that stir up and flush out insects from the vegetation.

(iv) Sea anemone that has stinging tentacles and the clown fish that lives among them to get protection from predators.

Scavenging is the act of feeding by scavenger like bacteria, fungi on the remain of dead animals.

Protocooperation is the type of relationship in which both partners mutually obtain benefits. But they associate purely to benefit from each other and can live without each other.

• Case Based Questions

1. Direction *Read the following passage and answer the questions that follows.*

Ecology is a vast arena in biology, which is a study of organisms, their distribution and interaction with each other and the environment. To study the relationship between prey, predators, other interactions and phenomenon like competition, camouflage, mimicry, etc., it is mandatory to study the theory of population interaction.

The interaction between nature, animals, plants and microbes to form a biological community is known as population interaction. These interactions can be intraspecific, i.e. existing between organisms of same population and interspecific, i.e. between members of different species.

(i) Name the association in which one species produces poisonous substance or a change in environmental conditions that is harmful to another species.

Ans. Amensalism is an interaction between different species, in which one species is harmed and the other is neither benefitted nor harmed, e.g. *Penicillium*, a mould secretes penicillin which kills bacteria, but the mould remains unaffected.

(ii) What do you mean by facultative mutualism?

Ans. Facultative mutualism is an interaction between two different species in which both are mutually benefitted but they can live without each other, e.g. sea anemone is carried from place to place by the moving crab and is benefitted by getting more places for the food. On the other hand, hermit crab also derives benefit through camouflage and protection provided by sea anemone because of the presence of stinging cells in the later.

(iii) Why did the Abingdon tortoise in Galapagos island become extinct?

Ans. The Abingdon tortoise in Galapagos island become extinct due to interference competition, i.e. the feeding efficiency of species A might be reduced due to the interfering and inhibitory presence of the speceis B. Therefore when goats were introduced in Galapagos island Abingdon tortoise become extinct due to greater browsing efficiency of the goats.

(iv) How will the ability to camouflage benefits the prey?

Ans. Camouflage is a phenomenon of blending of an organism with the surrounding due to similar colour, marking and shape, so as to avoid the predators, e.g. leaf-like insects such as grasshopper.

(v) Name the type of association that the genus– *Glomus* exhibits with higher plants.　(**All India 2014**)

Ans. Mycorrhizae show close mutual association between fungi and the roots of higher plants. Fungi help the plant in absorption of nutrients, while the plant provides food for the fungus, e.g. many members of genus–*Glomus*.

Thus, the genus–*Glomus* exhibits mutualism with higher plants.

2. Observe the diagram of the factors influencing population density and answer the questions that follows.

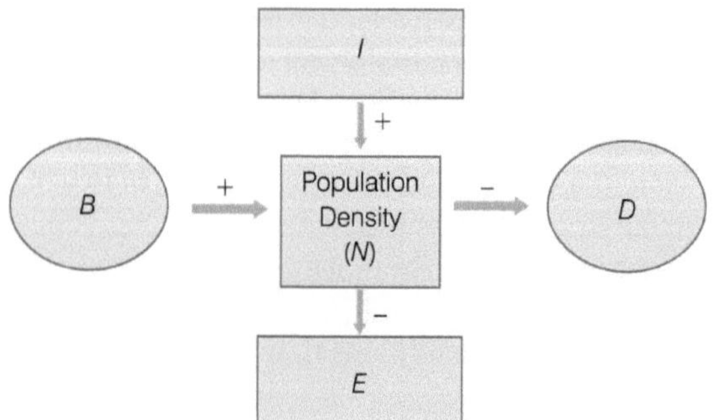

(i) What is the terminology for B and E ?

Ans. B in the diagram stands for Natality (Births) and E depicts Emigration.

(ii) If $B + I$ is more than $D + E$ then what will happen to population density?

Ans. If the sum of births and immigration $(B + I)$ exceeds the sum of deaths and emigration $(D + E)$ then the number of people added in the habitat will be more than the number of people moving out. Thus, the population density will increase.

(iii) What are the most important factors which influence a population density of an area under normal condition?

Ans. Under normal condition, number of births and deaths will influence or affect an area's population density.

(iv) If a habitat is being colonised recently then which factor contribute more to the population growth?

Ans. If a habitat is being colonised recently then the number of individuals of a same species that have come into the habitat from elsewhere during the time period contribute more to the population growth. So, it is known as immigration.

(v) If natality is represented by B, Mortality is represented by D, Immigration by I Emigration by E and population density by N. Then what will be the population density at time $(t + 1)$?

Ans. The population density at time $(t + 1)$ will be

$$N_{(t+1)} = N_t[(B+I)-(D+E)]$$

3. Study the graph given below and answer the questions that follows.　(**Delhi 2014**)

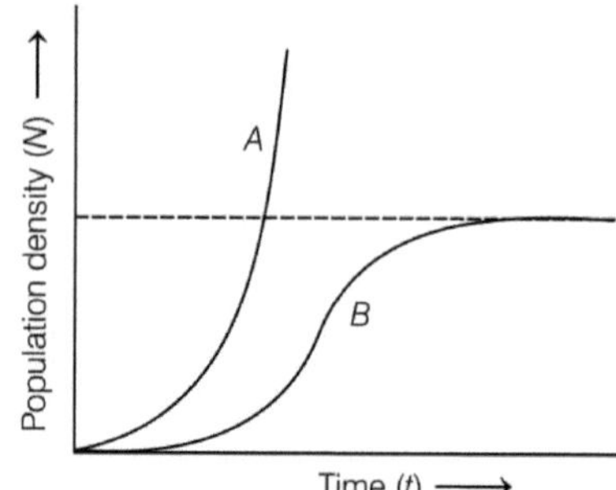

(i) Write the status of food and space in the curves A and B.

Ans. A–Unlimited food and space
B–Limited food and space

(ii) In the absence of predators, which one of the two curves would appropriately depict the prey population?

Ans. Curve B

(iii) Time has been shown on X-axis and there is a parallel dotted line above it. Give the significance of this dotted line.

Ans. The dotted line represents the carrying capacity. It is the capacity of a given habitat having enough resources to support maximum possible number, beyond which no further growth is possible.

4. Direction *Read the following passage and answer the questions given below.*

Ecological competition is the struggle between two organisms for the same resources within an environment. Resources are components of the environment they are required for survival and reproduction such as food, water, shelter, light, territory and substrate. The competitive exclusion principle sometimes referred to as Gause's law, of competitive exclusion or just Gause's law, states that two species that compete for the exact same resources cannot stably coexist. One of the two competitiors will always have an ever, so slight advantage over the other that leads to extinction of the second competitor in the long run or to an evolutionary shift of the inferior competitor towards a different ecological niche.

(i) In which process, the fitness of one species (measured in terms of its 'r' the intrinsic rate of increase) is significantly lower in the presence of another superior species?

Ans. Competition is best defined by the fitness of one species as compared to other competitive species. It is the process in which the fitness of one species is significantly lower in the presence of another superior competitior species.

(ii) In which mechanism, species facing competition might evolve mechanism that promotes co-existence rather than exclusion?

Ans. Species facing competition might evolve mechanism that promotes coexistence rather than exclusion. One such mechanism is resource partitioning.

(iii) Level of competition between species depends on which factors?

Ans. Level of competition between species depends on availability of resources, population density and group interaction of organism.

(iv) What is connel's elegant field experiment?

Ans. **Connel's elegant field experiments** showed that on the rocky sea coasts of Scotland, the larger and competitively superior barnacle *Balanus* dominates the intertidal area and excludes the smaller barnacle *Chathamalus* from that zone.

(v) In laboratory experiments, two species of the protist *Paramecium* (species 1 and 2) were grown alone and in the presence of the other species. The following graphs show growth of species 1 and 2, both alone and when in mixed culture with the other species.

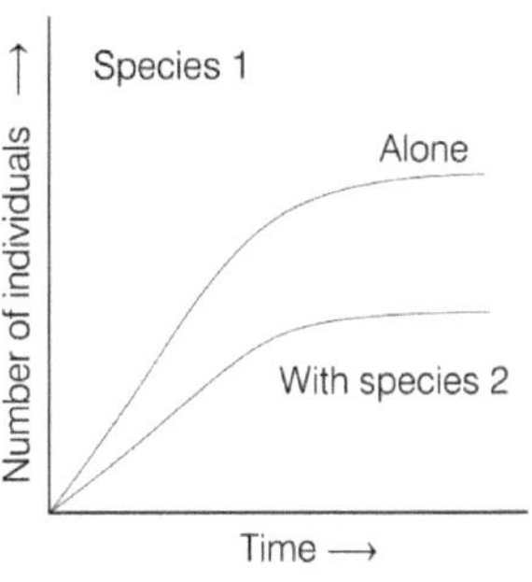

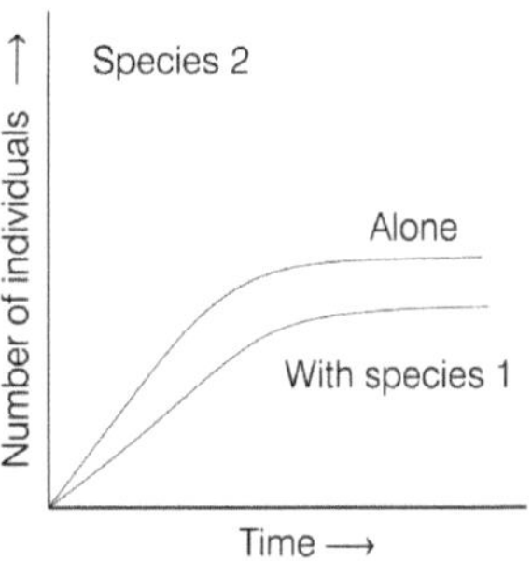

What conclusions can be drawn from the graphs?

Ans. When species 1 was kept with species 2, its number of individuals fell drastically while when species 2 was kept with species 1, its number of individuals was not much affected. Hence, both species are affected by interspecific competition, but species 2 is less affected.

Chapter Test

Multiple Choice Questions

1. Biotic community is the assemblage of populations of
(a) same species which live in particular area
(b) different species which live in particular area
(c) different species which live in different area
(d) same species which live in different area

2. Hydrophytes are characterised by the
(a) presence of sclerenchyma
(b) presence of aerenchyma
(c) absence of aerenchyma
(d) presence of root nodules

3. Competition of species leads to
(a) extinction
(b) mutation
(c) greater number of niches are formed
(d) symbiosis

4. *Cuscuta* is an example of
(a) ectoparasitism
(b) brood parasitism
(c) predation
(d) endoparasitism

5. The interdependent evolution of the flowering plants and pollinating insects together is known as
(a) mutualism
(b) coevolution
(c) commensalism
(d) cooperation

Assertion-Reasoning MCQs

Direction (Q. Nos. 1-3) *Each of these questions contains two statements, Assertion (A) and Reason (R). Each of these questions also has four alternative choices, any one of which is the correct answer. You have to select one of the codes (a), (b), (c) and (d) given below.*

(a) Both A and R are true and R is the correct explanation of A
(b) Both A and R are true, but R is not the correct explanation of A
(c) A is true, but R is false
(d) A is false, but R is true

1. Assertion (A) A mangrove tree growing in marshy place does not have pneumatophores.
Reason (R) Pneumatophores help in taking in air from atmosphere deficient saline soil.

2. Assertion (A) Sometimes one population adversely affects the other by direct attack, but yet depends upon them.
Reason (R) In predation, the contact is constant.

3. Assertion (A) Plants need the help of insects and animals for pollinating their flowers and dispersing their seeds.
Reason (R) Plants offer rewards in the form of pollen and nectar for pollinators and juicy and nutritious fruits for seed dispersers.

Short Answer Type Questions

1. Name two dominant plant species of mangroves.

2. Why are predators considered prudent in nature?

3. What is brood parasitism? Give one example of brood parasitism.

4. 'Predation is beneficial in long run'. Comment.

5. Name two basic types of competition among organisms. Which one of them is more intense and why?

Long Answer Type Questions

1. (i) What is metapopulation according to you as a biology student?
(ii) The size of a population for any species is not a static parameter'. Justify the statement with specific reference to fluctuations in the population density of a region in a given period of time. **(Delhi 2019)**

2. (i) What is parasitism? What are its types?
(ii) Name of the two intermediate hosts on which the human liver fluke depends to complete its life cycle so as to facilitate parasitisation of its primary host. **(Delhi 2014)**
(ii) Give the name of two parasitic plants and two parasitic animals.

Answers

Multiple Choice Questions

1. (b)   *2. (b)*   *3. (a)*   *4. (a)*   *5. (b)*

Assertion-Reasoning MCQs

1. (d)   *2. (a)*   *3. (b)*

For Detailed Solutions
Scan the code

CHAPTER 06

Biodiversity and its Conservation

In this Chapter...

- Biodiversity
- Magnitude of Biodiversity
- Patterns of Biodiversity
- Importance of Species Diversity to the Ecosystem
- Loss of Biodiversity
- Biodiversity Conservation

There are millions of plants and animals present on earth. Every distinct geographical location has its own set of flora and fauna. Immense diversity exists at all levels of biological organisation from micromolecules within cell to biomes. This staggering variety of life forms is referred to as **biodiversity**.

Biodiversity

It refers to the **variety** and **variability** of living organisms on the earth. It can also be defined as the variety of life forms, gene pools and habitats found in an area. The term 'biodiversity' was popularised by sociobiologist **Edward Wilson** to describe the combined diversity at all the levels of biological organisation.

The biodiversity can be described by the following three interrelated components or hierarchical levels of biological organisation.

Genetic Diversity

It is the measure of variety in genetic information contained in the organisms. It enables a population to adapt to its environment. A single species shows high diversity at the genetic level. There are more than 20,000 species of ants, 3,00,000 species of beetles, 28,000 species of fishes and nearly 20,000 species of orchids. Greater the genetic diversity among organisms of a species, more sustenance it has against the environment disturbances.

Genetic diversity within the species creates different subspecies, variety, breed, forms, etc.

For example,

(i) India has more than 50,000 genetically different strains of rice and 1,000 varieties of mango.

(ii) The genetic variation shown by the medicinal plant *Rauwolfia vomitoria*, growing in different Himalayan ranges can be in terms of concentration and potency of the active chemical reserpine that the plant produces.

Species Diversity

It is the diversity at the species level or the measure of the variety of species and their relative abundance within a region, e.g. Western Ghats have more amphibian species diversity than Eastern Ghats.

Two important measures of species diversity are

(i) **Species richness** It refers to the number of species per unit area. Species diversity increases, if the species richness is higher.

(ii) **Species evenness** It refers to the relative abundance of species in an area. The number of individuals and variety determine the level of diversity of an ecosystem.

Ecological Diversity

It refers to the diversity at ecosystem level. Due to the presence of more variety of ecosystems and habitats, i.e. rainforest, desert, wetlands, mangroves, coral reefs and alpine meadows. India has a greater ecological diversity than Scandinavian countries (e.g. Norway).

Magnitude of Biodiversity

- According to the **IUCN 2004**, more than 1.5 million species have been recorded in the world, but we have no idea of how many species are yet to be discovered and described. A sound estimate of global species diversity of about 7 million was given by **Robert May**.

- More than 70% of all the species recorded are animals, while plants comprise not more than 22%. Out of total animals recorded, 70% are insects (i.e. out of every 10 animals on this planet, 7 are insects).

- The number of fungi species is more than all the vertebrate species of fishes, amphibians, reptiles and mammals combined in the world and it is interesting to know that the diversity of microbial species alone might run into millions.

- **Indian biodiversity** India is one of the 12 megadiverse countries of the world. Though India has only 2.4% of the world's land but it shares an impressive 8.1% of the world's species diversity.

- There are about 45,000 species of plants and twice as many of animals have been recorded in India.

- India probably has more than 1,00,000 species of plants and 3,00,000 species of animals yet to be discovered and described. If we apply Robert May's global estimate then only 22% of species of the world have been recorded.

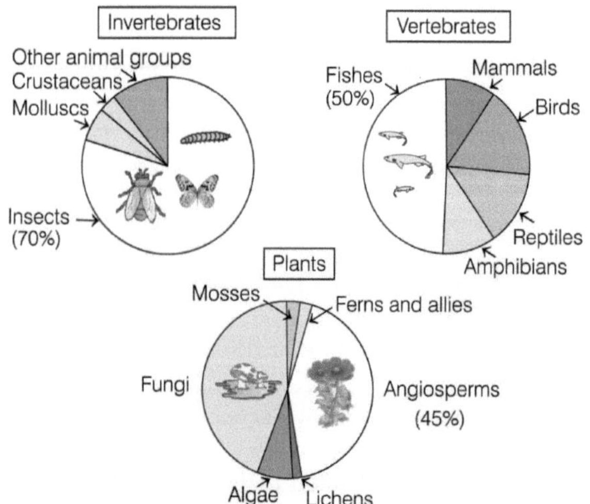

Representing global biodiversity : proportionate number of species of major taxa of plants, invertebrates and vertebrates

Patterns of Biodiversity

Biodiversity is not uniform throughout the world. It varies with the changes in latitude and altitude. For many groups of animals and plants, there are specific patterns in diversity based on the favourable environmental conditions as plants and animals are more diverse in areas, which are best suited for their survival.

Therefore, following patterns of biodiversity are seen

1. Latitudinal Gradients

- Species diversity decreases as we move away from the equator towards the poles. It means biodiversity is more at lower latitude (equator) than the higher latitude (poles). Tropics (latitudinal range of 23.5°N to 23.5°S) harbour more species than temperate or polar areas, e.g. Colombia located near the equator, has 1,400 species of birds, New York located at 41°N has 105 species of birds, while Greenland at 71°N has only 56 species of birds.

- India, with most of its area in tropical latitude has more than 1,200 species of birds. A forest of equal area in tropical region (like equator) has ten times more species of vascular plants than in temperate region (like Mid-West of USA).

- Amazonian rainforest in South America has the greatest biodiversity on the earth with more than 40,000 species of plants, 3,000 of fishes, 1,300 of birds, 427 of mammals and amphibians, 378 of reptiles and more than 1,25,000 of invertebrates. About 2 million species of insects are still waiting to be discovered and named in these rainforests as estimated by scientists.

Reasons for Greater Biodiversity in Tropics

Some hypothesis proposed by scientists to explain the rich biodiversity in tropical regions are

- The temperate regions were subjected to frequent glaciations in the past, whereas tropical latitudes have remained relatively undisturbed for millions of years.

- Tropical environments are less seasonal, relatively more constant and predictable than temperate region. This promotes niche specialisation and leads to a greater species diversity.

- Availability of more solar energy in the tropics, contributes to higher productivity, this in turn might contribute indirectly to greater species diversity.

2. Species-Area Relationships

- German naturalist and geographer **Alexander von Humboldt** observed that within a region, species richness increased with the increasing available area, but only upto a limit.

- The relation between species richness and area, for a wide variety of taxa (angiosperm plants, birds, bats, freshwater fishes) turns out to be a rectangular hyperbola.
- On a logarithmic scale, the relationship is a straight line described by the equation;

$$\log S = \log C + Z \log A$$

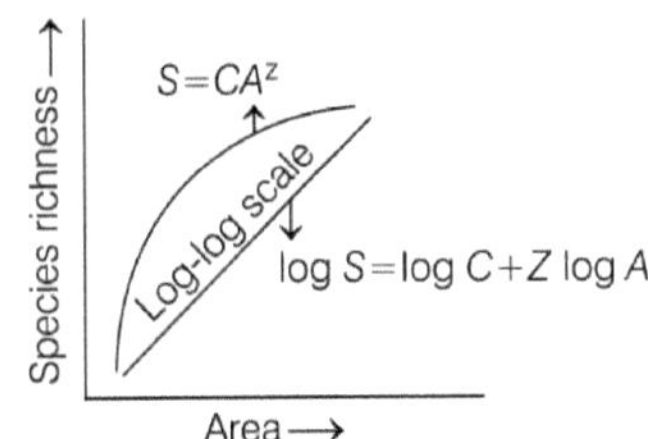

- Where, S = Species richness, A = Area, Z = Slope of the line (regression coefficient) and C = y-intercept.
- Ecologists have discovered that the value of Z lies in the range of 0.1 to 0.2, when analysis is done in small areas regardless of the taxonomic group or area. But the species-area relationships among very large areas (continents), will give a much steeper slope and Z values in the range of 0.6 to 1.2, e.g. for frugivorous birds and mammals in the tropical forests, the slope is found to be 1.15. Thus, it can be said that the larger the area, the steeper is the slope.

Importance of Species Diversity to the Ecosystem

- Communities with more species diversity, generally, tend to be more stable than those with less species. This is because such communities are more resistant or resilient to occasional disturbances (natural or man-made) and invasions by alien species.
- These communities do not show much variation in productivity from year to year.
- **David Tilman** discovered that increased diversity contributed to higher productivity and also proved that species richness is the key to the well-being of any ecosystem.
  It is also essential for the survival of man on this planet earth.
- **Ecosystem health** Ecologist **Paul Ehrlich** gave an analogy, **Rivet Popper hypothesis**, to understand the effect of loss of species biodiversity.
  - This hypothesis explain that ecosystem is an airplane and the species are the rivets joining all the parts together.
  - If every passenger travelling in the airplane starts taking rivets home (causing a species to become extinct), initially it may not affect flight safety, but as more and more rivets are removed, over a period of

time the plane becomes weak and poses threat to flight safety. However, if rivets on wings (keystone) species are removed, it would pose a more serious threat to flight safety.

Loss of Biodiversity

- Biological wealth of earth is declining rapidly and human activities are the major reasons for it, e.g. the colonisation of tropical Pacific Islands by humans has led to the extinction of more than 2,000 native bird species.
- **The International Union for Conservation of Nature and natural resources** (IUCN) was founded in 1948. Its headquarter is at Switzerland. It works in the field of nature conservation and sustainable use of natural resources.
- IUCN red list of threatened species is an inventory of global conservation status of biological species, which is compiled in **Red Data Book**. It was initiated in 1963.
- **IUCN Red List** (2004) enlists the extinction of 784 species (including 338 vertebrates, 359 invertebrates and 87 plants) in the last 500 years. The red list of 2012 contains 132 plant and animal species of India. Some examples of recent extinction are
  (i) Dodo (Mauritius), Quagga (Africa), Thylacine (Australia), Steller's sea cow (Russia) and three subspecies of tiger (Bali, Javan and Caspian).
  (ii) About 27 species have disappeared in the last 20 years in the world, with more than 15,500 species are endangered. Presently 12% of all bird species, 23% of all mammal species, 32% of all amphibian species and 31% of all gymnosperms are facing extinction threat with amphibians which are more vulnerable to extinction.
  (iii) **Endangered species** are those species which are facing a high risk of extinction in the near future due to decrease in its habitat, excessive predation or poaching. Some of the endangered species are Asiatic lion, Bengal tiger, Lion-tailed Macaque, Nilgiri Langur, Gangas river dolphin, etc.

Extinction in Biodiversity

- Study of fossil record reveals that large scale loss of species had also occurred earlier, even before humans appeared on the scene. There have been five episodes of **mass extinctions** during the long period of >3 billion years due to natural calamities, e.g. extinction of dinosaurs.
- Currently, the earth is heading towards the sixth extinction, which is different from the previous episodes in the rates. The **current species extinction rates** are estimated to be 100-1,000 times faster than in the prehuman times and human activities are responsible for the faster rates. If the present rate of species extinction goes on, 50% of the species might be wiped out within next 100 years.

- In general, loss of biodiversity may lead to
  - (i) Decline in plant production.
  - (ii) Lower resistance and resilience to environment perturbations such as drought.
  - (iii) Increased variability in ecosystem processes such as plant productivity, water use, pest and disease cycles, etc.

Causes of Biodiversity Loss

Habitat loss and fragmentation, overexploitation, alien-species invasion, coextinction are the four (Evil Quartet) major causes of loss of biodiversity.

1. **Habitat loss and fragmentation** occurs due to population explosion that has destroyed forest land, which leads to the **loss of habitat** of several species, e.g. once covering more than 14 % of the earth's land surface, the Amazonian rainforests ('lungs of the planet') now cover less than 6 % as they are being cut and cleared for cultivation of soybeans or conversion into grasslands for raising beef cattle. This has caused loss of habitat for lots of species and has put tremendous pressure on the ecosystem.

2. **Overexploitation** Uncontrolled or overuse of resources by humans leads to overexploitation of natural resources.
   Many species extinctions in the last 500 years such as of Steller's sea cow, passenger pigeon, etc., due to the overexploitation by humans.
   Currently, many marine fish populations are being over harvested, endangering the continued existence of some commercially important species.

3. **Alien-species invasions** When alien-species are introduced unintentionally or deliberately in a habitat, some of them turn invasive and can cause decline or extinction of indigenous species, e.g. the Nile perch introduced into lake Victoria (East Africa) cause extinction of cichlid fishes, invasive weed species like carrot grass (*Parthenium*), *Lantana* and water hyacinth (*Eichhornia*) also can cause environment damage and threaten the existence of native species. African catfish called, *Clarias gariepinus* is posing a threat to the indigenous catfish in our rivers.

4. **Coextinctions** When a species becomes extinct, the plant and animal species associated with it, in an obligatory way, also become extinct, e.g. when a host fish species becomes extinct, its parasites also vanish.

Biodiversity Conservation

Conservation of biodiversity is protection, upliftment and scientific management of biodiversity so as to maintain it at the optimum level and derive sustainable benefits for the present as well as future generations.

Reasons for Conserving Biodiversity

There are many reasons for conservation of biodiversity, but all reasons are equally important. They can be grouped into three categories which are as follows

1. Narrowly Utilitarian Argument

These are based on obvious reasons. Humans derive countless direct economic benefits from the nature like food (cereals, pulses and fruits), firewood, fibre, construction material, industrial products (tannins, lubricants, dyes, resins and perfumes) and products of medicinal importance.

More than 25% of the drugs currently sold in the market worldwide are derived from plants and 25,000 plant species are used in traditional medicines.

Moreover, biodiversity rich countries expect to reap more benefits from the increasing resources put into **bioprospecting**, i.e. exploration of molecular, genetic and species-level diversity for obtaining products of economic importance.

2. Broadly Utilitarian Argument

According to this argument, biodiversity plays a major role in ecosystem services that nature provides.
Some of these are

- (i) Production of oxygen, e.g. Amazon forests produce 20% of the total oxygen in the earth's atmosphere *via* photosynthesis.
- (ii) Pollination of flowers without which fruits and seeds are not produced, is provided by pollinator layer, i.e. bees, bumble bees, birds and bats.
- (iii) Control of floods and soil erosion.
- (iv) Intangible benefits of nature like aesthetic pleasures of watching spring flower in full bloom, walking through thick forest, listening to bulbul's song, etc.

3. Ethical Argument

Every species has an intrinsic value, even if it is not of any economic value to us. It is our moral duty to care for their well-being and pass on our biological legacy in good order to future generations. Moreover, many plants like tulsi and peepal have religious importance as well.

Approaches to Conserve Biodiversity

- Biodiversity can be conserved by protecting its whole ecosystem. There are two basic approaches for conservation of biodiversity.

Biodiversity Conservation

- In situ conservation
  - Biodiversity hotspots
  - Protected areas
    - National parks
    - Ramsar sites
    - Biosphere reserves
    - Wildlife sanctuaries
    - Sacred groves
- Ex situ conservation
  - Protection of gametes
    - Cryo-preservation
    - Seed banks
    - Tissue culture
      - Botanical gardens
      - Zoological parks
      - Wildlife safari park
  - Protection of threatened species

I. *In Situ* (On-site) Conservation

It is the conservation and protection of the whole ecosystem and its biodiversity at all levels in order to protect the threatened species. However, it is not economically feasible to conserve all the biological wealth at all the existing ecosystems. Methods used in *in situ* conservation are

1. Biodiversity Hotspots

These are regions with very high levels of species richness, high degree of **endemism** (species confined to a region and not found anywhere else) and accelerated habitat loss. Initially, 25 biodiversity hotspots were identified. Now, there are **34 hotspots** all over the world.

These hotspots are in India, i.e. Western Ghats and Sri Lanka, Indo-Burma and Eastern Himalaya. If all the biodiversity hotspots are put together, they cover less than 2% of the earth's land area, but harbour extremely high diversity. Ongoing mass extinctions could be reduced by 30% through strict protection of these hotspots.

2. Protected Areas

These are especially dedicated areas for protection and maintenance of ecologically unique and biodiversity rich regions. Protected areas are classified as

(i) **National parks** These are government maintained areas (90 in India), reserved for the betterment of wildlife and where activities such as cultivation, grazing, forestry and habitat manipulation are not allowed. The first National park was established in India in 1936, i.e. Hailey's National Park.

(ii) **Wildlife sanctuaries** They are tracts of land with or without lake where wild animals/fauna can take refuge without being hunted. There number is 448 in India. Other activities like collection of forest products, harvesting of timber, private ownership of land, tilling of land, etc., are allowed here.

(iii) **Biosphere reserves** These are large tracts of protected land with multiple use preserving the genetic diversity of ecosystem by protecting wildlife, traditional lifestyles of tribals and varied plants and animal genetic resources. They have been setup under **MAB** (Man and Biosphere) programme of **UNESCO**. There are **14** biosphere reserves in India. A biosphere reserve consists of three zones as shown below

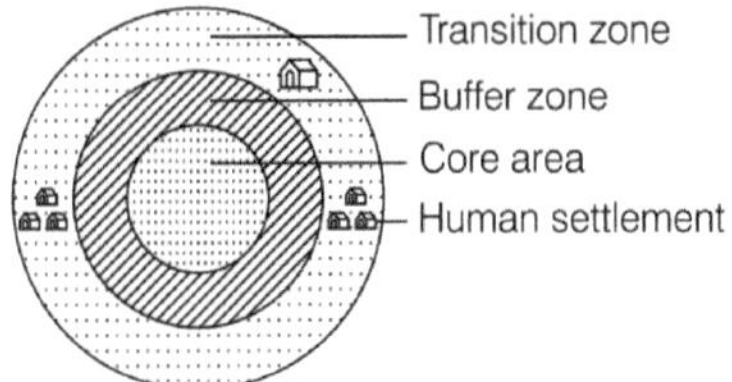

Zonation in terrestrial biosphere

MAB Programme

Man and Biosphere Programme is an international biological programme of UNESCO started in 1971 but introduced in India in 1986. MAB has studied human environment, impact of human interference and pollution on biotic and abiotic environments and conservation strategies for the present as well as future.

(iv) **Sacred groves** These are small groups of forests with special religious importance in a particular culture and are also of mythological importance.

- These are undisturbed forests without any human interventions and include a number of rare, endangered and endemic species.
- Sacred groves are found in Khasi and Jaintia Hills in Meghalaya, Aravalli Hills of Rajasthan, Western Ghat regions of Karnataka and Maharashtra and the Sarguja, Chanda and Bastar areas of Madhya Pradesh.
- These are protected by native people as a part of cultural traditions. In Meghalaya, the sacred groves are the last refuges for a large number of rare and threatened plants.

(v) **Ramsar sites** These are the wetlands designated as internationally important under the convention on wetlands held at Ramsar, Iran in 1971 for the conservation and wise use of wetlands. Thus, known as **Ramsar convention** The wise use of wetlands is defined as 'the maintenance of their ecological character achieved through the implementation of ecosystem approaches, within the context of sustainable development'.

It means wise use of wetlands and their resources, for the benefit of humankind. There are 26 Ramsar sites in India. Some of these are Ashtamudi wetland (Kerala), Sambhar lake (Rajasthan), Chilka lake (Odisha), Renuka wetland (Himachal Pradesh), etc.

II. *Ex Situ* (Off-site) **Conservation**

This approach involves placing the threatened animals and plants in special care units for their protection.
Ex situ conservation includes off-site collections and gene banks.

Protection of Threatened Species

It is done by live collections of wild and domesticated species in Botanical Gardens, Zoological Parks, Wildlife Safari Parks, etc. India has 355 Parks, where animals which have become extinct in the wild are continued to be maintained and has 35 Botanical Gardens where plant species are protected.

Protection of Gametes

The protection and maintenance of gametes is done by adopting following methods

1. **Seed banks** The storage of different genetic strains of commercially important plants in the form of seeds is one of the most widespread and valuable *ex situ* approaches of the conservation strategy.

2. **Tissue culture** Plant tissue culture is widely used to produce clones of a plant in a method known as **micropropagation**. This method is useful in maintaining a large number of genotypes in small area, rapid multiplication of even endangered species and for hybrid rescue, e.g. banana and potato.

3. **Cryopreservation** It is a method of *in vitro* conservation in liquid N_2 at temperature of $-196°C$ $(-130°F)$ in a controlled rate freezer for vegetatively propagated crops and storing other biological materials.

International Initiatives

- Biodiversity conservation is a collective responsibility of all the nations. Convention on Biological Diversity **(The Earth Summit)** held in Rio de Janeiro in 1992 called upon all the nations to take initiative in biodiversity conservation.

- In a follow up World Summit on Sustainable Development was held in 2002 in Johannesburg, South Africa.

- In this, 190 countries made commitments to significantly reduce the current rate of biodiversity loss at global, regional and local levels by 2010.

- In 2012, the United Nations Conference on Sustainable Development was again held at Rio and is called **Rio + 20** or **Rio Earth Summit 2012**.

Chapter Practice

Objective Questions

• Multiple Choice Questions

1. An ecologist uses the term biodiversity for the variety of species of
(a) All living plants
(b) All living animals
(c) Both (a) and (b)
(d) (a), (b) and microbes also living in their natural habitats

Ans. (*d*) Biodiversity can be defined as the variety of species of all living plants and animals and microbes also living in their natural habitats and the ecological complexes of which they are a part.

2. The active chemical drug reserpine is obtained form
(a) *Datura*
(b) *Rauwolfia*
(c) *Atropa*
(d) *Papaver*

Ans. (*b*) *Rauwolfia vomitoria* is the source of active chemical drug reserpine, which is prescribed in hypertension and acts as tranquilliser.

3. Which of the following refers to species diversity?
(a) Diversity in the amphibians between Western and Eastern ghats
(b) Genetic variation in the concentration and potency of chemical reserpine
(c) 1000 varieties of mangoes
(d) Presence of deserts, rainforests, coral reefs

Ans. (*a*) The Western ghats have a greater number of amphibians as compared to Eastern ghats, as the climatic conditions and other ecological factor favour species richness in Western ghats.

4. Which one of the following has the highest number of species in nature?
(a) Angiosperms
(b) Fungi
(c) Insects
(d) Birds

Ans. (*c*) Insects have the highest number of species in nature, making up more than 70% of the total. That means out of every 10 animals on this planet, 7 are insects.

5.
I. Higher latitude $\xrightarrow{\text{Biodiversity increases}}$ Lower latitude
(Poles) (Equator)

II. Higher latitude $\xrightarrow{\text{Biodiversity decreases}}$ Lower latitude
(Poles) (Equator)

III. Higher altitude $\xrightarrow{\text{Biodiversity increases}}$ Lower altitude
(Mountain top) (Sea level)

IV. Higher altitude $\xrightarrow{\text{Biodiversity decreases}}$ Lower altitude
(Mountain top) (Sea level)

Which of the matches above is/are correct?
(a) I and III
(b) I and II
(c) II and III
(d) III and IV

Ans. (*a*) Option (a) shows the correct match.

6. Which of the following countries has the highest biodiversity?
(a) Brazil
(b) South Africa
(c) Russia
(d) India

Ans. (*a*) Countries in tropical latitude like Brazil, climate remains relatively undisturbed, constant and predictable giving tune for diversification which favours rich biodiversity.

7. On a logarithmic scale, the species-area relationship is a straight line described by the equation

(a) $\log\ S = \dfrac{\log C}{\log A}$

(b) $Z \log A = \dfrac{\log C}{\log S}$

(c) $\log S = \log C + Z \log A$

(d) $\log S = \log C - Z \log A$

Ans. (*c*) On a logarithmic scale, the species-area relationship is a straight line described by the equation
$$\log S = \log C + Z \log A$$

8. Read the following statements regarding a stable community.

I. Must be resistant to occasional disturbances.

II. Should show much variation in productivity from year to year.

III. Must be resistant to invasions by alien species.

Choose the correct option.

(a) I and II (b) I, II and III

(c) Only I (d) I and III

Ans. (**d**) Statements I and III are correct, whereas statement II is incorrect regarding a stable community.

9. Rivet popper hypothesis assumes the ...A... to be an airplane and the ...B... to be the rivets joining all parts together. Here, A and B refer to

(a) A–species, B–ecosystem

(b) A–ecosystem, B–species

(c) A–species, B–community

(d) A–community, B–species

Ans. (**b**)

10. Match the animals given in Column I with their locations in Column II.

Column I		Column II	
A.	Dodo	1.	Africa
B.	Quagga	2.	Russia
C.	Thylacine	3.	Mauritius
D.	Stellar's sea cow	4.	Australia

Codes

	A	B	C	D			A	B	C	D
(a)	1	3	2	4		(b)	4	3	1	2
(c)	3	1	2	4		(d)	3	1	4	2

Ans. (**d**) A–3, B–1, C–4, D–2

11. The term 'The Evil Quartet' is related with

(a) four major causes of forest loss

(b) four major causes of population explosion

(c) four major causes of air pollution

(d) four major causes of biodiversity losses

Ans. (**d**)

12. In which of the following, both pairs have correct combination?

(a) *In situ* conservation : Seed bank
  Ex situ conservation : National park

(b) *In situ* conservation : Tissue culture
  Ex situ conservation : Sacred groves

(c) *In situ* conservation : National park
  Ex situ conservation : Botanical garden

(d) *In situ* conservation : Cryopreservation
  Ex situ conservation : Wildlife sanctuary

Ans. (**c**) The correct combination is option (c).

13. Which one of the following is not a feature of biodiversity hotspots?

(a) Large number of species

(b) Abundance of endemic species

(c) Mostly located in the tropics

(d) Mostly located in the polar regions

Ans. (**d**) Biodiversity hotspots are characterised by large number of flora and fauna, abundance of endemic species and also large number of alien or exotic species. They are mostly found in tropical and temperate regions. There are no biodiversity hotspots in polar regions. Thus, option (d) is not a feature of biodiversity hotspots.

14. Biosphere reserves differ from the national parks and wildife sanctuaries because in the former

(a) human beings are not allowed to enter

(b) people are an integral part of the ecosystem

(c) plants are paid greater attention than the animals

(d) living organisms are brought from all over the world and preseved for posterity

Ans. (**b**) Biosphere reserve differ from the national parks and wildife sanctuaries in that people are an integral part. But it is not the case in national parks and wildife sanctuaries, where flora and fauna are separately conserved.

15. Sacred groves are especially useful in

(a) preventing soil erosion

(b) year-round flow of water in rivers

(c) generating environmental awareness

(d) conserving rare and threatened species

Ans. (**d**)

• Assertion-Reasoning MCQs

Direction (Q. Nos. 1-5) *Each of these questions contains two statements, Assertion (A) and Reason (R). Each of these questions also has four alternative choices, any one of which is the correct answer. You have to select one of the codes (a), (b), (c) and (d) given below.*

(a) Both A and R are true and R is the correct explanation of A

(b) Both A and R are true, but R is not the correct explanation of A

(c) A is true, but R is false

(d) A is false, but R is true

1. Assertion (A) The great Indian bustard is a critically endangered bird found in India.

Reason (R) It is vulnerable to extinction in the future.

Ans. (**c**) A is true, but R is false because

The species which are facing, extremely high risk of extinction in the future are referred to as critically endangered species.

The great Indian bustard is a well-known bird which is categorised into critically endangered species. Threatened species are vulnerable to extinction in the future not, critically endangered species.

2. Assertion (A) If the species-area relationships are analysed among very large areas like the entire continents, the value of Z, i.e. slope of line lies in the range of 0.1 to 0.2.

Reason (R) Larger is the explored area more is the steepness of slope of line.

Ans. (*d*) A is false, but R is true. A can be corrected as

If the species-area relationship is for very large areas like the entire continent the slope of the line is much steeper with value of Z in the range of 0.6-1.2. The value of Z, i.e. slope of line (regression coefficient) of species-area relationship is similar and lies in the range of 0.1-0.2 when analysis is done among small areas.

3. Assertion (A) The presently occurring species extinction is different from the earlier mass extinction.

Reason (R) Present species extinction is due to natural causes, whereas the earlier extinction was due to the man-made causes.

Ans. (*c*) A is true, but R is false. R can be corrected as

The currently occurring species extinction is different from the earlier mass extinction as the present species extinction is due to man-made causes, whereas the earlier extinction was due to the natural causes.

4. Assertion (A) In case, a species becomes extinct, the plant and animal species associated within an obligatory way also become extinct.

Reason (R) When a host fish species becomes extinct, its unique assemblage of parasites also become extinct.

Ans. (*a*) Both A and R are true and R is the correct explanation of A.

5. Assertion (A) Zoological parks serve the purpose to protect the threatened species and provide special care.

Reason (R) Zoological parks are example of *in situ* conservation.

Ans. (*c*) A is true, but R is false because

Zoological parks serve the purpose to protect the threatened species and provide special care. Zoological parks are example of *ex situ* conservation.

• Case Based MCQ

1. Direction *Read the following passage and answer the questions that follows.*

When we conserve and protect the whole ecosystem, its biodiversity at all levels is protected, we save the entire forest to save the tiger. This approach is called *in situ* (on-site) conservation.

It includes biosphere reserves, national parks, wildlife sanctuaries and sacred groves. However, when these are situations where an animal or plant is endangered or threatened (organisms facing a very high risk of extinction in the wild in the near future) and needs urgent measures to save it from extinctions, *ex situ* (off-site) conservation is the desirable approach. It includes zoological parks, botanical gardens, gene banks, etc.

(i) The numbers of national parks, biosphere reserves and wildlife sanctuaries in India, respectively are
(a) 90, 14, 448 (b) 158, 62, 10
(c) 58, 412, 10 (d) 96, 412, 10

Ans. (*a*) In India, the numbers of national parks are 90, biosphere reserves are 14 and wildlife sanctuaries are 448.

(ii) In your opinion, which is the most effective way to conserve genetic diversity of the plant of an area?
(a) By tissue culture method
(b) By creating biosphere reserve
(c) By creating botanical garden
(d) By developing seed bank

Ans. (*b*) Biosphere reserve comes under *in situ* conservation method. Hence, it is the most effective way, for preserving genetic diversity of the plants by protecting wild population, traditional and domesticated plant genetic resources.

(iii) Sacred groves in India are related with
(a) aesthetic pleasure
(b) the place where threatened species are protected
(c) the place where only artificial plant breeding is allowed
(d) forest patches around the places of worship

Ans. (*d*) Sacred groves are forest patches around the places of worship, which are held in high esteem by tribal communities. These are found in several parts of India, e.g. Karnataka, Maharashtra, etc.

(iv) Cryopreservation of gametes of threatened species in viable and fertile condition can be referred to as
(a) *in situ* conservation of biodiversity
(b) advanced *ex situ* conservation of biodiversity
(c) *in situ* conservation by sacred groves
(d) *in situ* cryopreservation of biodiversity

Ans. (*b*) Cryopreservations of gametes of threatened species in viable and fertile condition is done by preservation at −196°C in liquid nitrogen and it is an advanced method for *ex situ* conservation of biodiversity for indefinite period of time. *In situ* conservation occurs at ecosystem level of threatened or endangered species.

(v) Refer to the given figure representing different zones of a biosphere reserve.

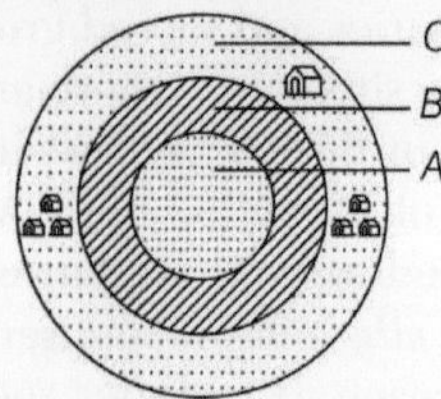

Choose the correct answer as per the statements given below.

I. Limited human activity is allowed such as for research and education.

II. An active cooperation occurs between reserve management and local people for activities like cropping, settlements, etc.

III. No human activity is allowed.

Codes

	I	II	III			I	II	III
(a)	A	B	C	(b)		B	C	A
(c)	C	A	B	(d)		C	B	A

Ans. (*b*) A–Core area, B–Buffer zone, C–Transition zone

PART 2
Subjective Questions

• Short Answer (SA) Type Questions

1. Explain the levels of biodiversity at genetic, specific and ecological levels with the help of one example each. **(Delhi 2016)**

Ans. (i) **Genetic diversity** A single species shows diversity at the genetic level over its distributional range. For example, the genetic variation showed by the plant *Rauwolfia vomitoria* growing in the different Himalayan ranges might be in terms of the potency and concentration of reserpine.

(ii) **Species diversity** It is the diversity at the species level or the measure of the variety of species and their relative abundance with the region. For example, the Western Ghats have a greater amphibian species diversity than the Eastern Ghats.

(iii) **Ecological diversity** It refers to the diversity at ecosystem level. It makes communities more productive and stable, e.g. India has a greater ecosystem diversity (in terms of variety of habitats in deserts, rainforests, mangroves, coral reefs, wetlands, estuaries and alpine meadows) than a Scandinavian country like Norway.

2. Mention the kind of biodiversity represented by more than a 1000 varieties of mangoes in India. How is it possible? **(Delhi 2016)**

Ans. The different varieties of mangoes in India represent genetic diversity. It occurs because India lies within tropical latitudes where the environment is constant and predictable. Also more amount of solar energy is available which leads to higher productivity.

3. How do scientists extrapolate the total number of species on earth? **(NCERT Exemplar)**

Ans. There are two methods to estimate and extrapolate the number of species on the earth.

(i) The primary method used by the scientists to extrapolate the number of species on earth is the estimation rate of discovery of new species.

(ii) Total number of species can also be extrapolated by the statistical comparison of the tropical and temperate species richness of exhaustively studied groups of insects.

The ratio is then extrapolated with existing species of plants and animals to predict the gross estimate of the number of species on the earth.

4. Species diversity decreases as we move away from the equator towards the poles. What could be the possible reasons? **(NCERT Exemplar)**

Ans. Species diversity decreases as we move toward the poles, because

(i) Temperature decreases and conditions become rough and harsh.

(ii) Both the amount and intensity of solar radiation decrease.

(iii) Vegetation decreases.

(iv) Less resources available to support species.

Speciation is generally a function of time and environmental stability, so if conditions are too harsh, it is difficult for the species to survive and adapt. This results in decrease in biodiversity towards the poles.

5. Write the importance of species diversity to the ecosystem. Support your answer with the finding of Tilman. **(Delhi 2016)**

Ans. Importance of species diversity for the ecosystem are
  (i) Ecologists for many years, believe that communities with species are more stable than those with less species.
  (ii) A stable biological community does not show too much variation in production from year-to-year. It must be resistant or resilient to occasional disturbance and must also be resistant to invasions by alien species.
  (iii) David Tilman's long term ecosystem experiments using outdoor plots provided answers to stability of a biological community and species richness in that community. Tilman found that plots with more species showed less year-to-year variation in total biomass. He also showed in his experiments that increased diversity contributed to higher productivity.

6. (i) 'India has greater ecosystem diversity than Norway.' Do you agree with the statement? Give reasons in support of your answer.
  (ii) Write the difference between genetic biodiversity and species biodiversity that exists at all the levels of biological organisation. **(All India 2018)**

Ans. (i) India is one of the twelve megadiversity regions of the world with 8.1% of genetic resources of the world. Since, India is placed in the tropical part of the world it exhibits more species diversity than the regions of temperate zones. India with much of its land area in the tropical latitudes, has more than 1200 species of birds. Greenland, Norway is away from tropics, so it exhibits less biodiversity.
  (ii) Differences between genetic and species diversity are as follows

Genetic diversity	Species diversity
It is related to the number of genes and their alleles found in organisms.	It is related to the number and distribution of species found in an area.
It is a trait of a species.	It is a trait of community.
It influences adaptability and distribution of species in diverse habitats.	It influences biotic interactions and stability of the community.

7. Give three reasons as to why prokaryotes are not given any figures for their diversity.

Ans. Three reasons are as follows
  (i) The conventional taxonomic methods are not sufficient for identifying these microbial species.
  (ii) Most of the species cannot be cultured under laboratory conditions.
  (iii) If molecular and biochemical criteria are adopted for delineating microbial species, this would put their diversity into millions.

8. Is it possible that productivity and diversity of a natural community remain constant over a time period of, say one hundred years?

Ans. No, it is not possible that productivity and diversity of a natural community remain constant over a certain time period.
  This is because
  (i) The natural habitat is never maintained in real.
  (ii) Abundant resources are never available, they are always in short supply or just enough.
  (iii) Environmental conditions for survival and reproduction are continuously changing.

9. Explain giving three reasons why tropics show, greatest level of species diversity. **(All India 2014)**

Or Give three hypothesis for explaining why tropics show greatest level of species richness. **(NCERT)**

Ans. Three reasons are as follows
  (i) Temperate regions were subjected to frequent glaciation in the past which had killed most of the species, but the tropics have remained undisturbed and hence, had evolved more species diversity.
  (ii) Tropical environments are less seasonal, relatively more constant and predictable than temperate regions. Such constant environments have promoted niche specialisation and thus, lead to greater species diversity.
  (iii) Resource availability is higher and rate of extinction is low in tropics.

10. Is it true that there is more solar energy available in the tropics? Explain briefly. **(NCERT Exemplar)**

Ans. Yes, there is more solar energy available in the tropics because
  (i) As one moves from equator to the polar regions, the length of the day decreases and the length of the night increases.
  (ii) In the tropical regions, the length of the day is almost equal to the length of the night, hence it has more solar energy available.

11. What is the significance of the slope of regression in a species-area relationship? **(NCERT)**

Ans. Slope of regression represents the changes in the species richness with the area. Species richness decreases with the decrease in area. The value of 'Z' (regression coefficient) lies between 0.1-0.2, regardless of the taxonomic groups in the region. For very large areas like continents, the slope of the line becomes much steep with the Z values in the range of 0.6-1.

12. Explain rivet popper hypothesis. Name the ecologist who proposed it.

Ans. The hypothesis was proposed by **Paul Ehrlich**. This hypothesis explains that ecosystem is an airplane and the species are the rivets joining all parts together.

If every passenger travelling in it, starts popping a rivet to take home (causing a species to become extinct), it may not affect the flight safety (proper functioning of ecosystem) initially, but as more and more rivets are removed, the plane becomes dangerously weak after some time.

Loss of rivets on the wings (key species that drive major ecosystem function) is obviously a more serious threat to flight safety than loss of a few rivets on the seats or windows inside the plane.

13. What characteristics make a community stable? **(NCERT Exemplar)**

Or List the features that make a stable biological community.

Ans. The characteristics/features that make a community stable are

(i) Less variation in productivity from year to year.

(ii) Resistance or resilience to occasional disturbances (natural or man-made).

(iii) Resistance to invasions by alien species.

14. Since the origin of life on earth, there were five episodes of mass extinction of species.

(i) How is the 'Sixth Extinction', presently in progress, different from the previous episodes?

(ii) Who is mainly responsible for the 'sixth extinction'?

(iii) List any four points that can help to overcome this disaster. **(All India 2014)**

Ans. (i) The current species extinction rates are estimated to be 100-1000 times faster than in pre-human times.

(ii) Human activities

(iii) To prevent sixth extinction to take place we would

(a) Preventing habitat loss and fragmentation

(b) Checking overexploitation

(c) Preventing alien-species invasion

(d) Preventing coextinction

(e) Conservation and preservation of species

15. What are the major causes of species losses in a geographical region? **(NCERT; Delhi 2008C)**

Or List four causes of biodiversity loss. **(Delhi 2014C)**

Ans. The major causes of species losses in a geographical region are

(i) Habitat loss and fragmentation.

(ii) Overexploitation of natural resources.

(iii) Alien-species invasions that can cause decline or extinction of indigenous species.

(iv) Coextinctions, i.e. when a species become extinct, the plant and animal species associated with it in an obligatory way, also become extinct.

16. Justify with the help of an example where a deliberate attempt by humans leads to the extinction of a particular species. **(Delhi 2011, 2008)**

Ans. When Nile perch, a large predator fish was introduced in Lake Victoria, it started feeding on native fish, i.e. cichlid fish. As a result, cichlid fish become extinct and due to scarcity of food predator, Nile perch, died too.

17. Explain how biodiversity is important for human.

Or Humans benefit from diversity of life. Give two examples. **(NCERT Exemplar)**

Ans. Humans derive numerous economic benefits directly from diversity of organisms.

(i) Food products (cereals, pulses and fruits), firewood and fibre (cotton, jute from plants and silk, wool from animals).

(ii) Construction material (timber for making furniture, houses and sports goods), industrial products (tannis, lubricant, dyes, resins and perfumes) and products of medicinal importance (about 25,000 plants are used in traditional medicine).

There are huge indirect benefits that humans derive from the diversity of life. These are, pure oxygen, natural pollinators, flood and soil erosion control, nutrient replenishment, waste recycling by microbes and aesthetic pleasure and mental peace.

18. Why should biodiversity be conserved? Explain giving three reasons. **(All India 2016C)**

Ans. Biodiversity should be conserved for the following reasons

(i) The broadly utilitarian argument says that biodiversity plays a major role in many ecosystem services that nature provides.

(ii) The narrow utilitarian argument says that humans derive countless direct economic benefits from nature and products of medicinal importance.

(iii) The ethical argument for conserving biodiversity relates to what we owe to millions of plant, animal and microbe species with whom we share this planet.

19. Express your opinion on removal of tribal people out of forest due to developmental activities in the forest.

Ans. Recently, it has been a trend of removing the tribal people out of the forest in the name of conservation measures. To ensure conservation of habitat and prevention of any sort of danger to biodiversity, government tends to seclude even tribal people from their home. It is an ethical issue. Tribal people are equally a part of the forest. They have lived there for years and have evolved along with the forest.

They share a mutual relationship with the biodiversity present there.

In their unique ways, they also conserve and protect the diversity. Therefore, we must make policies, which include tribals in the conservation measures and utilise their indigenous knowledge as a conservation tool.

20. Extinction of a species is classified into three types, i.e. natural extinction, mass extinction and anthropogenic extinction. Classify the following examples on this basis.

 (i) Animals lost due to inbreeding depression

 (ii) Disappearance of dinosaurs

 (iii) Extinction of passenger pigeon

 (iv) Extinction of marine invertebrates

 (v) Extinction of tiger

Ans. (i) Natural extinction
 (ii) Mass extinction
 (iii) Anthropogenic extinction
 (iv) Natural extinction
 (v) Anthropogenic extinction

21. What is an endangered species? Give an example of an endangered plant and animal species each?

Ans. An endangered species is a population of organisms, which is facing a high risk of becoming extinct because of following reasons

 (i) Its number being very low.

 (ii) It is threatened by changing environment.

 (iii) It is facing predator threat.

Endangered plant species-Venus fly trap

Endangered animal species-Siberian tiger

22. Suggest two practices giving one example of each, that help to protect rare or threatened species.

(All India 2017)

Ans. Practices that help to protect rare, threatened species are as follows

 (i) *In situ* (on-site) conservation which involves protection of species in their natural habitat. It involves biosphere reserves, national parks, wildlife sanctuaries, sacred groves, etc.

 (ii) *Ex situ* (off-site) conservation which involves placing of threatened animals and plants in special care units for their protection. Zoological parks, botanical gardens and wildlife safari parks serve this purpose.

23. '*In situ* conservation can help endangered / threatened species'. Justify the statement.

(Delhi 2017)

Ans. *In situ* conservation involves the protection of species in their natural habitats. It helps in the conservation of threatened/endangered species *via* following means

 (i) **Biodiversity hotspots** are regions with high levels of species richness and high degree of endemism (i.e.

species confined to that region are not found anywhere else). These hotspots can reduce the ongoing mass extinctions by almost 30%.

 (ii) **Protected areas** are ecologically unique and biodiversity rich regions. These are legally protected as biosphere reserves, national parks and sanctuaries. Hence, can help in conservation of endangered species.

 (iii) **Sacred groves** are forest areas set aside, all the trees and wildlife within it are venerated and given total protection. These are religious and cultural places, which are protected for conservation of endangered species.

24. (i) Explain the concept of endemism.
 (ii) Name four regions in and around our country that are considered hotspots. **(Delhi 2020)**

Ans. (i) Endemism means when a species of plant or animal is confined to a particular region and are not found anywhere else, e.g. biodiversity hotspots and species are called endemic species.

 (ii) India hosts 4 biodiversity hotspots, the Himalayas, the Western ghats, the Indo-Burma region and the sundaland (includes Nicobar group of Islands).

25. Mention the three zones of a biosphere reserve.

Ans. A biosphere reserve consists of three zones namely transition zone, core zone and buffer zone. They have been setup under MAB programme of UNESCO.

26. What are sacred groves? Where are they found in India? Explain their importance in conservation.

(NCERT)

Ans. Sacred groves are small groups of trees with special religious importance in a particular culture.

They are found in Khasi and Jaintia Hills in Meghalaya, Aravalli Hills of Rajasthan, Western ghat regions of Karnataka and Maharashtra and the Sarguja, Chanda and Bastar areas of Madhya Pradesh.

Sacred groves help in the protection of many rare, threatened and endemic species of plants and animals found in area. The process of deforestation is strictly prohibited in these regions.

27. Write in brief about Ramsar convention.

Ans. These are the wetlands designated as internationally important under the convention on wetlands held at Ramsar, Iran in 1971 for the conservation and wise use of wetlands. Thus, known as Ramsar convention. The wise use of wetlands is defined as 'the maintenance of their ecological character achieved through the implementation of ecosystem approaches, within the context of sustainable development'. It means wise use of wetlands and their resources, for the benefit of humankind. There are 26 Ramsar sites in India. Some of these are Ashtamudi wetland (Kerala), Sambhar lake (Rajasthan), Chilka lake (Odisha), Renuka wetland (Himachal Pradesh), etc.

28. List six advantages of 'ex situ' approach to conservation of biodiversity. **(Delhi 2019)**

Ans. Six advantages of *ex situ* approach to conservation of biodiversity are as follows

(i) To conserve those animals that have become extinct in wild, but can be maintained in zoological parks.

(ii) To preserve gametes of threatened species in viable condition through cryopreservation.

(iii) To propagate threatened plants *via* tissue culture.

(iv) To grow plants with recalcitrant seeds in orchards where all possible varieties are maintained.

(v) To conserve seed of commercially important plants in seed banks.

(vi) To save endangered or threatened plant that needs urgent measure to save it from extinction in botanical gardens.

29. Explain any three ways of *ex situ* other than zoological parks, botanical gardens and wildlife safaries, by which threatened species of plants and animals are being conserved. **(All India 2020)**

Ans. Three ways to conserve plants and animals are as follows

(i) **Seed banks** The storage of different genetic strains of commercially important plants in the form of seeds is one of the most widespread and valuable *ex situ* approaches of the conservation strategy.

(ii) **Tissue culture** Plant tissue culture is widely used to produce clones of a plant in a method known as **micropropagation**. This method is useful in maintaining a large number of genotypes in small area, rapid multiplication of even endangered species and for hybrid rescue, e.g. banana and potato.

(iii) **Cryopreservation** It is a method of *in vitro* conservation in liquid N_2 at temperature of $-196°C$ $(-130°F)$ in a controlled rate freezer for vegetatively propagated crops and storing other biological materials.

30. Differentiate between *in situ* and *ex situ* approaches of biodiversity conservation. **(All India 2011)**

Ans. Differences between *in situ* and *ex situ* conservation are as follows

In situ conservation	*Ex situ* conservation
It means 'on-site' conservation.	It means 'off-site' conservation.
It is the conservation of species in their natural habitats, i.e. their maintenance and recovery, especially of the endangered species.	This is the conservation of endangered species in man-made habitat that imitates their natural habitat.
e.g. National parks, wildlife sanctuaries, etc.	e.g. Zoo, aquarium, etc.

31. Many plant and animal species are on the verge of their extinction because of loss of forest land by indiscriminate use by the humans. As a biology student what method would you suggest along with its advantages that can protect such threatened species from getting extinct? **(Delhi 2015)**

Ans. As a biology student, I would suggest *ex situ* conservation approach for such animals. It involves placing the threatened animals and plants in special care units for their protection. It includes off-site collections (botanical gardens, zoological parks, etc.) and gene banks (seedbank, tissue culture, etc).

Advantages of *ex situ* conservation are

(i) Off-site collection can be used to restock depleted population, reintroduce species in the wild and restore degraded habitats.

(ii) It is useful in maintaining a large number of genotypes in small area, rapid multiplication of even endangered species, through tissue culture, etc.

• Long Answer (LA) Type Questions

1. Explain the status of Indian biodiversity. Give a brief account of causes of biodiversity loss.

Ans. India is one of the 12 megadiversity countries of the world. Though India has only 2.4% of the world's land, but it shares an impressive 8.1% of the world's species diversity.

There are about 45,000 species of plants and twice as many of animals have been recorded from India. India probably has more than 1,00,000 species of plants and 3,00,000 species of animals yet to be discovered and described. If we apply Robert May's global estimate then only 22% of species have been recorded.

Causes of biodiversity loss are as follows

1. **Habitat loss and fragmentation** Destruction of habitat is the most important cause of extinction of both plants and animals species, e.g. due to **habitat loss**, 14% of the earth's land surface that was covered by tropical rainforest is now limited to only 6% in the last few years.

   The **Amazon rainforest** (lungs of the planet) are also being cut and destroyed for cultivation of soybean or are converted to grasslands for raising beef cattle. Besides total loss, the degradation of many habitats by pollution also threatens the survival of many species.

   When large habitats are broken up into small fragments due to various human activities, mammals and birds requiring large territories and certain animals with migratory habits are badly affected, leading to their population decline.

2. **Overexploitation** Humans are always dependent on nature for food and shelter. But when human needs turn into greed, it leads to the degradation and

extinction of natural resources. Many species are extinct in last 500 years due to overexploitation, e.g. Steller's sea cow, passenger pigeon, etc.

3. **Alien (Exotic) species invasions** Introduction of **alien-species** also causes the risk of extinction. When alien-species are introduced, some of them turn invasive and cause decline or extinction of indigenous species, e.g **Nile perch**, a large predator fish, when introduced into the Lake Victoria in East Africa, eventually led to the extinction of an ecologically unique assemblage of more than 200 species of cichlid fish in the lake.

2. The relation between species richness and area for a wide variety of taxa turns out to be a rectangular hyperbola. Give a brief explanation.

(NCERT Exemplar)

Ans. According to **Av Humboldt**, a German scientist, 'within a region, species richness increases with increase in explored area (only upto a limit)'. Accordingly the relation between species richness and area for a wide variety of taxa (birds, bat, angiosperms, aquatic fishes) turns out to be a rectangular hyperbola. The relationship depicts a straight line on a logarithmic scale described by the following equation

$$\log S = \log C + Z \log A$$

Where, 'S' stands for species richness, 'A' is area and 'Z' and 'C' are slope of line (regression coefficient) and y intercept, respectively.

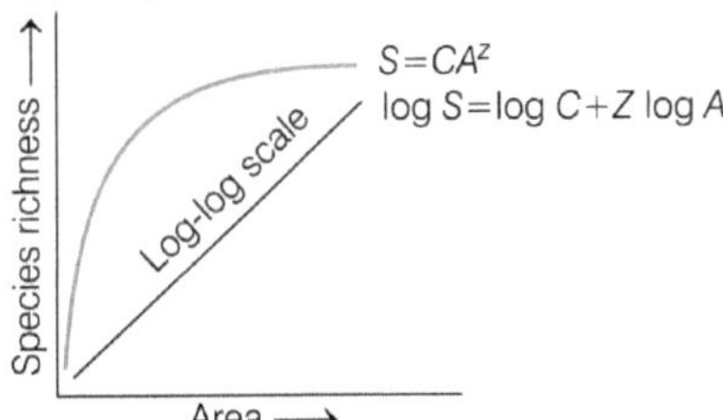

3. How is biodiversity important for ecosystem functioning? **(NCERT)**

Ans. Biodiversity is very important for ecosystem functioning. More diverse ecosystems are considered more stable. Stable communities are resilient and resistant to change.

Hence, diversity stabilises the community and also helps in increasing the productivity. Higher the biodiversity of an ecosystem, higher the number of species and therefore, lower is the rate of extinction. While in case of low biodiversity, there are higher chances of extinction.

Extinction of even one or two key species has negative impacts on the entire ecosystem.

Thus, the diversity ensures the stability and proper functioning of the entire ecosystem as explained *via* the 'Rivet popper hypothesis'.

- According to this hypothesis, ecosystem is like an aeroplane and all its parts are joined together using thousands of rivets (species).

- If every passenger, travelling in it, starts popping a rivet to take home (causing a species to become extinct), it may not affect flight safety (proper functioning of the ecosystem), but as more and more rivets are removed the plane becomes dangerously weak over a period of time.

- Moreover, which rivet is removed is also crucial, e.g. loss of rivet on the wings (key species that drive major ecosystem functions) is a more serious threat than loss of rivets on seats or windows inside the plane.

4. Describe the consumptive use value of biodiversity as food, drugs and medicines, fuel and fibre with suitable examples. **(NCERT Exemplar)**

Ans. Biological resources are the basis of life forms on our planet. The countries with maximum biodiversity possess better potential to compete with the rest of the world.

Biodiversity has great economic importance to mankind due to its many uses.

Some of the uses with consumptive value are as follows

(i) **Food** is obtained from biodiversity sources like livestock, forestry and fish. Biodiversity in modern agriculture is beneficial as a source of new crops, e.g. cereals crop like wheat, rice and maize account for about 55% of protein and 60% of calories in humans.

(ii) **Drugs** such as morphine (*Papaver somniferum*), quinine (*Cinchona ledgeriana*), reserpine (*Rauwolfia vomitoria*), belladonna (*Atropa belladonna*), aconite (*Aconitum napellus*), wintergreen and birth bark (*Gaultheria procumbens*) are derived from plants.

(iii) **Fuel and fibre** Plants like *Chorchorus*, *Gossypium* are sources of fibre while *Jatropha* is a source of biofuels. Fossils fuels are obtained from fossils of organisms.

5. How can you as an individual, prevent the loss of biodiversity? **(NCERT Exemplar)**

Ans. Biodiversity is the occurrence of different types of species, habitat, ecosystem, gene, gene pool in a particular place and various parts of earth. As an individual biodiversity can be conserved with conservation strategies and management of both biotic and abiotic resources.

Some of the conservation strategies are as follows

(i) Protection of useful animals and plants in their natural habitat or *in situ* conservation.

(ii) Preservation of critical habitats like feeding and breeding areas and resting area of endangered species to promote their growth and multiplication.

(iii) Hunting should be banned or regulated.

(iv) Habitat of migratory animals should be protected by bilateral or multilateral agreements.

(v) People should be made aware of the importance of biodiversity and its conservation.

(vi) Overexploitation of natural resources must be avoided.

(vii) Biodiversity plays an important role in maintaining and sustaining supply of goods and services.

(viii) Conservation of biodiversity ensures well-being of all the living creatures and their future generations.

• Case Based Questions

1. Observe the diagrams given below and answer the questions that follows.

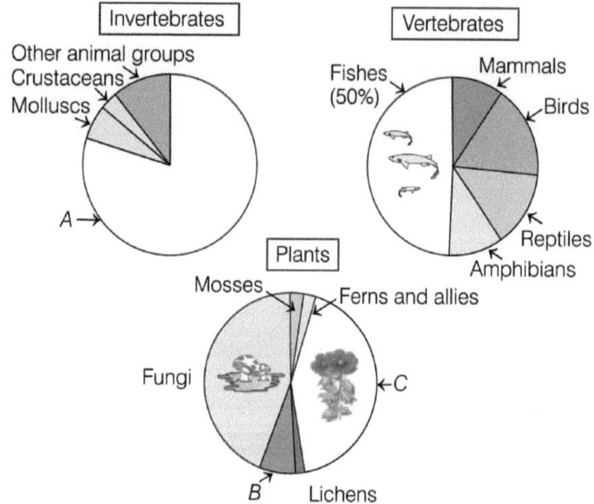

(i) What is being shown in the above representation?

Ans. The diagram shown in question depicts the global biodiversity of major taxa of invertebrates, vertebrates and plants.

(ii) What does the label *A* represents in the pie diagram of invertebrates?

Ans. Label *A* depicts insects which are the most species rich taxonomic group in the animal kingdom, constituting more than 70% of the total animals.

(iii) Which group of plants are the most endangered and why are they so few?

Ans. Ferns and allies are most endangered and they are few in number because they grow in humid and shady places and thus, need water for fertilisation. Due to high temperature and dry condition, few of them survived.

(iv) How do fungi that are saprotrophs sustain themselves as a large population?

Ans. Fungi has saprotrophic mode of nutrition they depend only on organic matter for their survival and hence, survive in any environment.

(v) Which group of plants is most advanced and which one is most primitive?

Ans. Group of plants labelled as *C* representing angiosperms, the most advanced taxonomic group and label *B* representing algae, most primitive taxonomic group of plant kingdom.

2. Observe the global biodiversity distribution of the major plant taxa in the given diagram and answer the questions accordingly.

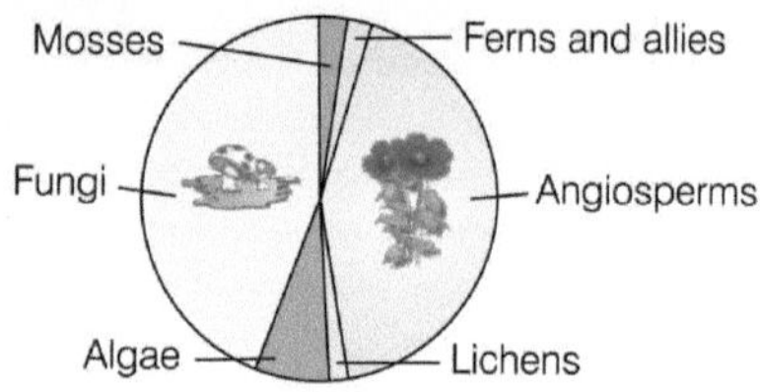

(i) Which group of plants are the most endangered?

Ans. Lichens

(ii) Why are mosses/ferns so few? Give reason.

Ans. Mosses and ferns are very few as they need humid conditions in forests and forests are disappearing.

(iii) How do fungi that are heterotrophs sustain themselves as a large population?

Ans. Fungi are able to sustain themselves as a large population because of their wider adaptability to the changing environment conditions.

3. The following graph shows the species-area relationship. Answer the following questions as directed.

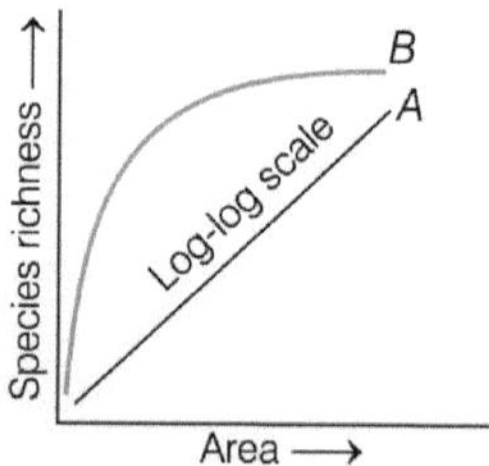

(i) Who studied the kind of relationship shown in the graph?

Ans. Alexander von Humboldt studied the relationship shown in the graph. He observed that species richness increased within an explored area, but only upto a limit.

(ii) In the species-area relationship, 'Z' represents.

Ans. In the species-area relationship, Z represents regression coefficient.

(iii) What is value of 'Z' regardless of the taxonomic group or the region?

Ans. Ecologists have discovered that the value of Z lies in the range of 0.1 to 0.2, regardless of the taxonomic group or the region whether it is the plants in Britain, birds in California or molluscs in New York state, the slopes of the regression line are amazingly similar.

(iv) What is the value of Z in species-area relationships among very large areas?

Ans. The species-area relationships among very large areas (continents), will give a much steeper slope and Z values in the range of 0.6 to 1.2

(v) If $\log A = 4$, $Z = 0.3$ and $\log C = 0.8$, find the value of log 'S'?

Ans. Given, $\log A = 4$, $Z = 0.3$ and $\log C = 0.8$

Putting these values in equation, $\log S = \log C + Z \log A$, i.e. species-area relationship equation, we will get the value of log S.

Thus, $\log S = 0.8 + 0.3 \times 4 = 0.8 + 1.2 = 2.0$

4. Direction *Read the following passage and answer the questions that follows.*

The loss of biological diversity is a global crisis with hardly any region on the earth not facing ecological catastrophes. Out of the 1.7 million species which are known to inhabit the earth, one-third to one-fourth is likely to get extinct with the coming decades. Man's intervention has speeded up the extinction rate from one species every 1000 years to one species every 10 years.

For most of the time man lived in a hunter-gatherer society, he depended entirely on biodiversity for sustenance. With the increased dependence on agriculture and industrialisation, the emphasis on biodiversity has decreased. Possible reasons behind the extinction of biodiversity are destruction of habitat, overexploitation, introduction of exotic species, deforestation, etc.

The phenomenon of biodiversity is very vast and complex with no single arching effect of diversity on either productivity or stability. However, biodiversity can be conserved by protecting its whole ecosystem with the two basic approaches *in situ* and *ex situ* conservation strategies.

(i) What do you understand by the term biodiversity?

Ans. Biodiversity may be defined as the variety and variability of living organisms on the earth. In other words, it is defined as the variety of life forms, gene pools and habitats found in an area.

(ii) State some of the possible reasons of depletion of biodiversity.

Ans. Some of the possible reasons why there is depletion of biodiversity are destruction of habitat, overexploitation of resources, introduction of alien or exotic species and coextinctions.

(iii) How has an increase in population led to an increased dependence on agriculture?

Ans. With an increase in population, there is an increased demand for food, energy and income. Increased population along with land degradation put forward the scenario of land degradation.

(iv) 'Extinction of one species leads to an extinction of the other'. Comment.

Ans. This statement means that when a species becomes extinct, the plant and animal species associated with it, in an obligatory way also becomes extinct, e.g. if a species of fish becomes extinct, all the parasites that are specific to it, also face extinction.

(v) Define sacred groves.

Ans. These are small group of forests with religious importance. They remain undisturbed and without any kind of human interference and includes a number of rare, endangered and endemic species. So, it is known as sacred groves.

Chapter Test

Multiple Choice Questions

1. The Western ghats have a greater amphibian diversity than the Eastern ghats. It is an example of
(a) species diversity
(b) genetic diversity
(c) ecological diversity
(d) None of the above

2. The organisation which publishes the Red List of species is
(a) ICFRE   (b) IUCN
(c) UNEP   (d) WWF

3. Which of the following statements describe natural extinction?
I. Extinctions abetted by human activities.
II. Slow replacement of existing species.
III. Also known as background extinction.
IV. A small population is most likely to be extinct.
Codes
(a) I and II   (b) I, II and III
(c) II, III and IV   (d) I, II, III and IV

4. Dodo, passenger pigeon and Steller's sea cow became extinct in the last 500 years due to
(a) habitat destruction
(b) overexploitation
(c) birdflu virus infection
(d) pollution

5. Sacred groves in India are related with
(a) cultural tradition
(b) it is the place where threatened species are protected
(c) it is the place where only artificial animal breeding is allowed
(d) forest patches around the places of worship

Assertion-Reasoning MCQs

Direction (Q. Nos. 1-3) *Each of these questions contains two statements, Assertion (A) and Reason (R). Each of these questions also has four alternative choices, any one of which is the correct answer. You have to select one of the codes (a), (b), (c) and (d) given below.*

(a) Both A and R are true and R is the correct explanation of A
(b) Both A and R are true, but R is not the correct explanation of A
(c) A is true, but R is false
(d) A is false, but R is true

1. Assertion (A) Tropical latitudes have greater biological diversity than temperate latitudes.
Reason (R) Tropical regions remain relatively undisturbed for millions of years.

2. Assertion (A) Species with low genetic variability are usually at a great risk of extinction.
Reason (R) Low genetic variability increases vulnerability to diseases, environmental changes and predators.

3. Assertion (A) The great Indian bustard is a critically endangered bird found in India.
Reason (R) It is vulnerable to extinction in the future.

Short Answer Type Questions

1. What accounts for the greater ecological diversity in India?   **(NCERT Exemplar)**

2. In what ways, can modern agriculture threaten the survival of species?

3. What is mass extinction? Give an example.

4. With an example explain latitude gradient, as a pattern of biodiversity.

5. What do you mean by fragmented habitat? Give one example.

6. (i) Explain two approaches of biodiversity conservation.
(ii) Which conservation method is used to maintain the species of wildlife in their natural habitats?

Long Answer Type Questions

1. (i) Seeds of different genetic strains are kept for long periods in seed banks. Explain the conservation strategy involved in this.
(ii) Can an extinction of one insect pollinator affect the whole ecosystem? If yes, explain.

2. Explain the importance of biodiversity.
(i) Hotspots and sacred groves.
(ii) What is the association between the bumble bee and its favourite orchid, *Ophrys*? How could extinction or change of one would affect the other?

Answers

Multiple Choice Questions

1. (a)   *2. (b)*   *3. (c)*   *4. (b)*   *5. (d)*

Assertion-Reasoning MCQs

1. (a)   *2. (a)*   *3. (c)*

For Detailed Solutions
Scan the code

Practice Paper 1*
(Solved)

General Instructions
- Time : 2 Hours
- Max. Marks : 35

1. There are 9 questions in the question paper. All questions are compulsory.
2. Question no. 1 is a Case Based Question, which has five MCQs. Each question carries one mark.
3. Question no. 2-6 are Short Answer Type Questions. Each question carries 3 marks.
4. Question no. 7-9 are Long Answer Type Questions. Each question carries 5 marks.
5. There is no overall choice. However, internal choices have been provided in some questions. Students have to attempt only one of the alternatives in such questions.

As exact Blue-print and Pattern for CBSE Term II exams is not released yet. So the pattern of this paper is designed by the author on the basis of trend of past CBSE Papers. Students are advised not to consider the pattern of this paper as official, it is just for practice purpose.

1. Direction *Read the following passage and answer the questions that follows.*

Rishi isolate the DNA from a source, then he used restriction endonuclease on it. He wants to separate the fragments of DNA. He asked to his teacher, what is the separation process of DNA. His teacher shows the given set upto him.

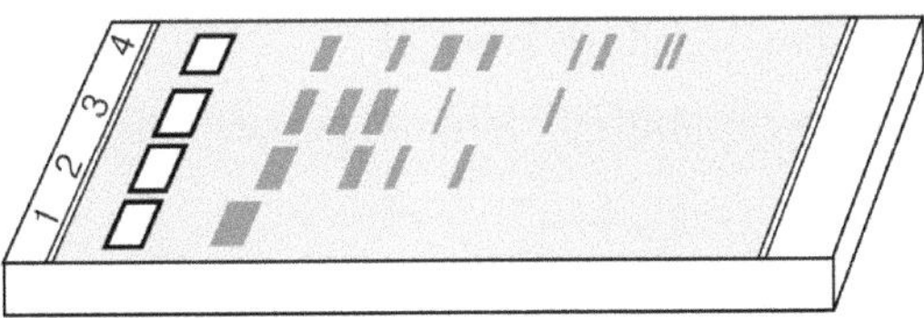

(i) The set up shown in the given figure is of
    (a) PCR   (b) bioreactor
    (c) gel electrophoresis   (d) vector

(ii) What is the role of restriction endonuclease enzyme?
    (a) It cut the DNA at specific position
    (b) It restricts the action of the enzyme DNA polymerase
    (c) It remove nucleotides from the ends of the DNA molecules
    (d) It repair broken DNA by joining two nucleotides

(iii) The dye which is used to stain DNA fragments in this technique is
    (a) agrose gel   (b) ethidium bromide
    (c) methyl orange   (d) azorubin

(iv) What is the principle of DNA fragments separation?
(a) DNA are negatively charged molecules, they move towards the anode under an electric field through a medium
(b) DNA are positively charged molecules, they move towards the anode under an electric field through a medium
(c) DNA are negatively charged molecules, they move towards the cathode under an electric field through a medium
(d) DNA are positively charged molecules, they move towards the cathode under an electric field through a medium

(v) The process by which separated strands of DNA are extracted is known as
(a) Competency
(b) Transformation
(c) Origin of replication
(d) Elution

2. What is GMO? List any five possible advantages of a GMO to a farmer.

Or How are transgenic animals used in chemical safety testing?

3. Explain the various steps involved in the production of artificial insulin.

4. When Ankit was diagnosed with AIDS, his colleagues wanted him to leave the workplace due to the fear of spread of AIDS. However, his boss was against their decision. He called a counsellor to setup a meeting with people to clear their misconceptions.

(i) Give the expanded form and causative agent of AIDS.

(ii) How does transmission of AIDS occur?

Or What measures would you take to prevent the water-borne diseases?

5. How do biocontrol agents control the target species? Explain by giving some important examples.

Or (i) What would happen if a large volume of untreated sewage is discharged into a river?
(ii) In what way anaerobic sludge digestion is important in the sewage treatment?

6. What are methanogens? How do they help to generate biogas?

7. Mention any four methods involved in the treatment of cancer.

Or What are biofertilisers and how do they enrich the fertility of the soil? Explain with the help of an example.

8. Extinction of a species is classified into three types, i.e. natural extinction, mass extinction and anthropogenic extinction. Classify the following examples on this basis.

(i) Animals lost due to inbreeding depression.
(ii) Disappearance of dinosaurs.
(iii) Extinction of passenger pigeon.
(iv) Extinction of marine invertebrates.
(v) Extinction of tiger.

Or Give the significance of predation in nature in detail.

9. The following diagrams are the age pyramids of different populations. Comment on the status of these populations.

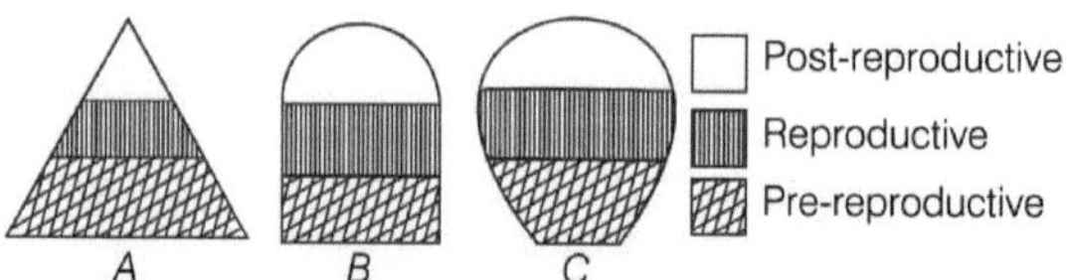

Or Discuss the various *in situ* and *ex situ* strategies for conservation of biodiversity.

Explanations

1. (i) (c) The given set up is of gel electrophoresis. It is used for the separation of DNA fragments.

   (ii) (a) Restriction endonuclease enzyme recognise a specific nucleotide sequence for binding and then cleave both the strands of DNA.

   (iii) (b) In gel electrophoresis, ethidium bromide is used to stain DNA fragments.

   (iv) (a) The principle of gel electrophoresis to separate DNA fragments is that DNA is a negatively charged molecules. They can be separated by forcing them to move towards the anode under an electric field through a medium (agrose gel).

   (v) (d) Elution is a process by which the separated strands of DNA are cut out from agarose gel and extracted from gel.

2. The plants, bacteria, fungi and animals whose genes have been altered are called Genetically Modified Organisms (GMOs).

   Advantages of GMOs to a Farmer

   (i) Crops become more tolerant to abiotic stresses like cold, drought, salt and heat.

   (ii) Dependence on chemical pesticides has reduced, i.e. pest-resistant crops.

   (iii) Enhanced nutritional value of food, e.g. vitamin-A enriched rice.

   Or Transgenic animals are employed for testing the safety of various chemicals (drugs, etc.) before being released for public use. It is also called as toxicity or safety testing. Transgenic animals are developed carrying the genes which make them more susceptible to the chemical substances than others.

   These animals are then exposed to the chemicals under test and effects generated are studied. These studies help in identifying the desirable and harmful effects of the chemical substances and their further improvement.

3. An American company Eli Lilly produced insulin *via* recombinant DNA technology in 1983. Insulin production by using recombinant DNA technology is shown in flow chart below

   DNA sequences corresponding to the two polypeptides, i.e. A and B-chains of insulin are synthesised *in vitro*

   ↓

   They are introduced into plasmid DNA of *E. coli*

   ↓

   This bacterium is cloned under suitable conditions

   ↓

   The transgene is expressed in the form of polypeptides, i.e. A and B-chains secreted into the medium

   ↓

   They are extracted and combined by creating disulphide bridge to form human insulin.

4. (i) AIDS is Acquired Immuno Deficiency Syndrome. It is caused by Human Immunodeficiency Virus (HIV).

   (ii) HIV gets transmitted by sexual contact with infected person, by sharing of infected needles, by transfusion of contaminated blood and from infected mother to her child through placenta.

Or To prevent water-borne diseases, water bodies, ponds, water tanks, reservoirs in the city or village should be cleaned periodically. The proper disposal of domestic waste, excreta, sewage should be done. At personal level, boiling of water, using water purifier, washing hands before meals should be practiced.

5. Biocontrol refers to the use of biological methods for controlling plant diseases, pests, etc. It relies on the natural control of pests, i.e. natural predation rather than introduced chemicals.

   Some examples of biological control agents are as follows

   (i) Ladybird and dragonfly are used to get rid of aphids and mosquitoes, respectively.

   (ii) *Bacillus thuringiensis* (*Bt*) is used to control bollworm insects.

   (iii) Free-living fungi like *Trichoderma* is common in root ecosystem and it is used for controlling several plant pathogens.

   (iv) Baculoviruses are used for species specific narrow spectrum insecticidal applications and is beneficial in IPM programme.

Or (i) If untreated sewage is discharged directly into the rivers, it will lead to serious pollution of the water bodies with organic matter and pathogenic bacteria, protozoans and many other disease causing microorganisms. This water, if used, will cause outbreaks of water borne diseases.

   (ii) In anaerobic sludge digestion, anaerobic bacteria digest aerobic bacteria and fungi in the sludge and the remaining organic matter.

   During this digestion, bacteria produce a mixture of gases such as methane, hydrogen, carbon dioxide and little amount of hydrogen sulphide. These gases (biogas) can be used as a source of energy as it is inflammable.

6. Certain bacteria which grow anaerobically on cellulosic material, produce large amounts of methane gas along with CO_2 and H_2.

   These bacteria are called methanogens (one of the common bacterium is *Methanobacterium*).

   Methanogens are commonly found in the anaerobic sludge during sewage treatment and are also present in the rumen (a part of stomach) of cattle.

   In rumen, methanogens help in the breakdown of cellulose and their excreta called gobar is rich in these bacteria. Therefore, dung can be used to produce biogas commonly called as **gobar gas**.

7. The methods involved in the treatment of cancer are as follows

   (i) **Surgery** It involves removal of the entire cancerous tissue. It is the easiest method of cancer treatment. However, it cannot be employed against all types of cancers.

   (ii) **Chemotherapy** Several chemotherapeutic drugs are used to kill cancerous cells. Some of these are specific for particular tumours. This therapy may lead to hair loss and anaemia.

   (iii) **Radiotherapy** It involves exposure of tumour to ionising radiations-like X-rays, which kill the cancerous cells.

Radiation therapy is employed in 80% of the cancer patients, but this approach may also cause damage to the adjoining normal tissues.

(iv) **Immunotherapy** In radio-immunotherapy, radioisotope-linked monoclonal antibodies are used for the treatment of cancer.

The patients are given substances, called biological response modifiers such as α-interferon, which activates their immune system and help in destroying the tumour cells.

Or Biofertilisers are living organisms that increase the fertility of the soil. These microbes help in supplying the nutrients to the plant. By their natural biological activity, they mobilise the availability of the nutrients to the plants thus, improving the fertility of the soil. Many species of bacteria and cyanobacteria help in fixing the nitrogen in the soil. Some bacteria stay in symbiotic relationship with legumes while, some are free-living nitrogen fixers. Biofertilisers have additional advantage of being eco-friendly and effective.

For example,

- Nitrogen-fixing bacteria fix atmospheric nitrogen into organic form, which is used by the plant as nutrient, e.g. *Rhizobium* is a symbiotic bacterium that lives in the root nodules of legumes and fixes atmospheric nitrogen into organic compounds.

- *Azotobacter* and *Azospirillum* are free-living bacteria, which absorb free nitrogen from the soil, air and convert it into salts of nitrogen compounds.

8.   (i) Natural extinction   (ii) Mass extinction
     (iii) Anthropogenic extinction   (iv) Natural extinction
     (v) Anthropogenic extinction

Or Significances of predation in nature are as follows

(i) **Control of prey population** In the absence of predators, prey species could achieve very high population densities and cause instability. So, besides acting as conduits for energy transfer across trophic levels. The predator keeps the population of the prey under check, so that an equilibrium is maintained.

The prey also maintains its optimum activity and efficiency since only weak and sick individuals are removed by the predators.

(ii) **Biological control of weeds and pests** It is largely based on predator prey relation. When certain exotic species are introduced into a geographical area, they become invasive and start spreading fast in the absence of natural predators, e.g. *Opuntia* turned out to be a serious weed in Australia.

It was brought under control when its natural herbivore *Cactoblastis* was introduced.

(iii) **Maintenance of species diversity** Predators help in maintaining species diversity in a community by reducing the intensity of competition among competing prey species.

(iv) **Vegetation** Predation helps in the growth of vegetation all over the globe by restricting the population of herbivores.

9. Figure *A* It is a 'pyramid'-shaped age pyramid. In this figure, the base, i.e. pre-reproductive stage is very large as compared with the reproductive and post-reproductive stages

of the population. This type of age structure indicates that the population would increase rapidly.

Figure *B* It is an 'inverted bell'-shaped pyramid. In this figure, the pre-reproductive and reproductive stages are same. This type of age structure indicates that the population is stable.

Figure *C* It is an urn-shaped pyramid. In the figure, the pre-reproductive and reproductive stages are less than the post-reproductive stages of this population. In this population, more older people are present. This type of age structure indicates that the population definitely is declining.

Or In order to conserve biodivesity two major approaches has been put forward, i.e. *in situ* and *ex situ* conservation.

1. ***In situ* conservation** It is the conservation of living resources through their maintenance within the natural habitat or ecosystem. *In situ* approach is preferable because much of the diversity can be conserved through protection of total ecosystem. Different methods used in *in situ* conservation are as follows

(i) **Protected areas** These are the part of land or sea especially dedicated to protection and maintenance of biological diversity and associated cultural resources. Protected areas are ecologically unique and biodiversity rich regions. These are legally protected as biosphere reserves, national parks and sanctuaries.

(a) **National park** It is an area strictly reserved for the betterment of wildlife where forestry, grazing are not permitted.

(b) **Biosphere reserves** These are the special category of protected areas of land and/or coastal environments, wherein people are an integral component of the system. These are the representative examples of natural biomes and contain unique biological communities within.

Biosphere reserves represent a specified area zonated for particular activity. These include

I. **Core zone** (No human activity is allowed in this zone)

II. **Buffer zone** (Limited activity is permitted)

III. **Manipulation zone** (Several human activities are allowed).

(c) **Wildlife sanctuaries** India has over 448 wildlife sanctuaries (IUCN category-IV protected area). Among these, the 28 tiger reserves are governed by **Project Tiger** and are of special significance in the conservation of the tiger. Some wildlife sanctuaries are specifically named **Bird Sanctuary**.

(ii) **Sacred groves** These forest are the undisturbed areas that are set aside without any human disturbance. All the trees and wildlife within it are venerated and given total protection.

2. ***Ex situ* conservation** It means conservation outside the habitats by perpetuating sample population in genetic resource centres, e.g. zoos, botanical gardens, culture collections, etc., or in the form of **gene pools** and **gametes** storage for fish, germplasm banks for seeds, pollen, semen, ova and cell, etc.

Genetic conservation It is an interdisciplinary science that aims to apply genetic method to conservation and restoration of biodiversity. It includes tissue culture, seed bank and gene banks.

Practice Paper 2*
(Unsolved)

General Instructions

- Time : 2 Hours
- Max. Marks : 35

1. There are 9 questions in the question paper. All questions are compulsory.
2. Question no. 1 is a Case Based Question, which has five MCQs. Each question carries one mark.
3. Question no. 2-6 are Short Answer Type Questions. Each question carries 3 marks.
4. Question no. 7-9 are Long Answer Type Questions. Each question carries 5 marks.
5. There is no overall choice. However, internal choices have been provided in some questions. Students have to attempt only one of the alternatives in such questions.

** As exact Blue-print and Pattern for CBSE Term II exams is not released yet. So the pattern of this paper is designed by the author on the basis of trend of past CBSE Papers. Students are advised not to consider the pattern of this paper as official, it is just for practice purpose.*

1. **Direction** *Read the following passage and answer the questions that follows.*

   During the unfortunate corona virus lockdown, Kavita started cursing the existence of microbes on earth. On hearing this, Deepak told Kavita that not all the microbes are harmful for us. Many microbes are useful in producing medicines, bioactive molecules and household products.

   (i) Microbes responsible for large holes in cheese belong to genes

       (a) *roqueforti*   (b) *cerevisiae*

       (c) *fumigatus*   (d) *shermanii*

   (ii) The microbes through which 'wonder drug' was derived was

       (a) *Aspergillus fumigatus*   (b) *Penicillium notatum*

       (c) *Penicillium chrysogenum*   (d) *Monascus purpureus*

   (iii) Beside making curd, which of the following is the correct function of the same bacteria?

       (a) Fermentation of fish

       (b) Inhancing the taste and texture of cheese

       (c) Increase vitamin-B_{12} content

       (d) Production of biogas

   (iv) *Nucleopolyhedrovirus* do not show

       (a) host specificity

       (b) narrow spectrum application

       (c) effect on non-targeted pathogen

       (d) utility in IPM programme

(v) Identify the correct source and function of cyclosporin-A.
   (a) *Monascus purpureus* – Suppresses immune system
   (b) *Trichoderma polysporum* – Activate immune system
   (c) *Monascus purpureus* – Activate immune system
   (d) *Trichoderma polysporum* – Suppresses immune system

2. (i) Cancer is one of the most dreaded disease. Explain 'contact inhibition' and 'metastasis' with respect to the disease.

   (ii) Why are cancer patients often given α-interferon as part of the treatment?

   Or An organic farmer relies on natural predation for controlling plant pests and diseases.

   Justify giving reasons why this is considered to be a holistic approach.

3. (i) Identify *A* and *B* illustrations in the following.

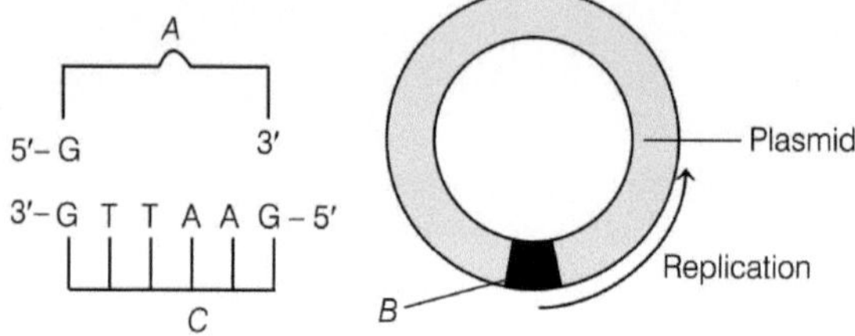

   (ii) Write the term given to *A* and *C* and why?

   (iii) Mention one importance of biotechnology.

   Or With respect to understanding diseases, discuss the importance of transgenic animal models.

4. What is addiction? State any four reasons of drug addiction.

5. Explain briefly

   (i) Restriction enzymes and DNA

   (ii) Chitinase

   Or What does '*Hind*' and 'III' refer to in the enzyme *Hind* III?

6. How does the human body protect itself from infections?

7. Describe the consumptive use value of biodiversity as food, drugs and medicines, fuel and fibre with suitable examples.

   Or How can you as an individual, prevent the loss of biodiversity?

8. What is genetic engineering? List the steps involved in *r*DNA technology.

   Or Compare and contrast the advantages and disadvantages of the production of genetically modified crops.

9. 'Analysis of age pyramids for human population can provide important inputs for long-term planning strategies'. Explain.

   Or (i) Compare giving reasons, the J-shaped and S-shaped models of population growth of a species.
   (ii) Explain 'fitness of a species', as mentioned by Darwin.

Answers

1. (i) (d)   (ii) (b)   (iii) (c)   (iv) (c)   (v) (d)

Biology
Class 12th (Term II)

Practice Paper 3*
(Unsolved)

1. **Direction** *Read the following passage and answer the questions that follows.*

   Biodiversity is not uniform throughout the world. It varies with the changes in latitude and altitude. For many groups of animals and plants, there are specific patterns in diversity based on the favourable environmental conditions as plants and animals are more diverse in areas, which are best suited for their survival.

   A German naturalist and geographer during his pioneering and extensive explorations in the wilderness of South American jungles, observed the pattern of biodiversity and described it through the following graph.

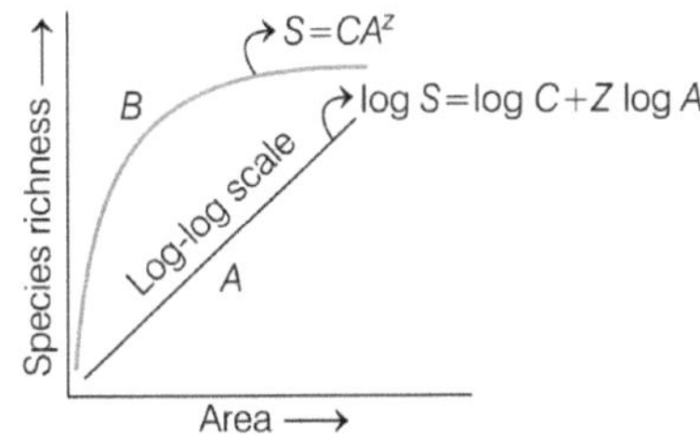

   (i) Name the naturalist who studied the kind of relationship shown in the graph.
   - (a) Robert May
   - (b) Alexander von Humboldt
   - (c) David Tilman
   - (d) Paul Ehrlich

   (ii) What does 'Z' stands for in the given equation of the graph?
   - (a) Species richness
   - (b) Intercept
   - (c) Area explored
   - (d) Regression coefficient

   (iii) The value of Z is
   - (a) constant
   - (b) zero
   - (c) one
   - (d) fluctuating

(iv) The slope of the line 'B' become steeper for
    (a) forest   (b) continents
    (c) small areas   (d) pond

(v) The given graph shows
    (a) the species richness decreased with increase in explored area
    (b) the species richness remain constant regardless of the region
    (c) the species richness increased with increasing explored area, but only upto a limit
    (d) there is no relation between species richness, taxonomic group and region to be explored

2. (i) How do organic farmers control pests? Give two examples.

(ii) State the difference in their approach from that of conventional pest control methods.

Or What is IPM? Give an example of bioinsecticides and bioherbicides and how do they help in pest control?

3. (i) It is generally observed that the children who had suffered from chickenpox in their childhood may not contract the same disease in their adulthood. Explain giving reasons the basis of such an immunity in an individual. Name this kind of immunity.

(ii) What are interferons? Mention their role.

4. Medically it is advised to all young mothers that breast-feeding is the best for their newborn babies. Do you agree? Give reasons in support of your answer.

5. What is gene therapy? Which disease can be cure by gene therapy?

Or The following illustrates the linking of DNA fragments

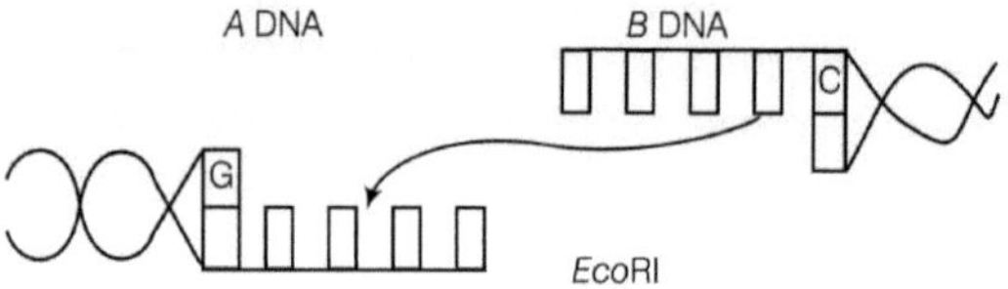

(i) Write the name of A and B.

(ii) Complete the palindrome, which is recognised by *Eco*RI.

(iii) Write the name of the enzyme that can link the two DNA fragments.

6. How has the study of biotechnology helped in developing pest resistant cotton crop? Explain.

Or (i) Mention the importance of gel-electrophoresis in biotechnology.

    (ii) Explain the process of this technique.

7. Mention any four methods involved in the treatment of cancer.

Or What do understand by recombinant DNA vaccines? Give two examples of such vaccines. Discuss their advantages.

8. Transgenic crops or Genetically Modified (GM) crops are being cultivated in many parts of the world. One of the main objectives of their production is to minimise the use of insecticides on cultivated crops. Explain with the help of a suitable example, how these genetically modified crops have been developed.

Or 'In some children, ADA deficiency can be cured by bone marrow transplantation or by enzyme replacement therapy, but both of these approaches are not completely curative'. Justify the statement.

9. How can we as a citizen of our country, prevent the loss of biodiversity?

Or Of the four major causes for the loss of biodiversity which according to you is the major cause for the loss of biodiversity? Give reasons in support.

Answers

1. *(i) (b)*   *(ii) (d)*   *(iii) (d)*   *(iv) (b)*   *(v) (c)*

Printed by Libri Plureos GmbH in Hamburg,
Germany